In a time of inflation, political uncertainty, and a changing global economy, I have not seen a better path to achieve the financial and emotional freedom needed to be the best version of yourself than Bryan Kuderna's book.

—Jim Campbell
syndicated radio host and author of *Madoff Talks*,
also a Netflix documentary series

Kuderna proves why economics makes the world turn round. From religion to big tech, this book highlights why things are the way they are, and how your money fits right in the center of it all.

—Frank O'Connell
former president of Reebok Brands and HBO Video
and author of *Jump First, Think Fast*

Sometimes the title of a book reaches out and demands that you immediately read it. That happened to me, as the question of "What should I do with my money?" has haunted me for years. Thanks to Bryan Kuderna and this book, now I can successfully answer that question for myself. I never saw the connection between my money and the global economy, but now I don't know how I ever missed it.

—Gregg Stebben
author of *White House Confidential*
and *Does Putin Have to Die?*

What Should I Do with My Money? is a "must-have" for investors in today's world. Bryan gives clear, easy-to-understand explanations of market conditions and shares his financial strategies. He managed to make economics entertaining and ultrarelevant. Everyone needs this book to develop a strong investing strategy for the future.

—Rick Grossmann
author of Entrepreneur Magazine's *Franchise Bible*

Whether conservative or liberal, your finances and well-being, and those of the country, can only be enriched by reading Bryan Kuderna's thought-provoking book. He brings big questions down to one simple, recurring one: "What should I do with my money?"

—Lee Barney
finance editor, Newsmax Media Inc.

WHAT SHOULD I DO WITH
MY MONEY?

ECONOMIC INSIGHTS
TO BUILD WEALTH AMID CHAOS

BRYAN M. KUDERNA, CFP®

HOST OF *THE KUDERNA PODCAST*

New York   Chicago   San Francisco   Athens   London   Madrid
Mexico City   Milan   New Delhi   Singapore   Sydney   Toronto

1 2 3 4 5 6 7 8 9   LCR   27 26 25 24 23

ISBN   978-1-264-85793-7
MHID   1-264-85793-4

e-ISBN   978-1-264-85802-6
e-MHID   1-264-85802-7

This publication is designed to provide accurate and authoritative information in regard to the subject matter covered. It is sold with the understanding that neither the author nor the publisher is engaged in rendering legal, accounting, securities trading, or other professional services. If legal advice or other expert assistance is required, the services of a competent professional person should be sought.
> —*From a Declaration of Principles Jointly Adopted by a Committee of the American Bar Association and a Committee of Publishers and Associations*

Library of Congress Cataloging-in-Publication Data

Names: Kuderna, Bryan M., author.
Title: What should I do with my money? : economic insights to build wealth amid chaos / Bryan M. Kuderna, CFP.
Description: New York : McGraw Hill, [2023] | Includes bibliographical references and index.
Identifiers: LCCN 2022046358 (print) | LCCN 2022046359 (ebook) | ISBN 9781264857937 (hardback) | ISBN 9781264858026 (ebook)
Subjects: LCSH: Finance, Personal. | Investments.
Classification: LCC HG179 .K83 2023 (print) | LCC HG179 (ebook) | DDC 332.0024—dc23/eng/20220928
LC record available at https://lccn.loc.gov/2022046358
LC ebook record available at https://lccn.loc.gov/2022046359

For all those who wonder why.
Never stop wondering.

CONTENTS

1. POPULATION   1

Can we afford to have more neighbors, or can we afford not to have more neighbors? Economics studies the behavior and interactions of economic agents, also known as humans. The shifting sands of a growing population give rise to every economic insight to follow. After all, a thing is a sum of its parts.

2. ENTITLEMENTS   21

What are you entitled to? Thomas Jefferson got off easy promising life, liberty, and the pursuit of happiness. Within every economy exist givers and takers, billions of scales balancing who should have what.

3. EDUCATION   49

An educated society is destined for greatness like a valedictorian is poised for success. But the costs of knowledge are not free, nor are the values of education guaranteed.

4. ECONOMIC PHILOSOPHY   73

The beliefs around the production, consumption, and transfer of wealth. To socialize or capitalize?

A NOTE FROM THE AUTHOR

I t all begins with a simple question.

"What should I do with my money?"

Seven words that sound so casual. This millennial couple is not the first to ask me. They are no different than clients of any other generation. They may have entered my office hoping to learn how to make more money, but whether they realize it or not, that's not their real motivation. They're after the same thing everyone else is—control, and equally as important, a sense of control. Money does not matter by itself, it's the things you can do with money, and the ability to do such things with confidence, that matter. That's why we're not going to talk about another popular question, "Do I have enough money?" Over 15 years of financial advising, I've met poor people who have "more than enough" and ultrarich people who will never have enough.

"What should I do with my money?" It is a question asked every day in every language in every corner of the globe, from the child at the snack stand deciding between chips and candy to CEOs in the board room debating billion-dollar acquisitions. A few moments of thought can transform this casual ask into something far more, turning simple answers into elusive solutions just beyond reach. When pressed a bit further, why chips over candy, why buy, hold, or sell, we suddenly learn the value of an outcome, and we learn even more about people. What if an answer does exist, one that not only helps you control your money, build wealth, and achieve financial freedom, but simultaneously builds a perfect economy? Imagine amid the infinite flows of money between eight billion people each day that you were able to highlight the path of your dollars.

Since 2008, I've navigated bull markets and bear markets, no inflation and record inflation, unprecedented employment and unprecedented unemployment, and added lots of letters after my name that a select few might recognize. I even came up with an answer to this couple's famous question, "What should I do with my money?" But if I share my answer, I can almost guarantee their follow-up question.

"Why?" Glenn is about to turn 40, newly married, works as a middle school teacher, and still isn't sure if he's ready for his first child. "Why do you suggest that?" he repeats. I met Glenn after he sent an email through my website with the subject line—"Help with student loans." We're in my office and he keeps shuffling with handwritten notes that his father told him to ask. Sometimes he puts the notes down and tosses in a question that he credits to his favorite podcast. His wife, Maria, is 33, a well-to-do private equity attorney in the city. She makes more than he does but is clearly not too concerned about financial planning, let alone hubby's fascination with crypto. I instinctively try to elicit her opinions on our conversation, not meaning to put her on the spot each time she jolts up from her phone and says, "Sure! If Glenn thinks so."

His reply, that impulsive "Why?," is proof my answer doesn't matter. My answer is not indisputable nor my words gospel. You see, it's not the initial question, "What should I do with my money?," that sparks debate between tens of thousands of books, shows, influencers, and professionals like me. It is the inevitable second question ... *Why?*

"Why should I do that with my money?" He tries again. Perhaps it's an intellectual challenge. Maybe my advice didn't agree with the note from his dad or the podcast tips. Glenn might just be confused by my answer, or perhaps he hoped for something sexier to call his buddy up about on the way home.

This, my friends, is where the fun starts. Pandora's box. The rabbit hole. A slippery slope. The ol' can of worms. The answer to "Why?" is what separates a robo-advisor from a financial advisor, artificial intelligence from intelligence. The ensuing game of ping-pong—why/answer, why/answer, why/answer—is the special opportunity in which individuals choose their own path, rather than follow the maze the world gives them.

Within minutes we are deep into the world's current events, peeling back each layer of macroeconomics (the universal circumstances of a structure seemingly designed by power brokers outside our realm) and how it affects microeconomics (the reality experienced by individuals and small busi-nesses in making decisions regarding the allocation of scarce resources). Glenn shares his worries about state pension funds going belly-up as his retiring coworkers flee the state for warm climates and lower property taxes. Maria, disinterested a moment ago, is suddenly on the edge of her seat shout-ing about China and Mexico's lack of concern for greenhouse gases giving an unfair financial advantage against the American companies her firm acquired. Somehow, we get to talking about the election in France and the possibility of welcoming socialism on our side of the pond. Answer/why, answer/why, answer/why. Personal finance has become personal.

It's not the answers of "buy this, sell that," but rather the *why* conversa-tions that impact real-life decisions about what people do with their money, how they feel about their money, and how they feel about control or a lack thereof. Day by day, I address these touchy subjects with clients ranging from those just getting by up to the rich and famous. They all speak as if econom-ics are far away, a chaos created by the privileged few while the real world watches from the nosebleed section. In this journey of life, people feel like the kid who won the chance to go into the money booth, ready to grab cash blowing all around him, only to step out 30 seconds later with five singles in his hands. Here exists a fundamental void, a misunderstanding of how money works.

We are all on this earth together, and so is our money. You must under-stand that money, your money, rests at the heart of every major issue in the world: entitlements, education, economics, environment, tech, war, religion, and finance. There are no exemptions, and everything comes at a cost. Each decision, no matter how big or small, requires a commitment of time and money, a trade-off or sacrifice of what is, to allow what can be.

There are two reasons why the answer to "What should I do with my money?" requires elaboration, to the tune of hundreds of forthcoming pages. First, everyone is unique. Therefore, a standard response cannot account for each client's personal priorities, causing the math involved in economics to equal a different value from one person to the next. We'll get into what forms priorities and costs in the next chapter. Second, nothing worthwhile is done without conviction. Never has a hall-of-fame running back tiptoed into the end zone with the game on the line; rather, he lowers his shoulder and blasts through the line with all his might. I would posit that this is the number one reason why so many expertly drafted plans never get implemented, because clients are not sure. My experience has shown that analysis does not cause paralysis; rather, lingering *whys* encourage more misguided analysis, and eventual paralysis. Conviction comes from confidence in the plan; confidence in the plan comes from an understanding of the macroeconomic circumstances (the world), microeconomic goals and concerns (the self), and the available levers to pull (the control).

Conviction begets speed, and speed of transaction is critical to success in finance, and, one might argue, to success in life. How quickly can you close the deal and move on to what is next? How quickly can you make the right choice before it becomes the wrong choice? How quickly can you right a wrong? Diving down the rabbit hole takes time, and sometimes it's hard to find a way back out. But your concerns are always valid, and curiosities deserve to be satisfied. The purpose of this book is not to know how to save, invest, spend, and learn for today and tomorrow, but how to do so for the rest of your life, no matter what tops your priority list. When you finish reading this book, you will understand how money works and why it works.

If you peeked at the index, you might be wondering where we are headed. How are education and religion economical? What does big tech have to do with socialism? Why does any of it matter to your financial plan? My answers on what you should do with your money may not always be what you want to hear, but are what I think you need to hear, and to be fair, you should want to hear what you need to hear. This act of humility is our first lesson in economics—needs always become wants. Circumstances transform into problems based on how long it takes to realize this truth.

As tempting as it may be to dive into a chapter that catches your interest, I'd encourage you to first go cover to cover. The answers to your *whys* often lie in hidden corners. Each topic is intimately related; no intricacy in economics is so generous as to operate in a vacuum.

Until your second question "Why?" is answered, financial recommendations are irrelevant. Your plans will float aimlessly like a lost ship at sea, its sails readjusting to whichever way the wind blows. Knowledge and the motivation to act in one's own best interests are mutually inclusive. The insights in this book are all about economics, but it just so happens that economics consciously and subconsciously touches every decision, opinion, and set of values a person sticks to. Conversely, each decision, opinion, and personal ethos generates economic consequence. You and the decision makers right around you form a pool of microeconomies, which if you follow will lead you to the sea of macroeconomies that make the world what it is. A society that chooses get-rich-quick schemes, seeks immediate gratification void of nuance, follows the latest fad, and ignores the importance of *why* is bound to manifest its own dysfunctional economy.

In the coming pages, you will learn about what's going on with our world, where we came from, where we are, and where we are going. You will learn what makes investments go up and down, why some things need to be taxed while others don't, whether college should be free or cost even more, what money to use for today versus tomorrow. Together, we will dissect America's problems, and in many respects, the world's. We'll observe macroeconomies from a telescope and microeconomies under a microscope. Some problems may seem inconceivable, while others might hit right at home.

This book is about thinking, engineering micro solutions to macro problems in that quiet time at night between your head hitting the pillow and your mind slipping into oblivion. These micro solutions are decisions you can make in your daily life to affect the same macro problems that make prime-time news.

The narrative around each chapter involves change and the costs of change. Without costs we would all constantly change to our immediate wants, living in a utopia bound for hysteria. The tension that defines cost, the compromise between two sides giving and taking, will invade every facet of economics. Change can appear to be the ultimate barrier to our control. Change is unpredictable, fast, and compounding. But really, that may be a better description of how change *feels*, not necessarily how it acts on its own. Change *feels* unpredictable if one chooses to ignore the proverbial writing on the wall, clinging to hope or a false sense of power. Someone in total control of a situation would never experience a bad change, so if they do, they know their sense of control was ill-perceived. If the same surprised individual looks back at whatever change occurred, it often appears apparent if not expected. Similarly, change *feels* fast if its progression is ignored until its completion. The only reason change *feels* compounded is that the last iteration was forgotten.

In order to use the tools in this book, remember that change may not always be an improvement, but an improvement is always a change. It is nice to have the serenity to embrace change, but nicer to have the ability to foresee change, and nicest to be an agent of change. This ability to change your own financial life while contributing to the world will all be possible with a greater understanding of how your microeconomies fit within their macro-economies, and the gains and losses inherent to both by everyday financial decisions.

If you feel out of control, you are right. If you feel in control, you are also right. Control is a freely chosen self-perception similar to happiness. Asking more *whys* and understanding each answer may help promote control, or it might open even more black holes. Such a conundrum might support the idea that ignorance is bliss, but it is only blissful until it ends up on your doorstep.

Good things are happening, bad things are happening, and a lot is happening that we don't understand enough about to classify. Join me as we fly through history and discover the economic insights to build wealth amid chaos!

Without wax,
B. K.

INTRODUCTION

The life of money-making is one undertaken under compulsion,
and wealth is evidently not the good we are seeking; for
it is merely useful and for the sake of something else.

—**Aristotle (384–322 BC)**

I f what to do with your money is based on economics, it's best to know what exactly economics is. Economics is the study of the production, consumption, and transfer of wealth. It is a definition that has been examined formally and informally since the beginning of time, equal parts elementary and mystifying. Each derivative comprises all that mankind relies upon:

1. **Production** is how everything is made, be it service or product. How did the print get on this page? Where did the watch on your wrist originate? Keep asking who, what, why, when, where, and how the coffee made its way into your mug, and you could write a book on international affairs.
2. **Consumption** is the use of any such product, service, or resource. What did you pay for this book? Your watch? That cup of coffee? Do you think it was worth it? Where else could your money have gone than toward your latest purchases?
3. **Transfer of wealth** refers to the connection between producers and consumers. Since nothing costs nothing, and everything costs something, every transaction implies a negotiated compromise. If

perfection, 100 percent efficiency, can never exist, does that mean every exchange of wealth results in a winner and loser, or is there a homeostasis eventually making producers and consumers equal beneficiaries?

Understanding these three building blocks of economics is the only way to correctly decide what to do with your money, or else unintended consequences will continue to surprise your plans. So far, economics appears pretty elementary. But just as thunder follows a bolt of lightning, elementary becomes mystifying once curiosity enters the scene. Asking why transforms an ordinary flash and a boom in the sky into a wonder of science. The same holds true in economics. *Consuming* and *producing* are no longer boring terms in a book when we ask why we consume and produce. Production and consumption represent unlimited marriages that build the greatest family tree ever recorded. They are each the outcome of the father of economics, Adam Smith's invisible hand working through a conglomeration of self-interested decisions.

However, it is the third phase of economics that is the game changer. Wealth, and the pursuit of it, answers the question why people do what they do with their money. Pursuit of wealth is the X factor. Wealth finds its etymology in the old English word *weal*, which refers to a state of well-being. This last definition might provide a new lens to look through when thinking about money. The world is producing and consuming everything imaginable, and it is doing so based on the exchange of well-being.

On July 4, 1776, Thomas Jefferson, assisted by his editors, John Adams and Benjamin Franklin, authored the Declaration of Independence.* Within the declaration, Jefferson famously wrote, "We hold these truths to be self-evident, that all men are created equal, that they are endowed by their Creator with certain unalienable Rights, that among these are Life, Liberty, and the pursuit of Happiness."

Could the US forefathers have included "wealth" in their declaration, clearly in pursuit of a better and more fair *weal* than the English crown was allowing? It is interesting that life and liberty are objective, but happiness, the

---

* The Continental Congress actually declared independence on July 2 and America's founding document was not signed until August 2, but let's not disturb the free world's proudest holiday.

one right not endowed but pursued, is subjective. As Honest Abe once said, "Happiness is a choice." Viewing the pursuit of wealth like happiness will provide a framework for economics and begin to answer the *whys* all around us.

Let's start small. Every individual within a microeconomy produces their craft with an expectation of some valuable result, monetary or otherwise. This result can then be used to finance or barter for some desired consumption. Each of these trades are rooted in motivation for an individual's pursuit of well-being. Macroeconomics may carry some grandiose appearance of being a higher-level course of study, but it is nothing more than a description of the motives behind a group of microeconomies, their combined priority lists. Now, there are times this can be distorted, times when macroeconomies do not represent their makeup but rather design their makeup, times when a minority rules the majority, but such discourse will be saved for later chapters.

Before investigating how money makes the world go round, there are a couple more economic definitions to grasp. Mankind must produce to then consume, with any gaps being filled through trade, all in reference to the pursuit of well-being. Every free-willed transaction is a form of quid pro quo, meaning "this for that." Here is where two very confusing terms enter the equation—**price** and **cost**. For the rest of this book, remember that these terms are *not* interchangeable.

Price Versus Cost

When a client hears a strategy for what to do with their money, their first follow-up question is typically, "What's it going to cost me?" This is when unintended disagreements can arise. The client usually means, "What is the price of your recommended strategy?" The financial advisor is prone to going astray by guessing whether the client meant price or cost. These terms will make perfect sense in a moment, but before going further, bear in mind that households, businesses, and national governments argue and confuse such basic language just the same.

Price is the quantifiable amount paid for something. It is simple, it is scientific, it is indisputable, it is what it is. The United States of America paid X dollars to Russia for Y barrels of oil. The car buyer paid more for a Mercedes instead of getting a Honda. The child paid the work of three mowed lawns for one month of Xbox Live.

It is ordinary for the bystander to ask in any of these scenarios, "Well, how much did it cost?" The United States, the car buyer, or the child would be expected to reply in a certain amount of dollars paid or lawns mowed. But doing so is only sharing the price of consumption for the other party's production. Little Mikey, the local lawnmower, is ignoring the most important feature in economics—wealth. This is because the worth of money, time, or any other figure is not in its possession, but in its use. The miser in Aesop's fable loved to stare at his buried gold each day, but it was only until it was stolen that he realized staring at an empty hole was no different. The exchange of wealth has something to do with price, but it has everything to do with cost.

Cost is the value given up for something else of different value. Sadly, for those scientists hoping for a black-and-white outcome, cost is not so quantifiable. It is correct that the cost of Xbox Live was the price of three yards, but if 100 hours of Xbox Live translate to laughter and fun warring over Fortnite with friends, then what a small cost it was. The car buyer may have paid $100,000 for his Mercedes as opposed to $25,000 for a Honda, but while the price was high, a decade of luxurious riding and durability might equate to a great value in the mind of its owner. If the United States pays Russia $90 per barrel of oil for 27 million barrels in a year, the price easily translates to over $2 billion, but the cost of funding an adversarial relationship in geopolitics has many layers of complexity.

In the pursuit of wealth, price is a given, but uncovering cost is what counts. Finding the true cost is where you will find well-being, or a lack thereof. We all know the scene where the old man proudly stomps his boot on the ground and shouts, "This ain't for sale!" and the cocky buyer replies, "Just wait, everyone has their price." This exemplifies the disconnect between price and cost in dealmaking. Cost is only an objection in the absence of value; the rub is that value can only be fairly defined by the beholder. This perpetual compromise between the cost one is willing to pay and the value one is willing to give up exists at the core of every chapter ahead. If price were the only value needed to transact, humans would live in a linear world like robots plodding away from one task to the next. This book would be nothing more than a marketplace listing prices of goods sold in various currencies. But price only represents the symbols and letters that fit into the languages of cost. Cost, and the cost of wealth, makes up the gray space in economics that forever challenges the gray matter of humankind.

The relationship that exists between producers and consumers, both striving for well-being, is what guides a fascinating subject known as economic behavior. This subject comprises the psychological, emotional, financial, social, and cultural views of the transfer of wealth. The fact that each individual is unique and has free will means that there is room for harmonious collaboration; not every squirrel is chasing the same nut. But when one party's pursuit of wealth is not found or satisfied, conflict can arise.

MICE

Understanding someone who defines wealth differently, as if they speak a different language, is not easy, but it is necessary for progress. The Central Intelligence Agency (CIA) may be known for breeding the world's greatest spies, but their training could be taught in any economics course. Spies are taught to find and use the MICE (not to be confused with moles or any other spy/rodent jargon). This acronym stands for money (M), ideology (I), compromise (C), and ego (E). Understanding what these values mean to you, your friend, and your foe can help craft a plan to achieve wealth. If you're still thinking microeconomies exist only in your world, and that macroeconomies are some incomprehensible and unchangeable circumstances forced upon us, remember that at the core of each are merely human beings and their thoughts about money, ideology, compromise, and ego (MICE). Just like business planning for a company quickly spills over to personal planning for its owners, so too do the MICE within macroeconomics weave their way down into microeconomics.

Money (M) may not buy happiness, but some extra cash can make life easier. Money may not be all a government thinks about, but when has the world's most powerful nation not been the richest? Ideology (I) is what defines a person's own wealth. It is the set of beliefs that drives economic behavior. Compromise (C) is the natural collision of ideologies surrounding wealth, the peaceful method that allows two different economies to obtain what they want from each other. Every leader in history that has ignored compromise, also known as dictators, has failed. Finally, there is ego (E), the element of MICE that never seems to make sense, the need for pride that makes humans human. *Ego* is the Latin word for *I*. Once the cards are on the table, money, ideology, and compromise have led me to buy this house or to sign this international peace treaty, but then I don't. There is something uniquely me that was left unsatisfied, and only I can feel my pride rise and fall.

Does using MICE for financial gain infer some form of manipulation, a word that sounds nefarious? Not necessarily. Many people who fail at wealth accumulation do so because they become trapped in their own cognitive loop, believing what they want to be true. The appropriate use of MICE should reveal the distinction between perception and perspective, allowing the user to stop relying on preconceived perceptions and begin understanding the other side's perspectives. Seeing from other perspectives is the magic that not only empowers you to foresee changes, but to become the coveted agent of change.

On the surface, each of the nine economic topics that comprise this book appears to represent a zero-sum game, meaning a win for one side equals a loss for the other side. For instance, allocating more money toward public education means less money for unemployment assistance, or money saved for retirement is money lost for college planning. Fortunately, MICE can multiply. Enhancing each economic tool enhances the ones that follow it (more people can support more entitlements, which can support more education, which can support greater economies, etc.).

Within every exchange of wealth, personal values and expectations of risk and reward encourage economic agents ranging from kids on the playground up to Fortune 500 CEOs and world leaders to nudge. Why not try to get just a little more for a little less? Nudges among eight billion people trying to do better form the interplay of economics. Eight billion people always boil down to two sides of a deal. Anyone who has ever offered a bid and received an immediate acceptance has felt the sting of being on the losing side of a bargain. "How low would you have gone?" the buyer ponders. "How high would you have gone?" the seller responds. This fear of missing out makes the allure of a nudge impossible to resist. But often one side nudges for slightly better terms, more value at less cost, until suddenly the other side has had enough.

Eight billion people might sound inconceivable, but it is actually an underrepresentation of economics. Each person does not live on their own island, transferring wealth with one person at a time without interference. In reality, people belong to a family, to a neighborhood, to a school, to a town, to a state, to a company, to a nation, to a race, and to a religion. The web of economic decisions looks like eight billion lights shooting into a prism.

POPULATION

Population tells a story about Earth, a story about people, and the adventures of how they coexist. Earth is static, finite, empirically measurable. People are dynamic, expansive. A common thread in population's storyline is money. Where exactly does money come from? Money is born from one person and then given to another person, then to another, and another. Money, like people, is never, ever static. It is dynamic and expansive.

One would have thought that it was even more necessary to limit population than property. . . . The neglect of this subject, which in existing states is so common, is a never-failing cause of poverty among citizens, and poverty is the parent of both revolution and crime.

—**Aristotle (384–322 BC)**

They comb through countless data points with a cadre of space measurement tools—satellite laser ranging, global positioning systems, Doppler orbitography, and radio positioning integration, to name a few. Together they form the International Terrestrial Reference Frame. Their vocation is the science of geodesy.

Tectonic forces. Hurricanes. Earthquakes. Volcanos. Change. There must be change. Change that is expansion. What isn't growing is dying.

Enter Xiaoping Wu of NASA's Jet Propulsion Laboratory in Pasadena, California, and his friends from Institut Geographique National in France and Delft University of Technology in the Netherlands. They are gathered to independently validate the study of the International Terrestrial Reference Frame and shed light on the earth expansion/contraction theory.

The fascination with planet Earth's boundaries is certainly not new. In 200 BC, the size of Earth was actually calculated to within one percent accuracy! Eratosthenes, a Greek astronomer, used Aristotle's idea that, if Earth was round, distant stars in the night sky would appear at different positions to observers at different latitudes. At noon on the first day of summer, the sun passed directly overhead the ancient city of Syene, Egypt (now known as Aswan, very near to the Tropic of Cancer). At this time, one could look down into the city's well and the sun reflected only the water, not casting any shadows on the well walls as it did every other day. At midday of the same day, Eratosthenes measured the angular displacement of the sun overhead at the city of Alexandria. He found that the angular displacement was 7.2 degrees, or 1/50 of a circle. Thus, the circumference of Earth could be estimated by multiplying the distance between the two cities by a multiple of 50.

As for the findings of twenty-first-century rocket scientists? NASA concludes the average change in Earth's radius to be +0.004 inches per year, approximately the thickness of a human hair. "Our study provides an independent confirmation that the solid earth is not getting larger at present, within current measurement uncertainties," says Wu.[1]

So much for change. A planet reputedly 4.54 billion years old not doing a whole lot of growing or shrinking. Planet Earth's surface may not be expanding, but if NASA's satellites were to zoom in, they will notice the earthlings certainly are.

MACRO

The most basic question of the economic prosperity of mankind comes back to supply and demand. Are there too many demands on Earth and its people or not enough? Is there a large enough supply of Earth's resources and people, or too much? History tells a clear story of the opportunities and threats presented by the supply and demand of population.

Humans hold dominion over 196.9 million square miles, most of which is covered by salty water. Since the beginning of time, the world's population took thousands of years, possibly millions, to finally reach one billion people in the year 1800. One century later, in 1900, the population had expanded over 50 percent to 1.65 billion.

Then some form of magic grasped the twentieth century. By 1928, two billion humans inhabited Earth. In other words, what took millennia to occur (population of one billion) was duplicated in the next 128 years. By 1975, another 47 years, the world's population doubled again to four billion. At the time of this writing, 2022, it has happened once more, a global population of roughly eight billion economic agents vying for wealth.[2] There are possibly more people on Earth today than in every prior century combined. (See Figure 1.1.)

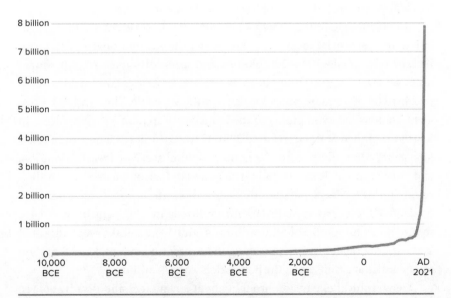

Figure 1.1   World population history (10,000 BCE to AD 2021)[3]

Certain mathematical trends have led to the exponential growth of mankind. According to the World Bank, the average international life expectancy in 1960 was 52 years old, in 2020 it was 73. During the same period, the infant mortality rate decreased from 6.45 percent to 2.70 percent.[4] Not only are there more earthly occupants, but durability is commensurate with multiplicity.

Old Borders

Where does everyone fit in as they pursue their MICE? Nations have some ability to cope with crowding, granted their efforts represent a redrawing of lines in a fixed container (Earth) of growing stimuli (people). This redistricting of the parameters in which economies belong are as dynamic as the people within them. To keep the history of maps in context, look back at the Treaty of Tordesillas. In 1494, Spain and Portugal, completely ignoring any indigenous peoples, split the New World in half. A north-south line was drawn through Brazil and everything to the west was Spain's, everything to the east was Portugal's. As the New World expanded west throughout all of South and North America, Spain was the lucky party in history's most lopsided arrangement. Of course, we all know that Spain does not single-handedly own the better part of the whole globe, far from it.

The United States of America provides the most recent study of population and territorial expansion. Following the Revolutionary War, Great Britain relinquished the 13 colonies and an additional 490,000 square miles westward in the Treaty of Paris in 1783. America's land mass covered roughly 865,000 square miles for its 3.9 million people. Then in 1803, President Thomas Jefferson brokered the Louisiana Purchase with Napoleon, in which the United States purchased 827,000 square miles of land from France for a paltry $15 million. After the Louisiana Purchase, Northwest Expansion, and annexation of Texas, in 1850 American land encompassed 2.94 million square miles for its population of 23.2 million. In its last great expansion, the United States purchased Alaska from Russia in 1867, acquiring 586,412 square miles for a total of $7.2 million.[5] Hawaii and Alaska were admitted as the last two states in 1959, bringing the American land total to 3.5 million square miles at a time when the population was 179 million.

Geographical expansion brought about advantages and disadvantages. Newfound territory revealed valuable natural resources and trade routes.

However, it also further separated economies and strained centers of control. Since 1959, America's land mass has remained relatively unchanged, while the population has climbed to over 330 million. Whether it was when there were few Americans or today when there are multitudes, the people of the United States have always been on the move.

Within the boundaries of nations, citizens will naturally follow the MICE; it is the sole reason for migration. Money, if not the first motivator, will eventually become so as a microeconomy realizes its necessity in order to consider ideology (I), compromise (C), or ego (E). In 1790, 90 percent of America's population lived on farms and ranches. Founders of the country enjoyed space, privacy, and land. Or so the modern city-dweller might assume. In old times distance was actually a detriment. Colonial Americans quickly realized the endless benefits of collaboration and the need for proximity. The result was urbanization, the movement of populations from rural areas to urban ones. Urbanization created more financial opportunity and the people followed. In 1810, there were only two cities with populations of more than 50,000, but by 1860 there were sixteen. Fast-forward to 1920, and for the first time in American history more people lived in cities than in rural areas.[6]

The trend gave rise to the industrial revolution and achievements that are still taught in social studies classes today. Names like Vanderbilt, Rockefeller, and Carnegie etched their place in history. When they asked, "What should I do with my money?" the answer always revolved around bringing people closer together. Railroads, skyscrapers, coal for trains, oil for cars. They wanted crowds, crowds that could come together faster and become bigger crowds. Economics demanded it, they supplied it. Cities became home to the wealthiest families not just in America, but in the world. However, these same cities created the greatest contrast in wealth disparity imaginable, a place in which the haves and have-nots brushed shoulders on busy sidewalks like ants on a molehill.

At the dawn of America, one of the main attractions of urban living was the exchange of information, a physical connection of producers and consumers. It could take days to relay sensitive information across a state, and weeks for it to travel coast to coast. History tells of battles being fought amid wars that had already ended and companies negotiating for the future that had already declared bankruptcy, all because of information lag. Cities cured this malady.

ECONOMIC INSIGHT

Innovation begins as a great risk in attempting to disrupt the norm, but with the potential for an enormous payoff. Visionaries from Don Pedro Menéndez de Avilés of Spain forming America's first city in 1565 in St. Augustine, Florida, to Henry Ford empowering travel, up to techies eliminating the need for travel altogether, all were able to lower the barriers of entry to finding wealth, in turn making them very wealthy.

For entrepreneurs and venture capitalists, the question is always which comes first, the chicken or the egg? Do you build it where they are going? Or if you build it, will they come? Was the world tired of slow, bumpy horse rides, unanimously yearning for Ford's new vehicle? Or did Ford create a product so revolutionary that people didn't even know what they really wanted until they hit the gas pedal? Producers spend fortunes predicting the future, studying consumer behavior, population trends, generational interests, and migration. Their goal is to mitigate risk by investing in products and services with a guaranteed customer base. This common exercise inherent in mature Fortune 500 companies is low risk/low reward, deploying resources to keep up with the pack. One could argue the icons of business ignore trends entirely, with what at first appears a foolish confidence to pursue the unthinkable, only later to be either forgotten or memorialized in history.

Stop and think, how many people lived in the wetlands of Orlando, Florida, let alone discussed its economics, before a man named Walt Disney decided to literally drain the swamp and cover it in steel and concrete? Just because an economy's demand isn't initially recognized does not mean it doesn't exist; sometimes it takes a pioneer to shine a light on it. The mature company can still achieve breakthroughs by incentivizing small divisions to take calculated risks, cultivating microeconomies hoping to make a name within the macroeconomy.

Knocking Down Borders

Nowadays, 5G and a good Wi-Fi signal have become as important as roads and bridges. Virtual pathways have knocked down borders between here and there. The explosion of remote working and learning during the Covid-19 pandemic amplified the opposite effect of urbanization; it is called ruralization. The locality factor in money (M) was largely negated as people looked further toward ICE. From 2010–2019, 60 percent of all metro areas experienced more growth in suburbs than in cities.[7] Home values soared during the pandemic, while commercial properties plummeted as people chose where to live and where not to work.

While global population growth is 100 percent organic (we've yet to import any aliens), national population growth can be part organic and part extraneous through immigration. Population dynamics within the United States are now attributed more to relocation than intrinsic growth. According to the 2021 US Census Bureau, of the 10 fastest-growing cities in the United States, 5 of them are in Texas. The majority of this growth is due to migration. Some of the major reasons credited for the influx are low crime rates, high-income opportunities, and top-ranked public education (people chasing MICE). If "the chicken or the egg" were framed as the business or the people, it has become clear the people are now coming first.

A good barometer of current and future growth is new residential construction. The top five cities spending the most on new residential construction are Austin, Texas; Nashville, Tennessee; Raleigh, North Carolina; Jacksonville, Florida; and Phoenix, Arizona, respectively.[8] By state, the list goes Idaho, Utah, Colorado, South Carolina, and Florida, respectively. It should come as no surprise that corporate relocations neatly coincide with migration trends, with Austin, Nashville, and Denver all being hotspots for corporate expansion. Companies share similar wants of financial incentives, travel convenience, and wide pools of talent.

One of Yogi Berra's classic lines goes, "Nobody goes there anymore. It's too crowded." Any restaurant, hotel, or other venue would love to face such a predicament. When an investor, developer, or government undertakes any project seeking a return, which is every project, they are focused on population.

Yes, they will obviously consider benefits of a certain locale (near the water, warm climate, efficient public transportation, business-friendly environment, etc.), but these are all just lures for more people. So as the stock market is considered a leading economic indicator, meaning the market's value is already reflecting anticipated events good and bad in the economy, so might population migration be a projection of an area's future worth. As was mentioned earlier, the concept of "If you build it, they will come," is one of speculation, high risk/high reward, versus the conservative approach of analyzing migration trends before jumping in.

The Roles of People

Whether it was when one billion people roamed Earth or today's eight billion, humans will always fulfill two roles simultaneously—"renters" and "users." No one claims immortality; therefore, everyone is renting some plot of dirt. As users, men and women are all using the resources Earth has provided to find sustenance and prosperity by any means necessary, through collaboration or domination.

While all humans qualify as renters and users of the Blue Planet, there exist subsets of "givers" and "takers." These terms are asynchronous. No one spends a lifetime being either, but rather wear both hats throughout the phases of life. Givers produce and takers reduce. Every economy across the globe must adjust its markets, services, governments, and inflows and outflows to accommodate these two opposing forces. Their existence is the foundation of each chapter to come.

Chapter 2, Entitlements, will show how government-provided benefits exist entirely for takers and are made possible by givers. But even this is not so binary. Florida, and its many seniors, may be identified as a population of takers of Social Security and Medicare, but their vast retirement incomes are a valuable source of giving to the state's economy. Chapter 3, Education, will illustrate the incubator in which takers are transformed into givers. Then Chapter 4, Economic Philosophy, will explore how the human finger presses upon each side of the scale of givers and takers. And so each chapter that follows shall address these stations of life intimately in a changing population.

It's fair to ask why all people can't simply operate at 100 percent productivity, as machinelike givers, but the world is not a fixed laboratory. Workers in their prime, feeling like they are literally giving their all each day, might think so, but not only is 100 percent productivity impossible, its appearance is temporary. A newborn is not a giver to the economy, nor can someone who

is disabled or elderly be asked to carry an unfair burden. Even after such realization, the monkey wrench in economic forecasting deals with assumption,
particularly in assuming that the healthy and capable individual must automatically be a giver. The identity of giver or taker is often left to choice. Just
because I can run does not mean I have to run. An imbalance of too many
takers and not enough givers, high demand and low supply, is what erodes
surplus and breeds deficiency.

It is better to see these two segments of society not as opposition, but as
natural realities. History proves collaboration is the only sustainable method
of progress, and it is necessary to the reality that takers must be allowed. The
rest of the book will show how people who collaborate to serve each other as
well as those on the other side of the fence are rewarded in more ways than
one. Groups, whether countries, religions, races, generations, or kingdoms,
need each other. Wealth needs both a home and a destination.

The ultimate benefit of collaboration is the forming of a macroeconomy.
There is no "chicken or egg" conundrum here; microeconomies always come
first. Some microeconomies stay that way forever, without any parent organization to ask for help. Others come together unintentionally, by virtue of
geography or some coincidence, or through force. Just as a young professional
looks to network and build human capital, so does a nation grow by adding
and connecting more people. A business needs more customers, a leader more
followers, a rock star more fans, and an economy more people.

The beauty of collaboration and expansion is that its benefits are exponential. More team members means more specialization. More specialization
means more experts. More experts means more advancement. More advancement means more efficiency and productivity. It's amazing how great a
pitcher can throw when he has a designated hitter to do the batting.

Bigger is better. Size creates economies of scale and leverage that a stand-
alone microeconomy can never enjoy. Show me the least populated city, the
smallest country, or a fledgling business, and I'll show you their mayor, president, or CEO wishing to become bigger and better. This may not always seem
true as some places can feel overcrowded, but within the right macroeconomy, such discomfort is only a temporary environment waiting to naturally
adjust. Growing population leads to excess success, which then allows givers
to embrace more takers.

The simultaneous rise in standards of living and global population support the "bigger is better" mantra. The innovations previously mentioned and

soon to be elaborated upon were not a simple result of the passage of time, but the collaboration of more people. It's nice to drink a glass of milk without having to milk the cow.

But is there a tipping point to global population? A time when the demands of humanity permanently outweigh the available supply. Is it 10 billion people, 15 billion, or maybe 20 billion? This is as important for world leaders to know as a pizzeria prepping for a busy Friday night; some advance notice for looming crowds can help economies prepare for stressors before they arrive. If such a tipping point does exist, what will it look like? More important for you and me, what will the course leading up to that tipping point look like? Perhaps humans will hover to and from housing projects elevated to the second story of the atmosphere, using a maps app on their phone to take into account vertical positioning on top of horizontal travel. Or as Lewis and Clark moved west, modern-day pioneers like Elon Musk and Jeff Bezos will put men and women on Mars. The answers to these hypothetical questions are what make yesterday's sci-fi today's reality and hint at what you should do with your money.

Population may already be imposing its own subliminal reaction. While it is true that people are living longer than ever, a counterbalance is present. Throughout the 1960s, women averaged roughly 5 births worldwide, whereas in 2020 women averaged 2.4 births in their lifetime. In America, the Centers for Disease Control and Prevention (CDC) reported an even more alarming figure of US women currently having 1.71 children in their lifetime, below the 2.1 figure considered for perfect population replacement.[9] How many millennials do you know who are one of seven children? The current global fertility decline could be a speed bump in the train of expansive progress or a success story preempting the troubles of overpopulation. The outcomes likely will not be witnessed by anyone walking today's Earth.

The next chapter will introduce the financial structure that previous generations of Americans designed based on *their* needs as givers and takers—entitlements. But as baby boomers transfer from being givers to takers, they will test the durability of healthcare and every other entitlement. The exploding use of nursing homes is already inferring an overwhelming strain. In 2020, private equity investments in nursing homes exceeded $1.5 billion.[10] For many homes, these buyouts were the only way to avoid going under, but ushered in new management focused more on investor performance than quality of care. Now, 11 percent of US nursing homes and 4 percent of hospitals are owned by private equity firms.[11]

The goal of balancing givers versus takers is omnipresent. Households, teams, businesses, states, and nations all face the challenge of providing for today while preparing for tomorrow. There will always be someone asking for something, and society needs to be able to reasonably answer that call. Buyers and sellers. Demanders and suppliers. Assets and liabilities. Givers and takers. The scales will never be perfectly balanced, but if progress means staying ahead, it implies a tilt toward giving. So long as an economy has more giving than taking, it will continue to move forward.

Maybe a crowded planet is much ado about nothing. After millennia of expansion, the world will now begin cycles of birthing booms and busts returning all disparities to homeostasis. It is a nice thought, but Figure 1.2, which shows population figures jumping from three billion to eight billion people in less than an average lifetime since the invention of color TV, contradicts the prediction.

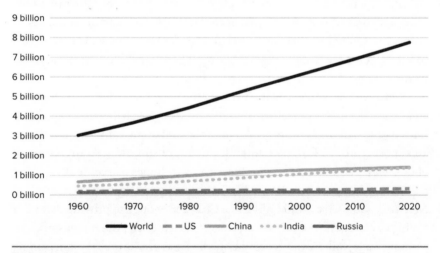

Figure 1.2   Population growth in major countries since 1960[12]

MICRO

24.9517° N, 67.0023° E: Little children run to and fro, zigzagging the dusty dirt road. Every few moments they lean against one of many dilapidated cardboard and aluminum structures, searching for a break from the relentless heat. Their faces glisten below matted black hair. It has not rained in over a month.

They must mind their step, for splashing through one of the soak pits is not only gross, but sure to bring a scolding from their mother. These pits are porous chambers out back in which human waste soaks into the ground. The boys and girls are accustomed to the foul odor, but Mother knows this is where mosquitos with malaria and dengue fever thrive.

This is a microeconomy that has grown. It is now bigger. It is not better. Orangi Town is the most crowded slum in the world. It is loosely governed by the macroeconomy of Karachi, Pakistan. Orangi spans about 8,000 acres (less than 1/25 of New York City) and is home to over 2.4 million people (same as Austin, Texas). There was a time not long ago when this maritime desert was abandoned.

Sewage is the most notable problem, which leads to the already scarce resource of water often being contaminated. Forty percent of the deaths in Pakistan stem from poor water quality. Housing is another dilemma only growing worse. It is expected that each two-bedroom apartment houses 10 occupants. Orangi has become a breeding ground for gang violence and turf conflicts. For three straight years, 77 percent of women in Orangi Town were victims of rape.[13]

Some residents stay, vowing to "help thy neighbor." They band together and undertake do-it-yourself projects, the most coveted being makeshift pipelines to alleviate the sewage problem. Others, like the minority Hindus in an almost entirely Muslim country, try to migrate to India. Many dream of obtaining a visa and moving to America, with hopes of eventually getting a green card or possibly citizenship. These lucky few reconnect in cities in New York, New Jersey, and California. Crowded enough to provide a familiar feeling of closeness, but not too crowded. The American dream tells of clean running water, toilets, and grocery stores being as ordinary as the sun coming up each morning.

Overcrowding

Overcrowding is an easy scapegoat for any problem of overdemand and undersupply. But is Orangi plagued with difficulties because so many people inhabit such a small space? If these people could spread out a bit more, would their problems be solved? Possibly rape, crime, gang violence, and poverty would somehow decline. Crowding was the universal goal that all the cities of America were founded on. Bring people together. Orangi illustrates the polarizing effect of population on the other side of town. Yes, population is what once launched New York City into becoming the financial capital of the world, but population is a two-sided coin that accelerates progress and destruction with equal potential.

A Manmade Detour in Population

Over 50 years ago, the threats of overpopulation caught the world's attention. Dr. Paul Ralph Elrich was a well-respected scientist, an entomologist specializing in the study of butterflies, to be exact. He taught as a professor at Stanford in the 1960s and later served as the president of Stanford's Center for Conservation Biology. What Dr. Elrich is best known for is not butterflies or his "arms race" between plants and insects, but rather a harrowing outlook on humanity. He sparked the controversial debate in 1968 with the release of his book, *The Population Bomb*, and its graphic descriptions of the possibly dire outcomes of an unchecked population. Around this time, many countries formally sounded the alarm.

In Egypt, Tunisia, Pakistan, South Korea, and Taiwan, health workers' salaries were tied to the number of intrauterine devices (IUDs) they inserted into women. In the Philippines, birth-control pills were literally thrown from helicopters over remote villages. Reports of millions of people being sterilized, sometimes illegally and coercively, came out of Mexico, Bolivia, Peru, Indonesia, and Bangladesh.

In the 1970s and 1980s, India, led by Prime Minister Indira Gandhi (the country's only female prime minister) and her son, Sanjay, enacted policies that required sterilization for men and women in order to obtain water, electricity, ration cards, medical care, and pay raises. Over eight million men and women were sterilized in 1975 alone. Robert McNamara, then head of the World Bank, said, "At long last, India is moving to effectively address its population problem."[14]

The most notable effort to control population growth in the modern era would be in 1980, when the Chinese Communist Party implemented the one-child policy. It would take a conspiracy theorist to propose if America's Supreme Court was considering population dynamics when it ruled in favor of protecting a woman's right to choose abortion in *Roe v. Wade* in 1973 and then overturned it in 2022, but like China's policy, it carried obvious population consequences.

How big a role national decrees have played in the worldwide decline in fertility is debatable and speculative. But the statistics are clear that the world is reacting to a crowded planet, whether consciously or not. (See Figure 1.3.) This is not the first time Earth has attempted to curb its population. The Bible shares several stories of resetting, whether it be the account of Noah in the book of Genesis, the plagues in the book of Exodus, or apocalyptic prophesies. Other religions and philosophies share similar parables of taking a pause when the planet becomes overwhelmed.

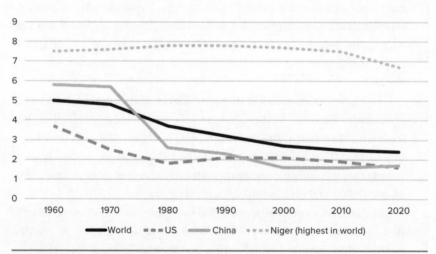

Figure 1.3   Fertility rate[15]

Stories about a place like Orangi might seem like way over "there," while we're right "here," but one must not forget how small the world really is. It's a common error to think of microeconomies as "me," "I," or "mine," and macroeconomies simply as what are not "me," "I," or "mine." Every macroeconomy is a collection of microeconomies, a collection of us and our lives. It is never way over there; it always ends up right here.

The most appalling statistics about Orangi are its prevalence of violent crime. For someone unfamiliar with the Middle East, an initial glimpse of Orangi might suggest its country of Pakistan to be third-worldly. However, painting with such a broad brush would ignore cities like Islamabad and Karachi with their megadevelopments, manufacturing hubs, and affluent tourist destinations. Similarly, the richest country in the world, the United States, still has cities like Detroit, Michigan; Memphis, Tennessee; Birmingham, Alabama; Baltimore, Maryland; and St. Louis, Missouri, the top five most dangerous cities in America, respectively.[16] While all five are urban areas, the largest, Detroit, is only the 27th most crowded city in America. This denotes that while overpopulation can be a detriment in an ill-prepared environment like Orangi, it by itself is not negative, as evidenced by the 26 larger, more peaceful cities than Detroit.

There are two obvious hypotheses to draw from population. One, bigger is better, but only within a developed economy. Two, bigger is worse within an emerging economy void of resources and proper social framework.

ECONOMIC INSIGHT

If birthing booms and busts don't efficiently manage population by itself, the Lone Star State provides an encouraging observation. Texas spans over 268,597 square miles of land, almost 7.5 trillion square feet. Earth's population is roughly eight billion people, meaning every individual on Earth could have approximately 938 square feet of living space if they lived in Texas, while leaving the rest of planet Earth vacant. For comparison's sake, there is about 531 square feet per person in New York City.[17] The wide-open plains of Texas prove that overpopulation does not create problems of space, per se, but rather problems of livability, zoning, environment, and the availability and usability of resources (these will come into focus in Chapter 5, Environment).

WHAT SHOULD I DO WITH MY MONEY?

Back to that question—why? Why do this or that with your money? If we were to play the old game from childhood, "I Spy with My Little Eye," we would start with a hint—person, place, or thing. At the end of the day, that is all an investor can invest in—people, places, or things. An investment, be it of any sort—stock, bond, real estate, and so on—is an allocation of money into an asset, with the hope of eventual appreciation and positive return. The determinant in an investment's success or failure is people. The outcome is completely dictated by people's expectations and realizations. People will look at prices, think about costs, ascribe a value, and then decide to buy or sell. People and their opinions on money, ideology, compromise, and ego are why this chapter is perhaps the least pragmatic, but the most relevant conversation in economics.

Rising and declining population figures are not good or bad in and of themselves. There is no fault in choosing to have two babies instead of three, or in a young generation someday growing old. Birth and aging are natural courses to embrace or contend with. Economic metrics such as the stock market or gross domestic product (GDP, the value of all goods and services generated by a country) have been enormous beneficiaries of population growth. When there are more people with more things to build, buy, and sell, GDP naturally rises. But when there are too many people wanting the same few things, inflation appears, causing everything to cost more than we can afford. If unchecked, this can morph into an even worse symptom of stagflation, high inflation combined with high unemployment.

If overpopulation, or rather imbalanced population, is preordained, does mankind have the power to fix population's woes? There may be a time when there are just too many people sucking the earth dry, or there might be a time when there are not enough people to work the land (more on this in Chapter 5, Environment), but until then, it's best to be an actor rather than a reactor. Prolonging Earth's resources and making life better for all comes back to finding equilibrium between givers and takers.

What They Should Do with Their Money

Consider what "they"—governments and politicians—do with their money to affect supply and demand. Supply-side economics, as the name implies, looks to control the supply chain to stimulate growth. From a financial standpoint, this theory includes tax cuts and decreased regulation to foster liquidity and business expansion. Someone concerned about the lack of population replacement and the issues around funding entitlement programs (Chapter 2, Entitlements) would look for ways to increase the supply of society's givers. Some ideas to address a shortage of human capital might include allocating resources toward childhood development and education, expanding immigration, and cultivating an economy conducive to large families. In essence, spur the supply of population and future workers.

Conversely, demand-side economics believes that increased demand equals increased growth since workers will be readily employed to fulfill such needs, and when supply is inadequate, reduce the demand. In an inflationary environment, the Federal Reserve can raise interest rates, in turn shrinking the money supply and lowering demand for goods and services (more on this in Chapter 4, Economic Philosophy.) A demand-side economist looking at population would study the demands of takers and investigate methods to increase or reduce their time in this phase in the context of how much givers can provide.

America, like any other democratic country, does have some control over its balance of givers and takers. It can ask its population to work sooner, longer, and harder to overcome any deficits. Accumulating and decumulating assets are the crux of Chapter 2, Entitlements, and something every worker thinking about retirement needs to recognize.

The United States is also fortunate to not have to depend solely on internal growth to generate givers. America is, at its core, a country of immigrants. An increase in immigration, particularly young immigrants, can be a much-needed enhancement to national productivity. In the 1930s, many of Germany's best scientists fled the Nazi regime and ended up in America (see Chapter 7, War). Albert Einstein was one of these refugees, landing at Princeton, by way of England. After World War II, it was the geniuses of eastern Europe and the Soviet Union who fled communism in search of the American dream. From 1943 to 1969, the United States won the Nobel Prize in physics an astounding 21 times; 11 of these winners were European refugees. Freedom is perhaps the greatest attractor of talented givers.

According to the United Nations report on International Migration, the world's 272 million immigrants reside in only 10 countries. (See Figure 1.4.) America is home to one-fifth of these immigrants, making it by far the most coveted destination on Earth. In 1970 there were 9.6 million immigrants in the United States, representing 4.7 percent of the population. As of 2022, there are an estimated 51 million immigrants, representing 15.5 percent of the population, the highest it has been since the turn of the twentieth century. In the twenty-first century, Mexicans and Asians each make up about a quarter of the population's immigrants. In every year since 2009, more Asian immigrants have arrived in the United States than Mexicans.[18]

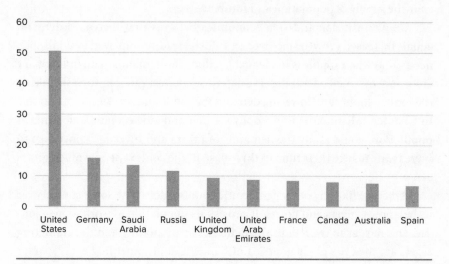

Figure 1.4   Top 10 countries with the most immigrants (millions)[19]

Back to What I Should Do

The first way to answer the magic question, "What should I do with my money?" is to find a place that offers you MICE, a place with good jobs or neighborhoods to raise the kids in. There are two types of residential real estate owners—homeowners and investors. Homeowners may be willing to pay what an investor could consider an irrational cost, as a homeowner's focus is more on ICE—job opportunities, closeness to family, school rankings, and personal preferences such as climate and lifestyle. Whereas an investor solely seeking financial gain, money (M), has a more limited view on the worth of property, fixating more on price than cost. Either way, homeowners and investors share parallel paths, as the end consumer is always a human looking for somewhere comfortable to live.

The most direct correlation in property values is the connection to population growth. Generally speaking, higher population growth equals higher home values, a classic illustration of supply and demand. A real estate investor who foresaw the California to Texas or Northeast to Florida pipelines and purchased in any of the cities referenced earlier a few years before they made the list has clearly been rewarded with a profit. The latest migration trends would suggest that a good financial indicator would be investing in young, liberal cities inside conservative states, such as Austin, Texas, or Nashville, Tennessee. From an international standpoint, capitalist economies in emerging markets have largely outperformed. Again, these tips communicate price via mathematical trends on paper, but tell little about the costs of moving a family or business here or there.

Last, successful people and businesses, both domestically and internationally, have always sought out low-tax environments with strong property rights. Governor Ricardo Rosselló of Puerto Rico signed the Incentives Act in 2019, which has successfully lured many wealthy Americans and businesses to relocate and drastically reduce their tax burden.

While it is true that God is not making any more land, migration can strip away value as quickly as it can add. One tropical storm might not scare away throngs of people dreaming of a beachfront property, but a few rough hurricane seasons might reframe the dream. The same could be said for retirees seeking "pension-friendly" states with little or no income tax who then meet a new governor that wants to change the rules. One can see how the price paid for a home is what it is, but the costs of ownership are varying and variable.

Most of the attention to real estate investing focuses on the demand side and predicting where people want to be. But the supply end of the equation is usually where things can go south, no pun intended. Real estate developers who bite off more than they can chew, such as those in Florida or Arizona leading up to 2008, can be left holding vacant, worthless properties when the economy makes other forms of wealth a priority.

When asking what you should do with your money, see what "they" did with theirs. They, being the government, installed entitlement programs based on healthcare and longevity. So plan to live a long time, longer than any of your ancestors. They, being Carnegie and Rockefeller, invested in everyday conveniences that the masses wanted, cities and rails connecting those cities. Look at what everyone wants but doesn't quite have. They, being the founders, built a framework based on freedom and property rights. Look for countries, states, and municipalities to invest, work, or live in with a structure that favors you and your microeconomy.

The twenty-first century is the by-product of extreme population growth. Relatively speaking, it's the best time to be alive. The autonomy and leverage afforded to each of us by this most advanced and high-tech era has deleted the prerequisites of time and place, allowing us to work and play when and where we want. Stop thinking eight billion people means too much competition, and start thinking about how to handle all the opportunity.

ENTITLEMENTS

Entitlements are a story about the philosophy of care. Each person feels entitled to some standard of living, to some basic security. Inalienable rights. It is the pride of every economy, "Live here and you'll never be cast astray." Where do entitlements come from? Per the eternal storyline of money, they are born from one person and then given to another person, then to another, and another. Since no on entitles themselves, learning what they do with their money often spells the answer to what you should do with your money.

You cannot help men permanently by doing for them what they could and should do for themselves.

—President Abraham Lincoln

O ctober 24, 1929—almost 13 million shares of stock are sold as investors wake up to the reality of overvaluation. The day of reckoning is called "Black Thursday." Five days later, on "Black Tuesday," the rest of the investment world follows suit and sells over 16 million shares. Companies go bankrupt overnight. Anyone who has ever put a dollar in the bank goes running to claim their cash, only to find the banks don't have it on hand. Bank runs sweep the country. The US Treasury tries to make emergency governmental loans to banks to keep them afloat, only to realize it no longer has enough money to pay its own government workers.

America is rocked by the Great Depression. By 1933, roughly 15 percent of America is completely broke, including over 18 million people who are either elderly, disabled, or a single mother. One out of four working Americans have lost their job.[1] The idea of a safety net does not even exist.

March 4, 1933—enter President Franklin D. Roosevelt. Within his first 100 days in office, FDR introduces the New Deal, a road to recovery. Fifteen major pieces of legislation aim to reestablish employment and financial security. Emergency assistance to climb out of the hole, and reforms to never ever go back in it. He takes action to provide immediate economic relief to the "forgotten man" and reorganize every major industry, all through vastly increasing the federal government's activities. The American people receive a panacea—hope. Rich or poor, white or Black, man or woman, help is on the way.

"The impact of all these forces [unemployment, bank failures, collapse of real estate and stock values] increasingly convinced the majority of the American people that individuals could not by themselves provide adequately for their old age, and that some form of greater security should be provided by society," writes Senator Paul Douglas of Illinois in 1936. However, at the time, government is struggling to survive itself, long past being able to assist the people.

FDR can sense the public morale coming back to life amid the New Deal, bolstering his administration, but wisely he takes pause; his ultimate responsibility belongs to the future. He worries what costs saving the present might lay upon tomorrow. "The lessons of history, confirmed by the evidence immediately before me, show conclusively that continued dependence upon relief induces a spiritual and moral disintegration fundamentally destructive to the national fiber," the president proclaims in his 1935 Annual Message to

Congress. "To dole out relief in this way is to administer a narcotic, a subtle destroyer of the human spirit."

ECONOMIC INSIGHT

The Great Depression is remembered as a time when all of America felt the pangs of poverty. While this is mostly true and the stock market, which was a haven for the country's richest, did lose almost 90 percent of its value from 1929 to 1932, not everyone suffered.

Walter Chrysler, head of Chrysler Corporation, wasted no time in leapfrogging the competition. He tasked his executives with devising drastic cost-cutting measures or face being laid off and focused resources toward his cheaper vehicles in the Plymouth brand. As a result, Chrysler overtook Ford as its market share rose from 9 percent in 1929 to 24 percent in 1933. He also positioned Chrysler perfectly for exiting the Depression by asking engineers to view the New Deal's national highway-expansion program, a project of FDR's Public Works Administration and Works Progress Administration, as an opportunity. Engineers responded by using wind tunnel testing to develop Chrysler's "Airflow" design. The aerodynamic approach to auto design ushered in more-fuel-efficient cars ready to travel beyond city limits at higher speeds.

Meanwhile, Joseph Kennedy Sr., patriarch of the Kennedy family, sold stocks prior to the crash, shorted stocks during it (betting share prices would fall), and signed contracts to become America's sole importer of Scotch whiskey and gin from Europe's largest distillers at the last moments of Prohibition. Others turned lemons into lemonade, such as J. Paul Getty buying up any cheap oil company he could find, Mae West seizing a chance to go from burlesque shows to Hollywood stardom, and Michael Kullin leaving Kroger Grocery with an idea to offer inexpensive goods and large inventory in the form of a "supermarket."[2]

MACRO

How ironic it is that money cannot buy happiness, but it can cause a great depression. The late 1920s and early 1930s underscored the harsh truth in studying MICE, that money (M) can blot out the rest of what makes an individual an individual. Worshipping an ideology, compromising with a neighbor, and fulfilling the passions of ego are all sidelined when we can't afford to put food on the table.

The most influential social programs in America today, which touch the financial plan of every household and business, stem from the Great Depression era. To be precise, the majority of these developments were born out of FDR's advisory group, known as the Brain Trust. In 1932, three very progressive professors from Columbia University guided the president-elect with the framework for FDR's New Deal, and a new enormous government.[3]

While economic survival dominated the country's mindset, FDR still found opportunity to fit in social reform. His forward-thinking administration quietly established a "Black Cabinet," led by Mary McLeod Bethune. Its purpose was to ensure that every New Deal agency had a Black advisor. The number of African American government workers instantly tripled.

The greatest of these initiatives was passed by Congress on August 14, 1935—the Social Security Act. Similar to its purpose today, the act aimed to address unemployment, disabilities, and retirement pensions. Old-Age, Survivors, and Disability Insurance (OASDI) as it's known entwined itself into the fabric of America. What many considered to be a temporary rescue package in a time of crisis, meant to relieve poor, older citizens no longer able to work and without kids around to care for them, became a new and permanent framework for American society. It is called welfare.

Before delving further into the history of America's entitlements, it is important to firmly understand what exactly an entitlement is. While the layperson might consider an entitlement to be any privilege one has a right to or is inherently deserving of, the Congressional Budget Office (CBO) defines it more technically. According to the CBO an entitlement is "a legal obligation of the federal government to make payments to a person, group of people, business, unit of government, or similar entity that meets the eligibility criteria set in law and for which the budget authority is not provided in advance in an appropriation act. Spending for entitlement programs is controlled through those programs' eligibility criteria and benefit or payment rules. The best-known entitlements are the government's major benefit programs, such as Social Security and Medicare."[4]

Conversely, welfare typically refers to a range of government programs that provide financial or other aid to individuals who cannot support themselves. As we'll see, Social Security and Medicare may have begun with the general intent of providing welfare, assisting older adults with inadequate income, but morphed into an entitlement not always connected to being needy. While the definitions are continually debated, one might assume that all welfare are entitlements, but not all entitlements are welfare.

The following breakdown of American entitlements is necessary to any financial plan as each program is for your benefit but also is your responsibility. They are 100 percent funded by your hard-earned dollars, you being the microeconomies of the United States and all of its parts, any person who has spent time being a taxpayer, a giver.

Social Security

At Social Security's inception, American employees and employers each paid into the system 1 percent of a worker's first $3,000 of wages. After almost three years of funding, the program got to work. As the Great Depression faded into the background, Social Security retirement benefits solidified the first federal government program not dependent on need, meaning whether poor or affluent, benefits would still be provided. While a concrete formula tying benefits to contributions did not exist, nor does it nearly a century later, FDR was wise enough to make every American emotionally vested in the program, labeling it an entitlement, not a charity.

Describing Social Security's political shield of having every worker's skin in the game, Roosevelt bragged, "We put those payroll contributions there so as to give the contributors a legal, moral, and political right to collect their pensions and their unemployment benefits. With those taxes [Social Security portion of income tax withholdings] in there, no damn politician can ever scrap my social security program. Those taxes aren't a matter of economics, they're straight politics."[5]

On January 31, 1940, Ida Fuller received the first Social Security check for $22.54 at the age of 65. She paid $24.75 into the system between 1937 and 1939 based on her total income of $2,484 in those few years. Ida went on to live to be 100 years old. She collected $22,889 from Social Security before her death in 1975, or 924 times what she contributed to the system.

Despite this ominous warning, Social Security initially appeared to be mathematically sustainable. In 1945, there were 41.9 tax-paying workers to every 1 Social Security beneficiary. Just 8 percent of the American population was over the age of 65, the normal retirement age (NRA) to collect benefits. The average life expectancy for men was 64 and for women, 68. America welcomed the growing program and its ability to help niche cases.

On the other end of the spectrum, the Fair Labor Standards Act in 1938 said that persons under 18 years old could no longer work in mining or manufacturing, but those older than 14 could work in any situations deemed not to be "oppressive." The need for this act illustrates just how many young people were seeking any work possible. In 1945, 52.1 percent of children dropped out of high school to pursue full-time work. In summary, there were a lot of people working for a long period of time to help a few people for a short period of time. It fit the population and the population fit it.

Fast-forward roughly 80 years, about one lifetime, and what was once an idea in a time of despair has become America's second-largest budget item, costing over $1 trillion annually. Over 64 million Americans are Social Security beneficiaries; that's more than half the entire population when the program began. The average retirement benefit in 2022 is $19,512 annually.[6, 7]

According to the Organization for Economic Co-Operation and Development, America's Social Security program is actually smaller than most other developed nations, in respect to replacement of career earnings. Social Security replaces close to 40 percent of wages, whereas the international average is 49 percent, and almost 80 percent in Italy.[8] (See Figure 2.1.)

Despite FDR's words of caution, Social Security has long passed the realm of niche assistance and morphed into what he could consider a "narcotic." The Center on Budget and Policy Priorities cites that 38 percent of seniors would live in poverty without Social Security. Nine out of ten Americans over the age of 65 receive benefits, accounting for the bulk of America's active beneficiaries. For half of America's older adults, it provides over half of their income.[9] Retirees expect their Social Security payment.

Can FDR's baby survive? The pessimist will point to the Social Security Administration's own admittance that trust funds, totaling $2.9 trillion in 2021, will be exhausted by 2033 if nothing changes. By the time this book sits on shelves, Social Security will dish out more benefits than it takes in. This imbalance occurred for the first time in 2021 and is projected to worsen every year moving forward. It is the unraveling of an evolving equation; as in 2022, there are only 2.8 taxpaying workers per beneficiary.

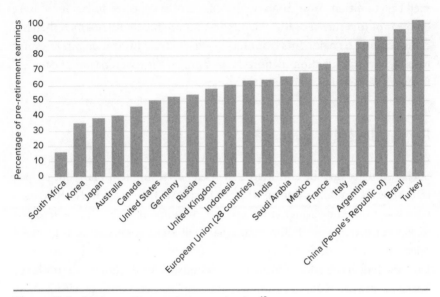

Figure 2.1   Net pension replacement rates[10]

But the optimist will note that the long-term gap between funds and benefits amounts to just 1 percent of annual gross domestic product (GDP) over the next 75 years. Not to mention if Congress opts to push forward without any changes to taxes or benefits, taxable income should cover 76 percent of projected benefits in each year after the trust funds are exhausted.[11]

While Social Security is most synonymous with retirement, it is not only for seniors. Of the nearly 65 million Social Security beneficiaries, 10 million of those are on disability. Fortunately, there has been a steady decline of Social Security Disability Insurance (SSDI) applications since 2010. These more favorable facts lead to projections of the Social Security Disability Insurance Trust Fund not being depleted until 2057.

Whereas Social Security provides citizens with confidence in collecting retiree benefits at a specified age (NRA), the definition of *disability* gives Social Security the leverage. In order to qualify for disability benefits, the beneficiary must be totally disabled; Social Security does not cover partial or short-term disabilities. This definition means the claimant must satisfy all of these three conditions: "You cannot do work that you did before because of your medical condition. You cannot adjust to other work because of your medical condition. Your disability has lasted or is expected to last for at least one year or to result in death."[12] If all three requirements are not met, then the claim will not be paid. This is similar to what private insurance carriers refer to as an "Any Occupation" definition, meaning if the covered worker can perform any occupation, they will not be paid.

Defined Benefit Pension Plans

Social Security may be considered the people's retirement plan, but corporate America actually came up with the idea first. The first private retirement plan was formed by American Express Company in 1875.[13] It was referred to as a defined benefit (DB) pension plan. DB plans are meant to continue a portion of the worker's salary into their retirement, indefinitely. Five years later, the Baltimore and Ohio Railroad established a DB plan more similar to Social Security in that both employer and employee contributions funded the plan. There is one stark difference in comparison to Social Security: corporate America does not have an Uncle Sam ready to bail out any shortfalls.

Private pension plans exploded onto the scene in 1950 with the signing of the Treaty of Detroit. Walter Reuther, president of the United Auto Workers (UAW) union, secured a deal with General Motors, and Ford and Chrysler shortly thereafter, which required fully funded pension plans set to the pensioner's life expectancy. Furthermore, these plans were to be noncontributory; employees would have no skin in the game as the funding would be fully borne by the company.[14]

In 1988, 236 companies in the Fortune 500 offered DB pension plans. Members of the Silent Generation, those born between 1928 and 1945, walked away from work with the assurance of both Social Security payments and DB pension income. They were arguably the first retirees to look forward to a long life without fear of running out of money. Now, only 13 of the Fortune 500 companies offer DB plans. In the early 1980s, roughly 60 percent of workers retired with a DB pension as their only form of retirement savings. Today, only 4 percent of retirees are relying on DB income alone. The majority of surviving

DB pensions in the private sector are negotiated by unions. These existing plans are under the normal pressures of financing lengthy and lofty guaranteed incomes, while their parent companies compete against globalization and nonunion competitors that drive innovation with lower labor costs.

Around the same time the private sector began implementing DB plans, the public sector adopted similar retirement packages for government workers to stay competitive in the workforce. In 1878, New York State became the first such provider when it revised its benefits for public employees to provide a lifetime pension for New York City police officers. The plan incorporated a formula referred to as "twenty-one and fifty-five," which stipulated the workers would be eligible to collect their benefits after 21 years of service and reaching age 55. The earliest municipal plan for teachers was set up in Manhattan in 1894. Many states and municipalities across the country followed suit in the first half of the twentieth century.[15]

As if the previous debate over Social Security retirement benefits is not enough for elected officials to navigate, the government is now the largest sponsor of the remaining DB plans. State and local governments are on the hook for over 5,500 different DB plans. According to the Bureau of Labor Statistics, 86 percent of state and local government workers still have some form of a DB pension. That should say something, when only 13 private companies in the Fortune 500, less than 3 percent, can stake the same claim.

This reality brings along with it an estimated $4.35 trillion deficit toward unfunded pension liabilities to state and local governments. All DB plans are designed by actuaries, mathematicians who factor in many different assumptions like retirees' life expectancies and investment returns on plan assets, to project how much money is needed today to satisfy tomorrow. Unfunded pension liabilities are the contributions required to be made to the plan to keep it actuarially sound and capable of upholding the retirement benefits it promises its employees, *unfunded* meaning they have not been made. A fully funded plan is one that has met the minimum requirements set by the actuaries to safely pay future retiree benefits. As of 2018, five states actually had less than half of their pension funded—Kentucky (33.9 percent funded), New Jersey (35.8 percent), Illinois (38.4 percent), Connecticut (43.8 percent), and Colorado (47.1 percent).[16] South Dakota and Wisconisn are the only two states currently fully funded.[17] Aside from population dynamics, public pension funds fluctuate as they invest about 50 percent of their assets in stocks, 25 percent in bonds, and the remaining 25 percent in private equity, hedge funds, and real estate.[18] The saving grace for these plans is that, unlike the private sector, they do have some taxing authority at their disposal.

Besides states and municipalities having access to less tax revenue than the federal government, and none at all for private sector plans, the other difference that makes funding DB pensions a taller order than Social Security is the payout amounts. The largest possible Social Security retirement benefit is $50,328 annually (maximum benefit deferred to age 70 and collected in 2022). For context, on the DB pension side, police officers receiving guaranteed lifetime payouts in excess of $200,000 annually are becoming more common. One of the country's largest programs, the New York State and Local Retirement System, has seen the number of retirees receiving six-figure pensions more than quadruple from 2010 to 2020.[19] As more baby boomers retire, these numbers will only increase.

Similar to Social Security being a provider of both retirement and disability benefits, most government pensions include a disability component too, which again is a richer benefit than Social Security's version. For a frame of reference, New Jersey's Police and Firemen's Retirement System (PRFRS) states that for an ordinary disability, "you must prove that you are physically or mentally incapacitated from performing your normal or assigned job duties, or any other position that your employer may assign." If the disabled party satisfies this definition, they may be eligible for a lifetime benefit equal to at least 40 percent of their final compensation. For an accidental disability (occurring on the job), the payout would be two-thirds of their compensation. Neither payout, ordinary disability or on-the-job, would be reduced for any other Social Security or private insurance benefits received, or earned income.[20] This type of definition of disability is more in line with what private insurance carriers define as "Own Occupation" language, meaning the inability to work at the claimant's current place of employment is sufficient to receive full benefits, regardless of other job opportunities or income. This is obviously much easier to qualify for than a nongovernment worker who applies for Social Security Disability Insurance and must prove that they cannot adjust to perform any job (keep these differences in mind when reading "Protection First, Fully, and Forever" in Chapter 9, Financial Literacy).

Medicare/Medicaid

If Social Security is the second-largest budget item for the US government, that means there is another, even larger obligation. That honor belongs to

Medicare/Medicaid. According to the US Office of Management and Budget, the 2021 budget for Medicare/Medicaid is $1.3 trillion.

America's largest expense came into existence in 1963. During the 1950s and 1960s, the main issue facing America's seniors was the cost of healthcare combined with a natural decline in income in retirement. Roughly half of the population over age 65 did not have any hospital insurance, and even fewer had insurance for surgery or out-of-hospital care. Private insurance companies, the only option for seniors before Medicare, had not only become unaffordable, but carriers were known for cancelling coverage for older adults, deeming their age "high risk." There were some federal-state programs of medical assistance before Medicare, but the scope of covered care was very limited, and due to a lack of funding, it was only for the country's poorest citizens.

If FDR opened the door to senior care, LBJ went barging through. In 1965, President Lyndon Baines Johnson's amendments to Social Security created Medicare. Medicare is a national social insurance program that subsidizes healthcare services for anyone age 65 or older (and now covers younger people with specific diseases and disabilities). Like most bills, it was founded on the best intentions, but littered with contradictions. It was and still is meant to provide the best quality care, but at the lowest price. It should encourage improvement in medicine, but not mandate any changes. It must remove barriers to health services, but avoid unnecessary services. It shall create shared responsibility via deductibles and coinsurance, but not create financial burdens.

In 1966, the most important part of Medicare, the Hospital Insurance Trust Fund, which receives payroll taxes and pays for Part A, Hospital Insurance, projected a shortfall.[21] Recall that Medicare started in 1965; in other words, what would become the biggest entitlement ever was immediately expected to present issues of insolvency.

Today, Medicare is made up of four parts: Part A (Hospital Insurance, or HI), which is funded through payroll taxes; Part B (Supplemental Medical Insurance), funded through premium payments; Part C (Medicare Advantage), an alternate private health plan; and Part D (Prescription Drug Benefit), funded by premium payments, state contributions, and general tax revenues. While Medicare is responsible for covering thousands of reimbursement codes, Medicare has the advantage of paying roughly half of what private insurers pay for hospital services.[22] This, in effect, gives Medicare a discounted rate and lessens the burden on an already stretched thin entitlement.

The 2021 Medicare Trustees Report projects the HI trust fund (Part A) to be insolvent by 2026. In plain English, this means Part A's "rainy day fund" would be empty, and Medicare would be existing "paycheck to paycheck," surviving on incoming tax and premium revenues. There are no provisions in the Social Security Act to address insolvency. In the event this comes to fruition, Congress would be forced to take legislative action or leave tens of millions of Medicare recipients with reduced coverage.

At the same time LBJ signed Medicare into law, he also included Medicaid in Title XIX of the Social Security Act, meant to provide healthcare to people with low income. Whereas Social Security and Medicare were two entitlements not based on need, somewhat based on personal contributions, and very based on age, Medicaid would be entirely based on need, somewhat based on age, but not at all based on personal contributions. However, there is some understandable confusion around Medicaid and helping people who are poor. While 11.4 percent of Americans live in poverty, Medicaid provides coverage to 97 million low-income Americans, or nearly one-third of the total population.[23]

Medicaid, by definition, is countercyclical to the economy. During a recession, when layoffs and job scarcity are higher, state and federal tax revenues available to fund Medicaid decrease, but expenses rise as more coverage is offered to the unemployed and new poor, a true double whammy.

Since the passage of the Affordable Care Act (Obamacare) in 2010, Medicaid has been expanded greatly and more responsibility has been shifted to the federal government. America's aging population has exaggerated this increase. (See Figure 2.2.) Seniors account for only one-fifth of Medicaid beneficiaries, but make up over half of the entire program's costs. Medicaid covers 60 percent of all nursing home residents and over half of all long-term care costs.[24]

Despite the gargantuan financial demands on Medicaid, the system's expenses are somewhat alleviated by paying lower reimbursements to healthcare providers than private health insurance companies would pay and significantly less than uncovered individuals would pay out-of-pocket. This is similar to Medicare, as they both can be viewed as the premier customers of the healthcare sector. However, Medicaid does not have the benefit of collecting premiums from its beneficiaries like parts of Medicare or normal private insurances. The plan's shortfalls are borne jointly by state and federal balance sheets.

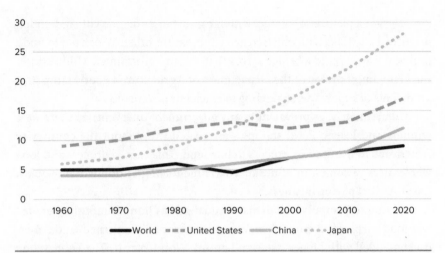

Figure 2.2   Percentage of population over age 65[25]

Food Stamps

Social Security and Medicare/Medicaid may dominate the American entitlement debate, but the idea of government assistance has many more tentacles. Leaving no man, woman, or child hungry has been about as American a concept as freedom itself. In 1939, under Henry Wallace, secretary of the US Department of Agriculture (USDA), the Food Stamp Program (now referred to as Supplemental Nutrtition Assistance Program—SNAP) was invented. People were permitted to buy orange food stamps equal to their normal food expenditures, and then for every dollar of orange food stamps purchased, 50 cents' worth of blue stamps were received for free and could be used to buy food the Department of Agriculture deemed to be at a surplus.

It was equal parts created to help feed the hungry and provide a buyer to farmers' overflows. Prior to this time, the agriculture industry had experienced such hardship in the Great Depression, and there was such a poor supply chain between farmers and people, that FDR filled the void by actually having the USDA pay farmers to plow their fields and slaughter pigs just to create scarcity and boost prices. The Federal Surplus Commodities Corporation, an agency of the New Deal, stepped in to buy any remaining surpluses and attempted to distribute them to the needy.

"We got a picture of a gorge, with farm surpluses on one cliff and undernourished city folks with outstretched hands on the other. We set out to find a practical way to build a bridge across that chasm," proclaimed Milo Perkins, the first administrator of the Department of Agriculture's Food Stamp Program. Lots of supply was struggling to reach lots of demand.

Unfortunately, as prevalent in any government intervention, there were winners and losers. Food stamps were issued throughout the country to Americans to use at their grocers to buy food. This caused grocers and food wholesalers to complain of unfair government competition while they lost much-needed paying business.

Fortunately, supply and demand equalized as hungry mouths were fed and food surpluses dwindled, employment eventually returned, and America contended with bigger issues in fighting World War II. The Food Stamp Program ended in 1943. FDR's mission was accomplished, a helping hand lent when needed and then removed once improved.

The Food Stamp Program reappeared sporadically in history as a political tool and eventually became a nationwide program yet again in 1974. Politicians had agreed it was a program proven to strengthen the agriculture economy and feed a rapidly growing country, and it won state support by authorizing that the Department of Agriculture would pay 50 percent of all states' costs for administering the program. By 1980, over 20 million Americans were receiving food stamps as it became a mainstay. The program peaked under President Barack Obama in 2013 when 47.6 million Americans received SNAP.[26]

President Donald Trump followed Obama with an about-face, searching for ways to reduce welfare. Before exiting, Trump proposed his 2021 budget to cut SNAP by $180 billion over the next 10 years, a 30 percent decrease. One of his primary cost-savings measure was to take SNAP away from adults who were not working at least 20 hours per week.

However, President Joe Biden's administration quickly reversed course by implementing the largest permanent increase in SNAP history by upping benefits by over 25 percent to its 42 million beneficiaries. Opponents of this measure argue SNAP, per its first initial, "S" for Supplemental, should not be meant to provide for all of a recipient's diet. Furthermore, the USDA reported that the second most purchased item with food stamps was sweetened beverages and that 20 percent of all assistance went to the dessert/snack category.[27] SNAP has yet to serve as many as the program's record number of recipients

in 2013, but a record financial amount of $108 billion of benefits were pro-
vided in 2021.

Unemployment

The other major form of welfare is unemployment insurance (UI), also created
by the New Deal. UI provides payments to workers who have become unemployed through no fault of their own. Upon its inception, UI provided for up to
16 weeks of benefits to those who lost their job. The program is overseen at the
federal level by the Department of Labor, but benefits are administered by each
state. It is funded jointly by state and federal governments and employer taxes.
Like Medicaid, it is also countercyclical to the economy—recession strikes,
unemployment rises, tax revenues decrease, UI benefits skyrocket.

UI teeters on the fine line of good and bad, rescuing the temporarily dis-
enfranchised on the good side and breeding moral hazard on the bad side.
Moral hazard is an economic term suggesting the lack of incentive to guard
against risk where one is protected from its negative consequences. The goal
of every economy is to achieve optimum efficiency and productivity through
as many self-sustaining citizens as possible. However, when workers notice
there exists a safety net—sometimes a safety net that provides even better
benefits than realized from a long day on the job—it can disincentivize rational behavior such as searching for a job, working hard to keep a job, and the
prudent financial planning needed to be financially independent. Not only
does this transform givers into takers, but it can rob marginalized workers of
the mentality needed to climb the economic ladder. Many movies set during
or before the Great Depression contain scenes of men running at the crack
of dawn to the docks, mines, or factories, shoving one another to get to the
front of the line as a foreman selects the last few workers needed for the day.
UI sought to prevent such scenes of desperation from ever happening again,
but it may have also have taken some of that same ambition and persistence
away with it.

Today, most states provide 26 weeks of benefits to those who are
unemployed or laid off, plus an extension by the federal government for
the long-term unemployed. During the Covid-19 pandemic, UI eligibility requirements were relaxed, and benefits were extended an additional 13
weeks and enhanced by an extra $600 weekly. From March 2020 to July 2021,

$794 billion of unemployment benefits were paid, more than six times what was paid out in 2009 during the Great Recession.[28]

Social Security, Medicare/Medicaid, SNAP (aka food stamps), and unemployment insurance are the largest and most recognized entitlements in the United States today, but there are plenty more—government funds paid toward housing, education, stimulus, business incentives, subsidies, and tax abatements (a reduction or exemption on the level of taxation normally faced by an individual or company) of every variety. It is hard to imagine life in America's first 150 years, a time before entitlements existed, a time when givers fended for themselves and takers were not yet takers, but rather an unfortunate class cast astray. Entitlements are no longer just about securing a baseline M (money) for a country's citizens, but have evolved into a debate of MICE between politicians, nations, businesses, unions, lobbyists, and employers and employees.

Welfare aims to enhance income, employment, healthcare, education, and other core economic benchmarks. But what is often seen as politically taboo, despite its obvious positive impact on every single economic indicator, is the nuclear family. In 1965, at the height of the civil rights movement, 7 percent of births were to unmarried women (24 percent of Black children were born out of wedlock compared to 3 percent of white children). By 1990, long after LBJ's "Great Society" plugged the New Deal's gaps, the rates had risen to 28 percent nationally (64 percent among Blacks and 18 percent for whites). According to the latest data in 2019, the national average rose to 40 percent (70 percent for Blacks and 28 percent for whites). The Hispanic nonmarital birth rate has increased to 52 percent, whereas Asians have held the lowest measure at 11 percent. While economics is not always linear, the connection between family and financial success may support why Asian Americans have routinely ranked at or near the bottom of recipients of public assistance by ethnicity, yet are the wealthiest race in the United States.[29]

The Costs of Entitling

The costs of entitling are immense. The 2023 budget of the US government projects a spending of $5.79 trillion. The costliest items are Medicare and Medicaid at $1.38 trillion (24 percent) and Social Security totaling $1.31

trillion (23 percent). For comparison's sake, the remainder of the US budget comprises defense spending at $795 billion (14 percent), nondefense discretionary (education, transportation, etc.) at $915 billion (16 percent), and other mandatory programs (health insurance subsidies, SNAP, housing assistance, federal civilian and military retirement, etc.) at $993 billion (17 percent).

Like any ledger, there are two sides. The projected government receipts total $4.64 trillion. The bulk of this comes from individual income tax revenue of $2.35 trillion, Social Security payroll taxes of $1.1 trillion, and corporate taxes totaling $501 billion.

If you reread these figures, you might be noticing what appear to be two mathematical errors. First, the breakdown of government expenditures does not total 100 percent. Second, the two sides of the ledger (income and expenses) are not close to equal; the budget projects a $1.15 trillion deficit. Both inconsistencies can be answered by one word—debt.

No different than a household or business, when inflows fall short of outflows, the federal government leverages debt to make ends meet. Debt, as anyone with a credit card knows, is not free. The missing expense that brings the federal budget to 100 percent is the cost of interest on debt. The annual interest on government debt is a projected expense of $396 billion (7 percent of 2023 total budget). While the Federal Reserve's decisions to raise or cut interest rates must fall within its dual mandate to monitor inflation and employment, the cost of servicing national debt certainly is not ignored. As interest rates rise, so too will rates on US Treasury securities. The White House projects annual net interest costs to triple over the 2022–2032 period, from $357 billion to $1.09 trillion, totaling $7.6 trillion over the next 10 years. If the Fed raises interest rates quicker than expected, these debt costs will only go higher.[30]

When average Americans hear the fractions and percentages spewed out in a report like this, it's easy to gloss over. One percent sounds so small. An investment portfolio can gain or lose 1 percent within a couple of hours of a trading day. However, because of the dynamics explained in Chapter 1, Population, shifting 1 percent of today's US entitlement plans would require extreme effort.

The comforts of the past century certainly owe a thank-you to the revolutionary leaders of FDR's time, but they may also owe the generations of the next century. Many of the improvements in standards of living are linked to welfare, but welfare has forever been linked to debt. An optimist can point to figures of billions becoming trillions as a natural symptom of inflation, but ratios do not mislead. In 1980, the federal debt-to-GDP ratio was 34.71 percent; it is now 127 percent. (See Figure 2.3.)

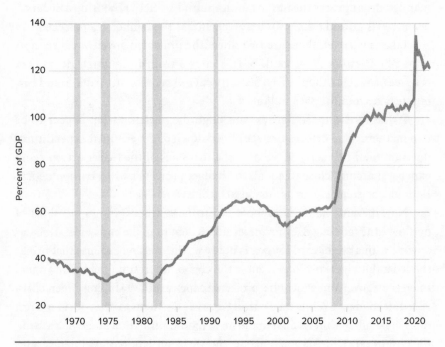

Figure 2.3 Total public debt as percent of gross domestic product (gray bars indicate recession years)

MICRO

"So, are we going to be OK?" he asks.

We've completed reviewing every nook and cranny of Mr. and Mrs. Retiree's financial world. Assets and liabilities. Possible inheritances and possible disinheritances. Inflows and outflows. Goals and concerns. Price and cost.

A sound retirement plan begins with an analysis of guaranteed income sources, such as Social Security or DB pension benefits, versus future obligations and expenses, like housing, food, and projected medical bills. From there, a myriad of strategies and assumptions can be implemented to fill any gaps. In Mr. and Mrs. Retiree's case, these gaps include covering expenses before he turns on Social Security and where the down payment will come from for their second home in Florida. We must devise a plan that works under the broadest amount of circumstances possible. Whether or not Mrs. Retiree finds another job substitute teaching, Mr. Retiree's IRA grows in value or gets hit with a market downturn, their primary residency sells in a few years for $2 million or just $1.5 million, or one of them lives to 90 or even longer. Step by step, eliminate each degree of uncertainty until the probability of success is overwhelming.

"Guaranteed income? I thought there were no guarantees in the world of finance," Mr. Retiree asks as he examines the Cash Flow Sources document that I've produced. *Fair point.* No one can guarantee tomorrow, so how can income guarantee anything further? Guaranteed income sources are better characterized as a series of "promises," with varying degrees of dependability by the source.

Take Mr. Retiree here, a 69-year-old healthy male born in 1952. He has been intentionally deferring Social Security past his full retirement age (FRA) of 66, opting to wait until age 70 to receive the maximum "guaranteed life-time payout" of $50,328. Could a hurricane next summer wipe out half of America and force a rescue effort that siphons every federal dollar from every program imaginable, leaving Mr. Retiree unentitled? *Sure, the* Titanic *did sink.* But in reality, he has an extremely high level of confidence in the realization of this "promised" entitlement, backed by the full faith and credit of the US government.

Furthermore, Mr. Retiree has been collecting a pension since he turned 60 from his career as an elementary school gym teacher just across the state line. He worked there for 30 years with a finishing salary of $50,000, which entitles him to a lifetime payout of $27,272.[31] In addition, over the past 10 years, Mr. Retiree worked as his hometown's borough administrator with a salary of $100,000. Upon his retirement next year, he'll be entitled to another pension of $16,666, or 16.6 percent of his previous five years' average salary.

Are these two pensions "guaranteed" like Social Security? *Sort of.* State and local governments across the country are facing dire straits with their unfunded pension liabilities, which have prompted modifications such as higher employee contribution requirements, phasing out newer employees from existing DB pension plans, new calculation methods suggesting lower and later payouts, and so forth. Such pensions are still "promises," albeit morphing ones.

So once fully retired, Mr. Retiree can "assume" with a great degree of certainty a fixed income of $94,266 annually from his two pensions and Social Security combined. Fully aware of the protections afforded by the Pension Source Tax Act of 1996 (PL 104-95), Mr. and Mrs. Retiree hop on the Northeast-to-Southeast pipeline and flee the high-tax state in which he earned these benefits for a "pension-friendly" state with no income tax and lower property taxes. Their former home state is left paying out enormous benefits without recouping any further tax revenue. The state has transitioned into a pure giver, while Mr. and Mrs. Retiree enjoy becoming takers.

Never fans of investing or following the markets, Mr. and Mrs. Retiree comfortably enter their golden years without having given much thought to financial planning over their career. They have Social Security, pensions, and a nice chunk of cash in their savings. There is one aspect of this last phase of life that does garner their attention, probably piqued by one of the million pesky commercials, and that is the cost of healthcare.

Fortunately, Medicare is in place as a primary payer and backed up by the lifetime health coverage afforded by Mr. Retiree's former workplace. In addition, Medicaid could swoop in if private long-term care proves too expensive in those final years. Mr. and Mrs. Retiree are ready to set sail toward the retirement they deserve. Their ship has few leaks to plug, if any.

WHAT SHOULD I DO WITH MY MONEY?

The perception of control can be seen as identifying as either a victim or a beneficiary of one's circumstances. Therefore, it's necessary to understand the financial construct we live in and how we arrived here. For roughly half of America's history, individuals had to fend for themselves or collaborate with friends, family, and neighbors to survive. For the latter half of American history, systems have been created to share the burdens of life. The largest US budget items did not even exist one century ago, so how can one predict what they will be when your grandkids are your age? Whether the trend continues toward more assistance or begins to return toward individual responsibility, neither should affect what you should do with your money.

If you are wondering how circumstances seem to no longer matter, let me put it to you this way. . . . If I were your parent and I bluntly stated that paying for next year's summer vacation was entirely on you, how might you begin to prepare? What if for this summer vacation you so badly want, I tell you that maybe, if I can afford to, maybe I will pay for it. Now, what's your plan? In scenario one, you work and save all year, and you go on your dream vacation. Choose not to work and save, then no surprise—no vacation. In scenario two, you work and save all year, and you go on your dream vacation with the possibility of having some of my change in your pocket for extra fun. Choose not to work and save, then a surprise awaits—maybe vacation and you have no money left, or maybe no vacation at all.

You may feel the uncertainty of entitlements is unfair, the suspense too much to handle. But it is uncertainty, that tinge of anxiety, that can push you to be responsible when complacency teases you, whereas the certainty we all equally crave teases society with moral hazard. This catch-22 is why entitlements, particularly forms of welfare in which the costs are borne more by givers than takers, must exist in such a way that taking from them is nearly as painful as the alternative. It is best to accept circumstances as they are, or whatever they will be, and in the meantime create your own certainty.

What They Do with Their Money

As in all issues of wealth, there are financial and emotional concerns surrounding entitlements. The proposal to quit any major financial habit cold turkey might work on paper, but in practice may not be reasonable. The collapse of Enron Corporation and the accompanying loss of employees' retirement savings is a prime example. That would be like me telling you I promise to pay for next summer's vacation, only to tell you weeks before vacation that I have no money. Therefore, providers of entitlements can decide to continue such plans at all costs, mentally converting "privileges" to "rights," or choose to abandon their existence in an organized fashion.

The "organized fashion" wording cannot be overlooked. Humans may be creatures of habits, but this does not imply an inability to adapt or resile. People like good news and dislike bad news, but no news leads to surprises that require costly bailouts or failure. In short, tell the worker how and when they are going to get hit, while providing some self-defense training in the interim, rather than throw a sucker punch.

Here is the rub. Democracy is an incredible structure, but the ever-present tension between doing what is needed and what is wanted makes clear communication a paradox. Decision makers, whether in the government or private company, will always engage in debate, which inevitably leaves people to form "what if" retirement plans. If two opposing sides could convey one universally agreed-upon approach, fact could at last be separated from fiction. As Republicans and Democrats in Congress prove each year, the larger the organization, the harder this will be.

Entitlements can continue to be appreciated in the form of guaranteed benefits provided by the system, or restructured and rebranded as a return of hard-earned dollars to the people with the freedom to choose how to plan their individual future. Medicare/Medicaid, Social Security, and DB pensions are at their core the same thing. Save today and prepare for tomorrow. Just as a family reviewing their budget in a pinch must decide to either make more or spend less, so must the providers of entitlements weigh these options:

1. Shorten Today and Lengthen Tomorrow

If the savings today are inadequate for the needs of tomorrow, one must lengthen the today and shorten the tomorrow. This exercise does have precedent in America, particularly with the full retirement age (FRA) for Social Security. There are seven different payout ages for people born between 1943 and 1960, but there are no changes thereafter. With babies being born in 2023, that is a 63-year gap that desperately needs addressing. A solution could be more longevity indexing, deferring the FRA further. This effectively makes the today of working and paying tax into the system longer, and the tomorrow of collecting benefits shorter.

The same strategy of longevity indexing could be applied to Medicare/Medicaid or even unemployment benefit durations. Ongoing longevity indexing could salvage entitlements by maintaining consistency with life expectancy and life events. As mentioned in the last chapter on population, there are more people inhabiting America now than ever before, and that population growth is weighted heavily toward seniors. The systems that make up America need to reflect the people that make up America.

2. Contribute More Today

Over the past few decades, Americans have been doing the opposite in aiming to retire early, a shorter today and longer tomorrow. Entitlements can match this trend by taxing more income today to fulfill more benefits for tomorrow. The equivalent "tax" for a private pension would be to reduce pay raises, benefits, and bonuses, while increasing employee contributions, to sustain the DB plan.

If it feels too late to ask a retiree to pick up the slack, federal, state, and local governments can change their laws to effectively move money from one pocket to another once workers are past the payroll tax phase of their career. As of 2021, there is over $11.8 trillion sitting in IRAs, and over 28,600 taxpayers have IRAs worth over $5 million.[32] These tax-deferred retirement accounts can be taxed in different manners to offer future revenue in step with market growth as a way to subsidize faltering pensions.

Social Security seized this opportunity in 1984 when President Ronald Reagan's administration began taxing Social Security annuities, which were then taxed even more in 1993 under President Bill Clinton. Raising taxes on Social Security benefits to maintain the system may appear to be simple window dressing, which it is, but it can provide the mental assurance to future retirees that the system will still be there.

These super-complex programs boil down to basic math. But since what is given cannot be taken away, everyone who is a part of a system feels duly entitled, like FDR intimated earlier. Deficits can only be financed through debt, until someday they can't.

ECONOMIC INSIGHT

Investment vehicles should be analyzed like a stool with three legs—market risk, liquidity, and tax consequence. Retirement plans may contain varying levels of risk, with a DB pension being relatively safe and a 401(k) or IRA being as conservative or aggressive as the participant desires. Liquidity is often a major issue with retirement accounts, as most qualified plans stipulate the participant can't access the funds before age 59.5

without incurring a 10 percent premature distribution tax (certain exceptions may apply).[33]

Investors who are concerned about the unfunded liabilities introduced thus far, and their role in the federal government's $31 trillion national debt, may fear tax volatility and potential tax increases (See Figure 2.4). This is where Roth contributions, as opposed to pretax contributions, can allow the retirement saver to swallow their medicine today by contributing to retirement on a posttax basis with the opportunity for tax-free growth thereafter (when used as a qualified distribution according to IRS guidelines).[34]

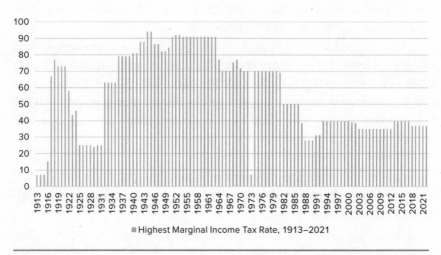

■ Highest Marginal Income Tax Rate, 1913–2021

Figure 2.4   US historical marginal income tax rate[35]

3. Transition from DB to DC

If the first two options are not feasible for the pension sponsor, DB pensions can be abandoned altogether. This solution is to return earnings back to the worker, empowering them with the freedom to choose and making retirement their own responsibility. The private sector has been tinkering with this for decades, as discussed earlier in the massive shift from company DB plans to defined contribution (DC) plans, such as the 401(k), 403(b), and IRAs. Company leaders and their human resources departments can market this transition however they see fit. Rather than tell an employee they are "forced out of the pension," they can tout how each employee is now "afforded the option to keep their money and invest freely." As an extra carrot, companies often use the recaptured expenses from funding a DB plan to offer a new employer match on company retirement plans.

For readers in the public sector yearning for such freedom of choice, the writing is on the wall. But beware, duplicating guaranteed lifetime income is not an easy task. Under certain circumstances, New York City employees have this option by exempting themselves from Social Security and/or Medicare taxes. To do so, such employees must contribute at least 7.5 percent of pay to a defined contribution plan (403(b), tax deferred annuity, 457 plan, etc.).[36] The same money that would have gone to Social Security and Medicare is recaptured and placed in a retirement account in the employee's name, giving them flexibility in investment decisions and eventual distribution options. The Big Apple's Social Security exemption could be expanded upon for the rest of the United States and immediately ease the burden on Social Security. However, society must realize this shifting of risk is just that, risk transferred from the government to the individual.

4. The Buyout

Another iteration of the DB-to-DC transition is the buyout. This is a strategy that has become fairly common in the private sector, but unexplored by the much larger public pensions. There are two methods for this approach. One is to transfer the pension liability to an insurance company. Insurance companies are well suited for providing retirement income due to their experience issuing annuities. A prominent example occurred in 2020 when GE transferred 70,000 employees' pension plans, or $1.7 billion of obligations, to Athene Annuity and Life Insurance Company.[37]

According to the Mercer US Pension Buyout Index, which compares the cost of transferring a pension to an insurance company versus the economic cost of retaining the pension obligations, the hypothetical cost of purchasing annuities from an insurer was 99.5 percent of the accounting liability versus 105.2 percent of the liability to maintain the plan. The higher cost to retain the plan is due to administrative costs, investment expenses, and increasing future PBGC (Pension Benefit Guaranty Corporation) premiums.[38] Beyond the potential cost savings to the plan sponsor is the peace of mind achieved by offloading one of the biggest and most uncertain liabilities on an organization's balance sheet.

The second method of completing a buyout is to offer a lump-sum payment directly to the employee. Large corporations such as ATT, Boeing, Honda, Toyota, and GE have altered their pension plans in hopes of shedding its weight. The employee is tasked with calculating whether the lump sum is worth more than the present value of their DB pension payments.

Conversely, the company may be required to immediately shell out large one-time payments through current assets or financing versus staggered payments over decades as a pension. The victory of erasing uncertain future liabilities (pension payments) could come at the cost of a liquidity crunch if all the employees were to choose the lump-sum option.

There may be several more variables to consider beyond pure math. The most popular concern for employees is if their former employer can remain in good financial standing for the next 30 years of their retirement. Another is that many employers require the retired employee to maintain a pension in order to qualify for ongoing health benefits. Last, aside from "joint life" or "period certain" options, most pensions do not have a death benefit, meaning once the employee and their spouse have passed away, the checks stop. Suddenly, a DB pension valued as a multimillion-dollar benefit is not so valuable if the employee dies early in retirement. On the flip side, a lump-sum payout can be bequeathed to anyone and possibly last generations. This caveat is why many employees set on collecting their DB pension in the future, purchase permanent life insurance to protect their spouse and family legacy.

5. Other Fringe Benefits

Retirement benefits hog the conversation for baby boomers, rightfully so as most people work a normal career and do survive to retirement age, but the disability component of Social Security and other pension programs cannot be overlooked. Social Security Disability Insurance may not be seen as heavy a burden compared to the disability benefits tied to pensions, since it uses the "any occupation" type of language. This high bar for disability claims has led to only 35.25 percent of applications being approved. Furthermore, the average disability benefit in 2021 was $1,462 monthly.[39]

A key to lessening the load placed on state and local pension's disability trust funds would be to bring their disability language more in line with that of the Social Security Administration. The coupling of an easier path to disability approval with much richer benefits for police and firefighters causes a disproportionate load on their pension programs. States might also consider taxing these awarded benefits and/or imposing offsets for other employment income or benefits received so as not to create an overinsurance effect, another moral hazard that allows an employee to claim disability knowing the benefits can be near equal to their normal earnings.

6. The Temporary Fix

The fix most politicians have grown to appreciate is the temporary fix, which often leads to the worst long-term outcomes. The temporary fix is to kick the can down the road, keep providing loftier benefits while letting whoever's up next fix the liability column. In the early 1980s the Social Security Trust Funds experienced severe cash flow issues as a result of the stagflation of the 1970s. Congress passed legislation that permitted interfund borrowing among the three trust funds (Old-Age and Survivors, Disability, and Medicare). On two separate occasions, in November of 1982 and December of 1982, the Old-Age and Survivors fund borrowed $5.1 billion from Disability and $12.4 billion from Medicare. Fortunately, both debts were paid off in full by 1986.[40]

This is a dangerous game of switching money from one pocket to another to plug growing leaks that should not be allowed. States and municipalities have exercised the same solutions, but without the great taxing powers of the federal government and usually resulting in mounting debt.

Back to What I Should Do

As they decide what to do with your money, it is appropriate you continue to ask the questions, "What should I do with my money?" and follow it up with "Why?" The answers to why, when contemplating retirement, healthcare, and safety nets, will inevitably draw back in entitlements. But for most workers, certainly millennials and future generations, there will be ample room for personal choices within macro circumstances.

If you believe the current system works, in providing an adequate level of care for workers and retirees, but realize that it may not always be possible, then you should use your money to create your own security system. This can be done by owning individual life and disability insurance throughout your career, rather than depending on Social Security and evolving pension or group employer plans. Retiree benefits can be duplicated through a strong savings rate of 20 percent of earnings, some pretax and some post-tax or Roth to mitigate future tax bills. A portfolio suitable to your risk tolerance and time horizon can be maintained to keep up with inflation and build capital. Some of this can be transitioned to an income annuity later in life to provide guaranteed lifetime income similar to Social Security and DB plans. Financial vehicles and products will continue to change, adapting to the wants and needs of the population, providing opportunities to those who stay in the know.

Millennials are popularizing the term *FIRE* (financial independence, retire early) across blogs and podcasts, many hoping to be done with the workforce by their 40th birthday. While financial independence is a goal shared by all financial advisors, a true early retirement represents a subtraction from the productivity column, possibly destabilizing the scales of givers and takers. Workers pursuing FIRE should consider what that long retirement will look like, remembering that money (M) is only a part of what makes up MICE.

Just like the story that opened this section, a child can bank on their parents paying for vacation, or they can hope for the best and prepare for the worst. Financial independence is an incredible feeling that allows you to truly choose your day's course without the infamous stress of worrying how long your dollars will last. But financial independence starts with being financially independent.

EDUCATION

Education is a story about the past, present, and future. A story about wealth, making things better, making life better, the universal desire for well-being. Education comes from a wise uncle, a dusty children's book, the hallowed halls of illustrious universities. Sometimes the price is high, other times it's free, but every lesson has its costs.

After God had carried us safe to New England, and we had builded our houses, provided necessaries for our livelihood, reared convenient places for God's worship, and settled the civil government, one of the next things we longed for and looked after was to advance learning and perpetuate it to posterity, dreading to leave an illiterate ministry to the churches when our present ministers shall lie in dust.

—Harvard University, *New England First Fruits* (1643)

"**M**om!" Tom, a boy about to turn 18, yells upstairs. "Did you get the mail today?"

It's a fun sort of suspense, but the wait for a response is too much. He runs out front to the mailbox. There they are, three oversized envelopes. He leaves the bills and coupons and dashes back into the house with his prize.

Each package is torn open, revealing all that future should be. Young adults smiling, laughing together on a picnic blanket amid perfectly manicured lawns flanked by feats of architecture. Boys and girls, of every different complexion, tinkering with the latest gadgetry and technology under the guidance of seasoned professionals.

Senior year is a breeze, aside from that one AP Lit course. All the days are half-days, except Thursdays have only one block so it's over by 10 a.m. Remote learning is the way to go on Thursdays. Senioritis. He is already checked out. College calls his name.

"So, what do you want to be when you grow up?" Tom's teacher casually asks each student by name, alternating between the few in-person and those at home learning from their bed.

"A nurse," says one.

"I dunno. Whatever," mumbles a remote boy with a blacked-out screen.

"Something in business," shouts another.

Tom skips the SATs. *I'm really a good student, just not a good test taker,* he reassures himself and his parents. Fortunately, many of the pamphlets mention that they are optional now. He is in good company since having read about the 2019 lawsuit levied by a coalition of Black and Latino students against the University of California, the most prestigious public university system in America with over 226,000 undergrads, which successfully removed SAT and ACT consideration from university admissions and scholarship decisions by arguing that testing illegally discriminates based on race and wealth.[1] Formal tests aside, his grades have been slipping over the past year too, but that's OK since the school district announced they will no longer be assigning class rank to students.

Not only is it unfair to be penalized by a college for just missing a class percentile, but it's a matter of self-esteem, reads a letter from the superintendent. The loosening of requirements and standardized testing help colleges broaden their enrollment. Proponents refer to it as a growing student body. Opponents call it a bigger customer base.

"Did you see the price tag on the one in the lead now?" Tom's mother whispers to his father after dinner is cleared.

"Yeah . . . well, you know they say you never actually pay that price," he responds.

"Well, even if it's half that price, then what?"

"We'll just have to figure it out. Loans. You know," trying to make sense of it between cleaning dishes. "Did he even decide what he wants to study?"

"Ha, who knows," she says with a smile. "Hopefully software engineering or medicine. I read they're the most demanded degrees in America."[2]

"All I know," his father grumbles while drying his hands, "is he better not end up like Joey next door." Joey is their 26-year-old neighbor still living at home. He never settled on a particular major, even though his parents and academic counselor agreed to a fifth year on campus, a "Super Senior," they called it. Joey's parents worried that his friends might get a head start and grab the jobs he could have had, as they tack on another student loan, but the counselor eased their concerns with a study from the National Center for Education Statistics that showed only 41 percent of college students finish in four years.[3]

"I guess we'll have to wait and see," Tom's mom says with a shrug.

MACRO

Most 18-year-olds are not sure what exactly they want to be when they grow up. It's a conundrum even many adults face. *Choices.* The freedom to choose is forever a blessing and a curse. Sixty-seven percent of high school grads choose college as the next stop.[4] Four additional years, possibly six, or eight, should buy some time and clarity around one's own MICE.

College expands the mind, opens new doors, and broadens choices before hopefully narrowing them down, all the while providing a comfortable place to grow. That last fragment, suggesting the mutual existence of comfort and growth, may serve as a point of contention, but that can be saved for later. College certainly is not the only form of education worth discussing, but in the present economy, it is embraced as the final bridge toward becoming a full-time giver to society.

Some high school graduates take the path of higher education because they should, and other uncertain students simply because they can. The financial rewards of higher education are real, if not always realized. Eighty-seven percent of college grads land employment as opposed to 74 percent of those with solely a high school diploma.[5] The median earnings for an adult between the ages of 25 and 34 with a high school degree are $36,600, whereas those with a bachelor's degree make $59,600, and graduates with an advanced degree average $69,700.[6]

Diplomas, of course, do come at a price. As of 2022, the tuition for a private four-year college averages $38,185 annually (this does not include the room and board expenses). Public in-state colleges average a more palatable $10,338 tuition expense per year.[7]

The economic consequences of higher education are not without trade-off. America's student loans are spread across 46 million borrowers and total over $1.7 trillion of outstanding debt. The average student loan debt held by college graduates is $37,584. Young professionals in the States may be jealous of their European peers, as many colleges in countries like Germany, Norway, and Iceland do not charge for tuition, but the average student loan debt in the United Kingdom dwarfs the United States at £45,800, or roughly $48,000.[8] These huge figures by themselves are not an epidemic; rather, it's the inordinate weight they place on young professionals' budgets, and the corresponding weight society places on the government to do something about it.

This data all speaks to price, but not yet cost. The long-term costs to the two different cohorts, students who should study versus uncertain students who default to study, are as different as night and day. The former should be empowered toward college, whereas the latter may be better redirected toward alternative paths. A 4.0 high school student intensely interested in a subject that must be taught, such as engineering or medicine, can pay a lofty price for education, but a low cost if they find themselves immediately on the right side of the income spectrum after graduation.

Conversely, misguided college students run the risk of paying a much greater cost over time. This cohort can present itself in two forms. First is the student who is ready to learn and get to work, but has no idea what they want to do. Finding one's purpose should not come with a six-figure price tag. The second form is the student who pursues a skill that is better to be learned than taught, perhaps destined for the trades or entering the service. Even someone interested in sales or communications might have more success waiting tables at a fancy restaurant than in reading a textbook. The number of uncertain students who default to college solely because they can has been growing exponentially. They likely skew the popular fact that only one in four college graduates goes on to work in a field related to their major.[9]

The previous chapter introduced some of the gargantuan expenses of the US government for entitling. Student loan repayments are another significant line item, as 92 percent of student loan debt is borrowed from the US Department of Education (ED), a branch of the federal government. Heading into the coronavirus pandemic, 20 percent of borrowers were late on their repayments.[10] In March of 2020, the ED paused federal student loan repayments, suspended all interest, and stopped collections on defaulted loans. While not as apparent as the Fed rate cuts, stimulus packages, and enhanced unemployment benefits, this was another measure that inflated America's money supply. Over 43 million federal borrowers were able to invest and spend their money into the economy, rather than repay the government. The student loan relief was temporary and pandemic-related; however, its deadline was extended several times, eventually into 2023. The Congressional Budget Office (CBO) estimated the student loan forbearance period cost the federal government $4.3 billion per month, totaling over $150 billion.[11]

ECONOMIC INSIGHT

Bill Gates, Paul Allen, Mary Kay, Richard Branson, James Cameron, Simon Cowell, Michael Dell, Ellen DeGeneres, LeBron James, Larry Ellison, Steve Jobs, Jake Paul, Wolfgang Puck, Ted Turner, and Mark Zuckerberg. These people share several similarities. They are all extremely successful and recognized as thought leaders within their industries, some of which they created. While they come from diverse backgrounds and made their mark in different pursuits, ranging from tech to entertainment, they do all belong to the same fraternity—the nongrads. Some never tried college, others dropped out halfway through, and some even got expelled.

Are they natural outliers? Sure, Bill Gates has a higher IQ than average and not everyone can be six-foot-nine and fly through the air like LeBron, but much of their success is attributed to normal human decision-making. The relatable trait is in each of their abilities to identify and supply, sometimes even invent, what is necessary to fulfill a very broad demand. Furthermore, most of them chased their pursuits with a reckless abandon at a young age, some as teenagers, which made college an obstacle to becoming first to market. They thought about what to do with their money, but more important, what to do with their time.

Uncertain students hoping to find their calling without spending a fortune can be thankful for the evolutions of podcasts. It was not until 2004 when Adam Curry, a former MTV video jockey, and software developer Dave Winer coded a program called iPodder and brought internet radio broadcasts in the form of podcasts to the masses. Now there are over two million podcast shows available not only for free entertainment, but that share expert knowledge on nearly every field of study imaginable.

The path these superstars took can be termed high risk/high reward, as earning a college diploma does offer much greater employability and security. However, you should note that most business icons are leaders not overly concerned by employability and security and likely to label the common collegiate message of a "comfortable place to learn" an oxymoron. While many would be uncomfortable taking the unbeaten path as an entrepreneur, these legends may consider the employability and security of a nine-to-five job a risky trap of the worst discomfort.

The Costs of Teaching

A stroll through one of America's pristine campuses can help justify steep charges for room and board, *comfortable growth*. There is the unlimited cafeteria plan and alternate dining options including favorite chains such as Chick-Fil-A, Smoothie King, Panera, and more. It seems each year brings about brand-new, fully furnished townhomes that older siblings are sure to envy. The perfectly manicured lawns and gardens don't happen by themselves. These eternal construction sites warrant their bill.

The tuition piece is where critics begin to struggle with the math (see Figure 3.1). Nearly 80 percent of college professors are adjunct, or part-time, teachers. Most of these adjunct professors make a few thousand dollars per course taught. Forty percent of adjunct professors admit to difficulty covering basic household expenses.[12]

If the average private tuition expense is $38,185 and assuming the average student takes eight classes per year, that is a cost of $4,773 per class. Students are typically left paying their own laboratory fees and costs of books (often authored by their same professors). If the average college class size is 30 students (some introductory university classes can be in the hundreds), that would equal a per-class revenue of $143,190. This equation is a simplification, but a rational one. The simple subtraction of adjunct teaching costs from class revenue leaves a surplus of over $130,000 in this case.

Knowing that adjuncts, graduate assistants, even tenured professors are not to blame for the student loan epidemic, it appears the biggest expenses to a college point to the top administrators. In 2019, nineteen presidents of public universities made over $1 million, with an average compensation of $544,136.[13] The president of the University of Southern California, C. L. Max Nikias, was paid $7.6 million in 2018. For context, the most powerful position in the free world, the president of the United States, makes $400,000 annually.

The media also likes to pick on big-time athletic departments as culprits for the high costs of higher education. Sixty-seven athletic coaches, mostly football and basketball coaches, make more than their school's president. The University of Alabama's board of trustees approved an eight-year contract extension in 2021 for their legendary football coach, Nick Saban, which averages $11.7 million annually.[14] However, such coaches have had an easier time justifying their compensation than administrators because their revenues are outside of student expenses (ticket sales, television rights, team paraphernalia, etc.). For instance, the University of Texas's athletics raked in over $223 million of revenue in 2020.[15]

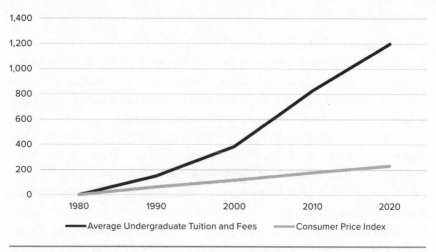

Figure 3.1 College inflation versus overall inflation (% change)[16]

ECONOMIC INSIGHT

One of the more confusing conceptsfor anyone paying a tuition bill or student loan to understand is the existence of college endowment funds. Families struggle to get their kids through college, students struggle to pay for their books, young professionals struggle to repay their debt, and politicians struggle to find more ways to help by shifting tax dollars. Meanwhile, some of the largest investment accounts in the world are owned by the same institutions behind these exorbitant bills.

As of fiscal year 2021, national college endowment assets totaled $821 billion.[17] For context, there are roughly 19.8 million students enrolled in college in the United States. If all the accounts were instantly liquidated, about $42,000 would be available to each student. But just as the Pareto principal (80/20 rule) applies to so many other areas of economics, so it appears in college funding. About 19 percent of endowments are worth more than $1 billion, accounting for 83.7 percent of all endowment assets. Harvard University has the largest endowment, worth over $51 billion at the end of fiscal year 2021, followed by the University of Texas system at $42.9 billion. Using the prior equation, Harvard has approximately 30,000 students, meaning each student could have about $1.7 million at their disposal if the account was emptied for their benefit.[18]

Most people would assume any financial aid created by these endowments would favor students from low-income households. However, as Charlie Eaton, an assistant professor of sociology at the University of California, noted, "In recent years, [the University of California] Berkeley has enrolled more low-income students than the entire Ivy League combined. Economist Raj Chetty and his collaborators have shown that thirty-eight of the top private colleges and universities—many with large endowments—enroll more students from the top one percent of the income spectrum than from the bottom sixty percent combined."[19]

The National Association of College and University Business Officers (NACUBO) has begun asking institutions how much of the gifts received for their endowments are earmarked specifically for diversity, equity, and inclusion initiatives (DEI). In 2021, 65 percent of reported gifts were for DEI.

It's understandable to not understand how an institution with a huge endowment can routinely raise its cost of tuition. The ambition to stay ahead of the curve can be a double-edged sword. Some of the most notable gifts, such as a famous alumnus donating a state-of-the-art building to campus, might cover the cost of construction. But all the future upkeep and maintenance for a hi-tech facility and the professors therein represent new liabilities. All unfunded costs must be passed on.

So why not open the coffers and start sending kids to school for free? College endowments are tasked with helping the current generation as much as possible without diminishing resources for future generations. As such, trustees of colleges and universities establish spending policies that allow their institutions to spend endowment earnings equal to about 4 to 5 percent of the endowment.[20] This long-range planning is meant to provide stability to the college or university for generations to come.

This is no different from a wealthy family drafting an estate plan. The patriarch and matriarch may have worked and saved since childhood to build their fortune. In their later years as they mull their legacy, strategies including terms like a dynasty trust, a legal document utilized to transfer wealth through generations, may be utilized. The general purpose of this planning is to allocate assets for future heirs while preserving the nest egg for as long as possible. It's common for such trusts to use strict rules regarding the disposition of assets. However, some include emergency access for occasions like health, education, maintenance, and support (HEMS). College endowment policies may also incorporate similar provisions in times of crisis.

The Evolution of College

Colleges go back further than America itself, but aside from the name, little else would be identifiable by today's students. If college is a primer to a productive economy, a primer on college's beginnings is in order. One of the main questions a potential college student in the nineteenth century had to ask himself was if he could commit to celibacy. Furthermore, could the young man forgo earthly possessions and commit to this path forever? College meant going to the seminary.

Nearly all the major universities in America are an offshoot of churches. Higher education once connoted a further pursuit of getting to know God. At the time of the Civil War, 262 of 288 college presidents were clergy.[21] This did not last long, though.

"In its religious life the college should be as little as possible denominational. The narrowness of sectarianism and the breadth of the college outlook are utterly incompatible. Denominations may lay the eggs of colleges; indeed, most of our colleges owe their inception to such denominational zeal. But as soon as the college develops strength, it passes inevitably beyond mere denominational control. Church schools are often conspicuous successes. Church colleges are usually conspicuous failures. A church university is a contradiction in terms," William DeWitt Hyde, the 26-year-old Liberal Protestant and president of Bowdoin College, proclaimed in 1885.

As subsidies to colleges from the church began to dwindle, either due to financial strain or on purpose, new college presidents found more opportunities to distance themselves from the ways of old. Around the same time, the Carnegie Foundation, with a mission to improve the science of education, started disbursing its enormous funds. In addition to Andrew Carnegie's famed libraries, the foundation rolled out a program to fund professional pensions for educators. One of the caveats for qualification was that receiving institutions must be nondenominational. Despite his legendary penchant for philanthropy stemming from his Scottish Presbyterian upbringing, Carnegie struggled throughout his life with religion. "I give money for church organs," Carnegie said in 1901 after selling his steel company to J.P. Morgan, "in the hope the organ music will distract the congregation's attention from the rest of the service." Carnegie dedicated part of his legacy to facilitating competence, but competence detached from religion.

And so, nearing the twentieth century, colleges became universities, and the new academic guild quickly replaced men of the cloth. The original universities of America, mostly Ivy League schools, carried some Christian influence, but more as a matter of tradition than practice. Even so, at the turn of the century formal education remained a novelty. In 1900, 78 percent of children between the ages of five and seventeen were enrolled in school, but few progressed to college. Most formal education was geared toward learning English and acclimating to American customs as the country became flooded by immigrants from Europe. Universities found their major sources of funding from philanthropists, like Carnegie and Rockefeller, and through the federal government via the Morrill Land Grant Colleges Act of 1862, which set aside federal lands to build colleges for agriculture and engineering.

In 1929, the Great Depression struck, and as FDR eyed the seemingly lifesaving measures of entitlements, the ideal of higher education was seen as far too elitist. Remember that the New Deal sought to relieve the unemployed and poor, restore the economy, and reform financial systems. Higher education was not even on the radar. Aside from a few universities with endowment funds, notably Harvard, most colleges watched enrollment and fundraising drop and were faced with dire straits.

Alas, the college experience that millennials and following generations enjoy today finally found its footing in 1944 with the GI Bill. The new bill gave veterans returning from World War II the chance at a free education.

Between 1939 and 1969 the number of 18- to 24-year-olds in college quadrupled.[22] Finally, the stigma of higher education existing for religious leaders, agriculturalists, or a vocation for the wealthy vanished. Veterans, which the majority of America's young men had been after World War II, came from every walk of life to pursue higher education. This kick-started an economy that would soon be based on brains instead of brawn.

While veterans matriculated in and out of the classroom, the enrollment momentum did not slow thanks to a booming postwar economy. States found themselves able to allocate surplus funds to their own colleges. Bustling campuses across the country received their ultimate shot in the arm in 1965 with the introduction of Federal Family Education Loans (FFEL). For the first time in history, private and state lenders could issue loans that were guaranteed by the US government, meaning if a borrower defaulted, the government would pay the lender to make up for the loss. These loans gave hope to every American youth.

Expansion inevitably leads to entanglement. Higher learning became so prominent as to be directly correlated to the ebbs and flows of the economy. Tuition and student loans found their way into kitchen table conversations across the country and as growing line items in state and federal budgets. In the 1970s inflation spiked, college costs soared, and subsidized loans largely replaced federal grants. At the same time, Americans felt the pain of a weakened economy and costly oil embargo, putting education on the back burner for most Americans.

Fortunately for everyone, this era served merely as a speed bump as economic prosperity soon returned and college enrollment and revenues flourished for the next few decades. The 1980s saw female students come to equal the number of male ones. The expansion of college campuses certainly added to Congress's reasoning for the National Minimum Drinking Age Act of 1984, raising the legal drinking age to 21. In the 1990s Hispanic enrollment rose 68 percent and African American enrollment by 31 percent.[23] College continued to become more widely accessible, but still at a level that a diploma was uncommon enough to almost guarantee a job upon graduation.

Affirmative Action

The current makeup of college student bodies owes much of its credit to affirmative action. Affirmative action, a result of the Civil Rights Act of 1964, is "the use of policies, legislation, programs, and procedures to improve the educational or employment opportunities of members of certain demographic groups (such as minority groups, women, and older people) as a remedy to the effects of long-standing discrimination against such groups."[24] In the 1960s and 1970s, racial quotas began to be used in college admissions as a form of reverse discrimination for women and people of color. Aiming for diversity in the classroom created the ultimate paradox—the only way to look past race was to always look at race.

In 1978, the Supreme Court heard its first challenge to affirmative action in college with *Regents of the University of California v. Bakke*. Allan Bakke, a white male, was denied admission to University of California at Davis's medical school, which had set aside 16 of its 100 seats for members of a minority group. In a five-to-four ruling, Justice Lewis F. Powell Jr. cast the deciding vote in favor of Bakke. The court outlawed quotas, but allowed colleges to use race as a factor in making admission decisions.[25] California eventually passed Proposition 209 in 1996, which outlawed affirmative action, prohibiting government agencies and institutions (including colleges) from giving preferential treatment to individuals on the basis of their race or sex.

Affirmative action has been successful in diversifying higher education, as in 1976, white students made up 80 percent of US college students, and in 2016, that percentage dropped to 57 percent. However, what advantages some prospective students naturally must disadvantage others. In 2019, 37 percent of Blacks between the ages of 18 and 24 years old were enrolled in college or graduate school, not far from the ratio of 41 percent of whites and the 41 percent national average. The biggest outlier was Asian Americans at 62 percent.[26] In 2013, Harvard conducted its own internal investigation and found a bias against Asian American applicants in its admissions process. If Harvard looked solely at academics, the investigation found 43 percent of its incoming freshmen should be Asian American. The true figure that year was 18.6 percent. The university did not act on these results or make them public until the case went to court in *Students for Fair Admissions, Inc. v. President and Fellows of Harvard College.*[27]

In the 2007 US Supreme Court case *Parents Involved in Community Schools v. Seattle School District No. 1*, the court found it unconstitutional to use race as a factor in assigning certain students to certain K–12 schools within a district to prevent racial isolation. Chief Justice John Roberts's opinion famously concluded: "The way to stop discrimination on the basis of race is to stop discriminating on the basis of race." As another reminder to the constant struggle on the subject, his colleague, then-Justice Ruth Bader Ginsburg, said during oral arguments, "It's very hard for me to see how you can have a racial objective but a nonracial means to get there." An insight from the American people was equally opaque as a 2016 Gallup poll revealed that 60 percent of Americans support affirmative action, but 70 percent don't believe race should be a factor in college admissions.[28]

Fast-forward to the Great Recession of 2008, and states primarily responsible for their own public schools were forced to cut funding. Colleges responded by raising tuition rates to cover gaps, enrollment spiked amid a labor shortage, parents navigating the subprime mortgage crisis struggled to foot the college bill, and *boom* . . . large student loans transformed into a necessary evil.

The growth of higher education is clearly a blessing, but not one without its pitfalls. College is now its own sector of the economy and an enormous multitrillion-dollar one at that. (See Figure 3.2.) But like most of America's growing industries, it rests heavily on the back of leverage.

ECONOMIC INSIGHT

The majority of consumer debt is "secured" debt. This means that there is an asset backing the associated loan. A mortgage is backed by a house; foreclose and the bank takes your home. An auto loan is backed by a car; default and the repo man arrives. This provides the lender with some assurance, and therefore the loan can often be offered at a lower interest rate.

The other type of debt is "unsecured," meaning there is no asset securing the loan. The most common form of this type of debt is the credit card. If a credit card holder cannot make their minimum monthly payment, they may go into collections and watch their credit score tank, but the lender has little other power to recoup their loan. Oftentimes in dire circumstances, the credit card lender will negotiate a reduced payment to work with the borrower, or if the borrower were to declare bankruptcy, there is a chance this debt could be discharged completely (subject to certain conditions). To offset this risk, credit cards often carry the highest variable rate of interest.

Student loans represent an intangible hybrid of the forms of debt. Literally, it is unsecured in the sense that a diploma does not have much of a trade-in value, assuming the borrower graduates. Figuratively, it can be argued that it is secure, as the borrower is securing a future stable income achieved through higher education. This hope of a secure income and corresponding on-time student loan repayments is what can allow a young adult to acquire an almost unlimited amount of debt, to finance a huge educational system, backed by the US government.

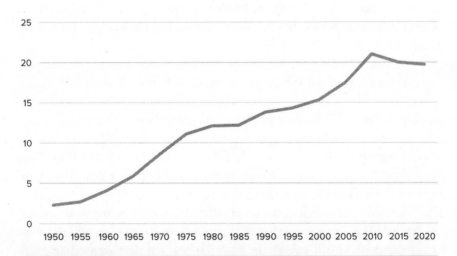

Figure 3.2   Total US college enrollment (millions)[29]

WHAT SHOULD I DO WITH MY MONEY?

Youth is bestowed but once, and never again. The costs of squandered opportunities are magnified by time as much as the value of those capitalized upon. In the realm of education, price is transparent. Prospective students can type into Google any college and filter by majors, state, region, public or private, and instantly see the current prices for tuition and room and board. But the costs to each person who pursues knowledge are entirely unique. Should parents' money go in the 529 college savings plan or the 401(k) retirement plan? Should a loan be taken against the house or from Sallie Mae? Should four years be spent in the army or in the university? Education presents a litany of "this or that" decisions full of costs for young students.

Economists are quick to point out the swinging pendulum, that every sector contracts and expands on its way to reverting to average. But not every sector of the economy finds well-balanced moderation; some disappear while others just keep moving forward. It would be impossible for a 16-year-old of the early 1900s to have even imagined pursuing a graduate degree at a college across the country, no less funded by money the family did not have. Their dinnertime conversations with Mom and Dad likely involved having to drop out of school to start working the farm.

Does the pendulum theory mean American youth will eventually be choosing work over education in their teens yet again? Or maybe progressing sectors, like education, ignore the pendulum, offering only anecdotal reflections of what once was. Grandpa's story about hitting the streets as a cop at 18 years old might never be seen again.

The student loan epidemic, masses of young professionals falling behind on debt they can't afford and postponing major life events like buying a home, is forcing students, parents, and educators to revisit their financial goals in reverse order. Can those eventual results satisfy these here costs? The college brochures that high school students swim through are full of statistics describing career results and alumni achievements. With life after graduation being the true measure of success, the aim of college is then to see how quickly students can get to where they need to be.

As previously mentioned, the median salary for a young professional with a bachelor's degree is $59,600. However, some trades can skip the education debate and still scratch the financial itch. An elevator mechanic has a median salary of $97,860. Not to mention, their "students" do not pay for education but are paid to learn, as an apprenticeship is the only educational requirement.[30] The rising demand and salaries of workers in the trades would seem to nullify the premise that college is the ticket to financial freedom.

Community colleges, trade schools, even some specialized high schools are seizing this argument. As of 2021, the national average total annual cost for in-district community college is $3,730.[31] Some states may offer completely free tuition based on the student's high school grades. The usual four-year campus luxuries and Greek life may not be the same, but it is a serious consideration for knocking out 101-level courses that can eventually offer the same diploma as a peer paying 10 times as much. The controversy over universities choosing which course credits completed at community college to accept is desperately in need of a standard outline.

What to Major In

Price aside, America is certainly not the only country that has experienced an educational revolution over the past century. It is worth noting that the majority of American colleges and universities subscribe to a liberal arts approach, cultivating the student as a whole. On the contrary, countries such as China adhere to a major declaration policy in which only the top high school students can choose a major prior to college and the rest are entered into a lottery. Once the major is determined, the student usually is not allowed to switch thereafter.

The more restrictive approach of the Chinese Communist Party allows the government to guide its future toward areas of study deemed most necessary, whereas the freedom of America's democratic system relies on the hope that capitalistic incentives will prompt youth to choose majors that the economy deems critical. China might be seen as the arranged marriage, the parent knowing what is best for the child, versus America empowering its children to pursue their own love.

America has made a noticeable push toward STEM subjects (science, technology, engineering, and mathematics), though, and many states offer their own scholarships for students headed in this direction. On the flip side, China has experimented with some liberal arts philosophies. Geoff Hall, dean of humanities and social sciences at the University of Nottingham Ningbo China, has said that the Chinese government has enabled his school to explore courses unchartered by state schools. "This has to do with the whole campaign of moving from 'Made in China' to 'Designed in China' . . . just creating scientists is not enough, you need thinkers," Hall said.[32]

In comparing the two superpowers' philosophies, it appears America has some catching up to do. The Organization for Economic Co-Operation and Development's Programme for International Student Assessment (PSIA) measures 15-year-olds' ability to use their reading, mathematical, and science knowledge and skills. The latest scores show America coming in 13th in reading, 36th in math, and 18th in science, among tested countries. China ranks first in each category.[33]

Is there one philosophy that holds the key to an ideal future workforce? It depends on what the ideal economy is supposed to look like. One might aim for the maximum number of graduates achieving financial independence while paying their fair share in taxes. Another economy might seek the road of innovation, producing graduates bred for the greater good of country and mankind. Or is each student's individual happiness the only true goal? One can hope that a democratic, capitalist American economy should continually autocorrect the educational landscape, allowing teenagers to pursue their MICE in an efficient manner.

Get Up and Go

Education can be viewed in a similar way a saver looks at their "rainy day" fund. Most wealth management professionals consider cash to be a necessary evil. It provides security, guarantees, liquidity, flexibility, and the capital needed to maximize opportunities or handle unfortunate surprises. However, by itself, cash does not provide the saver with much ability to grow their wealth, let alone keep up with inflation. Growth occurs through investing. Therefore, a rainy-day fund should be big enough to satisfy all basic requirements, but not any larger.

A life in education, like a life's earnings in cash, cannot get the job done by itself. Any accomplishment in wealth or the individual's pursuit of MICE occurs outside the walls of education and beyond a checking account. This is not at all to downplay either's priority, as we know cash and education are necessary, and in some instances, like the down payment for starting a new business or the student becoming a surgeon, its requirement might be significant. But an efficient savings and an efficient education are key to obtaining more wealth sooner. The quickest way to reaching a destination is by spending more money and time in drive, and less in neutral.

If the well-educated lifelong student (a client with all his money in cash) sits on one side of the spectrum, an entrepreneur that can't sit still stands on the other side. Between the two ends lies the harmonious collision of employment.

What can the Elon Musks, Bill Gateses, and Mark Zuckerbergs of the world, who all cut their education short in the pursuit of enterprise, teach the economy? The aim is not only success, as failure is an ingredient baked into any success, but rather the issue at hand is a need for speed. Competitive economies require learners to get up and go. *Wait, patience is a virtue, do not race to your death,* the teacher says. True, but time cannot afford to be wasted in an efficient economy.

Once students get just enough education to be let loose on the world, where should they work? There are ultimately two outcomes, the business or the government. According to the Small Business Administration, 99 percent of all businesses in America qualify as small business, and 100 percent of the other 1 percent began as small businesses. Furthermore, small businesses employ over two-thirds of new jobs and account for almost half of America's GDP.[34]

The average life span of a family business is 24 years. Only 13 percent of such businesses will be able to go from grandparent to grandchild, and less than 3 percent will ever survive to a great-grandchild.[35] Most of the deceased companies do not speed to their demise overnight, but rather slow to a halt while plundering generations of wealth. There is a form of complacency that creates an environment in which the offspring do not jibe with the business or the business does not jibe with the offspring.

How do the stories of today's greatest innovators running away from college to create businesses that likely will implode by the time they are grandparents relate to four years on campus? A key to educating an effective and efficient workforce is to look at college like a business. Amid the countless ratings assigned to institutions of higher learning, a measurable and meaningful barometer would be to survey alumni, asking four simple questions that every prospective student must be thinking about. This survey could be sent out every decade to its alumni to capture the college's lasting impact on the various stations of life:

1. Are you financially independent?
2. Have you achieved your professional goals?
3. Are you happy?
4. Rate how large an impact your time in college had on these three metrics.

What About the Debt?

The decisions thus far about where to learn, how to learn, and how to pay for it all, are all microeconomic. They might revolve around macro circumstances, like tuition, loan interest rates, and affirmative action, but every graduating class is a microeconomy formed by individual decisions. Any change on the macroeconomic side, what "they" can do with their money, will be influenced by the proverbial elephant in the room—national debt. A trillion dollars used to make headlines. Contemplating that sentence for a moment might assuage the anguish of student loans by itself. Yes, 1.7 trillion is a big number; only math fanatics would know there are 11 zeros in the figure without typing it out. But remember, there are a lot of people now, a lot of graduates making up over 46 million borrowers. This translates to the most formally educated workforce in American history.

Big numbers drag inflation back into the conversation. Along with inflated college costs and student loan debt comes an inflated number of college students, followed by inflated incomes. Fortunately for borrowers, this trend has coincided with a long period of historically low interest rates. The interest rate on federal direct loans for undergraduate borrowers in the academic year 2021–2022 was 3.73 percent.[36] Rates throughout the 2000s can make borrowers' respective debts feel "cheaper" than comparable amounts taken out, say, in the 1980s (or new rates at the time you read this book). The pausing of all accruing interest on federal student loan debt during and after the Covid-19 pandemic only exaggerated this feeling. So what's the big deal?

The message is that student loan debt may be an epidemic, but a surmountable one spread among millions of very educated citizens with lots of time on their side. This could be one financial solution; simply let it play out. Community colleges and specialized schools can continue competing with four-year universities for frugal students, while society pushes its graduates to put their diplomas to use and repay their debts.

The more popular answer involves monetary and fiscal intervention. Low interest rates were just referenced in the appeal of student loans. As the economy fluctuates, such as the recent 2022 introduction of red-hot inflation on the back of stimulus and low interest rates, the Fed stepped in to rapidly raise interest rates and curtail inflation. This will translate to higher costs to service student loan debt at higher interest rates across the board, possibly reducing demand for formal education as it does to every service or asset requiring financing. Colleges may have to reduce tuition rates and slow their campus expansions to continue attracting students and their parents' funds. The pool of uncertain students at college because they could be, rather than should be, will likely shrink. A swinging pendulum.

The formal education train could plow forward in spite of high interest rates or a faltering economy if fiscal intervention deems college a priority (i.e., continuing student loan forbearance or even forgiving some student loan debt). You can decide if political opinions on the matter are economically driven, altruistic to America's youth, or just plain politics. Proponents of student loan forgiveness and other forms of relief can satisfy all three of these motives simultaneously, at least at face value. First, plenty of charts can be made available to placate capitalists by likening its economic boost to that of a tax cut; youngsters will have newfound surpluses to pay down other debts or buy houses, start families, and spend in the economy. Second, it is an obvious help to any borrower feeling cash strapped. Last, there are 43 million votes that could be swayed by such a helping hand.

Why then would a politician not want to keep feeding the monster? *If it sounds too good to be true*, the contrarian rebuts. The equal and opposite reactions of physics remain present in shifting line items on any balance sheet. In a country already drawing criticism for its ballooning debt and budget deficits, America could stand to lose $1.7 trillion of "accounts receivable," plus interest. Next, the altruistic rationale can quickly be debunked by claiming moral hazard. The necessary work ethic and discipline regarding debt management and budgeting could fade with the removal of natural consequences, such as repaying what is owed. Finally, on the point of appealing to voters every couple of years, prior generations may perceive an attack on both sides—having paid the full sticker price yesterday, only to be taxed tomorrow for a novel entitlement.

While education planning may be a primary goal of financial planning, the scientific truths of nature versus nurture still persist. If Tiger Woods' father never showed him how to golf, he still likely would have been able to best any country club hack spending thousands of dollars each year on lessons. Nature, or informal nurture, might explain why Richard Schulze could skip college and found a company called Best Buy, while a graduate from Wharton might struggle to find a perfect career. A college, like any organization, must then investigate its role in recruiting good students versus creating good students.

Colleges have unquestionably provided great incubators for professional advancement, and the United States plays host to most of the best in the world, but economics continue to ask educators and students alike to prove its costs. No matter its form, education espoused around a campfire or from PhDs at Yale, the driver of innovation and prosperity must always prove its costs. To ignore the economics of learning is as foolhardy as to ignore the learning of economics.

ECONOMIC INSIGHT

The best way to avoid the student loan epidemic is to avoid student loans. While loans are necessary for the majority of students, the burden can be alleviated, like most financial woes, by planning ahead. Not every new mom and dad have the means to start thinking about college planning with toddlers crawling around, which underscores why it is so important to fold college into an overall financial plan.

Early in my career, I was referred to a woman who had recently lost her husband. Aside from being devastated by losing the love of her life, she had to immediately fill his role as breadwinner and financial decision maker, while still being mom to her high school daughter. The last thing she wanted to do was interrupt her daughter's ambition for going to college.

I sat down at her kitchen table and learned about their family. As I began fact-finding the widow's financial situation, I was disheartened to learn her late husband did not carry any life insurance. He did at one time, but when he got sick and had to leave his job, he lost the Group Term Life Insurance he had considered adequate throughout his career. They had limited savings, a couple of auto loans, some small credit card debt, and a fair amount of equity in their home. I quickly noticed his primary financial plan was maxing out his 401(k). They shied away from ever doing a 529 College Savings Plan as they were turned off by the possible penalties subject to withdrawals that weren't for "qualified education expenses."

Her daughter joined us halfway through our meeting and expressed how badly she wanted to go to college next year and that she was near the top of her class. Her mom, juggling emotions of total pride in her girl with the sadness of their situation, said she would do whatever it takes. They both joked that it seemed they were poor, but not poor enough for many of the scholarships and financial aid applications.

When the first tuition bill came, to avoid depleting her limited savings, we were forced to turn to her late husband's 401(k), which we had since rolled over into an IRA in her name. The funds were available penalty free, but still fully taxable as ordinary income. The tax deductions their accountant had promoted for so many years were now acting like a morphine drip to a dying patient. Every dollar withdrawn pushed her toward a higher tax bracket, lowered her tax refund, and made any financial aid less likely.

Despite her late husband's efforts, his lack of diversity in account holdings, which were focused so heavily in retirement plans, led to a liquidity crunch and unfavorable tax ramifications when it came to college. The small saving grace was the home equity line of credit (HELOC) we were able to access to provide much-needed tax-free cash to help with college and clear up their lingering credit card debt. Her story is a stark reminder to the importance of individual life insurance to provide an influx of capital when life needs it most.

ECONOMIC PHILOSOPHY

Economic philosophy tells a story much greater than money, beyond inflows and outflows, or rich versus poor. It is a story about the human mind, the way people are raised, the groups they form, the thoughts they share. How people think about how people think. Economics creates the echo chambers standing between here and there, us and them. Another story from one person to another, and another, then another.

It's the economy, stupid.

—James Carville

J eff walks across the sprawling campus on a late-August day, taking time to appreciate the shimmering ponds flanked by historic buildings. It is enough to inspire any youth toward higher education. Over 40,000 students, faculty, and staff from across the world move to and fro. A passing student smiles and lifts her Starbucks cup, "caramel macchiato," he guesses. But most have their heads down, engulfed in the newest iPhone, sensory deprivation induced by AirPods.

Jeff notices the famed auditorium on his left, imagining who he could listen to one day at graduation—a celebrity, the president, business icons, perhaps someone controversial. After all, this was the same building that hosted Mahmoud Ahmadinejad when he was president of Iran. Inside is the same stage where he claimed homosexuals did not exist in his country, denounced Israel, and called the Holocaust a theory without fact.

Jeff notices the same pamphlet plastered on each lamppost: ABOLISH CAPITALISM!! At the bottom, in fine print—*Sponsored by Columbia Socialist Club*. Entitlements. Education. Economics. Here, youth converge ready to fix the Three Big Es.

The other four of the top-five ranked schools in America—Princeton, Harvard, Massachusetts Institute of Technology, and Yale—each have their own socialist club too. Most are divisions of the Democratic Socialists of America. Many campuses also have Young Republican organizations, although they are noticeably smaller, not enough to create a capitalist subset. In 1994, 39 percent of college graduates identified as Democrat; in 2019, 57 percent of graduates were Democrat. Voters with postgraduate degrees lean even further Democrat (61 percent).[1] The liberal agenda of most college campuses is no secret. Since Senator Bernie Sanders ran for president on a socialist campaign, what was once thought of as a dirty word has become hip.

These hallowed halls welcome the brightest minds not just in America, but from around the globe. They contain the promise of the future. Academia plays host to the collision of preconceived notions, economics, and politics, all wrapped under the umbrella of learning.

Caught daydreaming about debates with his new roommates, Jeff snaps himself out of the fog. Tomorrow is the first real day of college:

8:00 a.m. . . . . . Intro to Robotics 101
10:30 a.m. . . . Analytical Physics Lab 102

2:30 p.m. . . . . Biokinetics and Thermo 201

6:30 p.m. . . . . Gender Classification and Inclusion 101

The lamppost draws Jeff back. He takes a mental note of the meeting place and time for the Socialist Club's first meet-and-greet of the semester. *Definitely not something I'll learn as a biomedical engineering major.* He imagines how angry his parents would be about his getting sidetracked already.

It is an opportunity to make new friends, learn some new ideas, and maybe catch an argument that will make YouTube. He has not picked up his books yet for his first fall semester and already the urge to belong to a group is playing head games.

MACRO

Trade-offs, *incentives*, and *economics* are terms that can easily blur together. The previous two chapters on entitlements and education already displayed the persistent nature of quid pro quo, that there is no free lunch, and every decision will boil down to a compromise. The point of economic thinking, though, is to assign value to each and every undertaking—a monetary value and an emotional value.

The monetary aspect in a decision can be apparent, such as an expected expense or profit of doing business. It is price. It is the money (M) in MICE. Aside from scams and misrepresentation, the only extra layer in money comes in the form of a lost opportunity cost, defined as the missing of an otherwise potential profit, investment, or period of productivity and all its returns or losses thereafter. The limited scope of money means that monetary consequences offer the benefit of being measurable, just as all parties to the equation can agree that one plus one equals two.

Emotional components are often far more complex as their economic value is ascertainable only to the beholder. It is the ideology (I), compromise (C), and ego (E) found within MICE. There is no exchange of agreed-upon prices for these three domains. Simply put, emotion measures how badly the individual decision maker wants a certain outcome. It has little to do with price, but everything to do with cost. As mentioned in the Introduction, only *you* can define cost. The emotional component of wealth is what can appear to stump basic math in any compromise, because to the other side, one and one may come together to make eleven.

Since the world acts as a perpetual market, directed by the supply and demand of every endeavor, the blind pursuit of emotion is impossible. Entitle everyone, educate everyone, tax nothing. Utopia. Impossible. Emotional desires cannot be addressed if financial prerequisites are not satisfied. This is the reality economics teaches. Financial freedom is a part of emotional freedom.

In order to answer the second question from which this book began— why any financial recommendation is the right one—it is critical that individuals and companies rank the nonfinancial outcomes of financial decisions, and vice versa. An economy purely chasing profit, in the best case, is bound to lose sight of its purpose, and in the worst case may be motivated to take immoral or unethical action. Whereas an economy fixated on ICE is on borrowed time from anyone with a financial interest. Even the most noble charities will agree that just because *nonprofit* implies not making profits, it does not mean making losses. This ranking and prioritizing of goals and their costs is what starts a financial plan, molds a microeconomy, and changes the way a macroeconomy governs itself.

Starting from the top, recognize that macroeconomics are a lagging indicator of people's wants and needs; they are the circumstances thrust upon us by everything up to this moment in time. They are the agreements and disagreements of prior generations of givers and takers. In order to take advantage of the situation one must understand the origin of circumstances, why such rules and norms exist, the intent of their makeup, and the ripple effect of macroeconomics.

Macroeconomics are most identifiable by nation, as a government's stance on economics dictates the character of a country. Such a statement may sound extreme against the context of winning and losing wars, social policy, and other identities, but the undertone that affects its citizens' daily lives is a nation's stance on finance. Like a painter who cannot afford a brush, a country without financial backing cannot afford to provide for its people.

Capitalism Versus Socialism

To prevent the dreaded argument between two likeminded parties misinterpreting each other's words, this chapter must begin with a set of agreed-upon definitions. As Thomas Jefferson once said, "Every difference in opinion is not a difference in principle." The easiest way to begin analyzing an economy is by its tilt toward capitalism or socialism. These are two extremes, perhaps sparking emotional or political biases merely by their mention. It has become protocol to tag each nation as one or the other, but in reality, almost all nations are a combination of the two philosophies. Not only that, but time has a way of rewriting each government's mantra. For instance, the world knows Italy as a democratic republic, not the autocracy of Emperor Caesar's ancient Rome.

Merriam-Webster defines *capitalism* as "an economic system characterized by private or corporate ownership of capital goods, by investments that are determined by private decision, and by prices, production, and the distribution of goods that are determined mainly by competition in a free market."[2] Capitalists focus on incentives, people responding rationally to natural motives. The harder one works, the more one deserves. The better one is, the more one gets. Its protagonist says capitalism is fair and worthy, assuming everyone will play by the rules. The antagonist says capitalism is cutthroat and greedy, assuming people's lust for power and money makes corruption inevitable. Competition is the lifeblood of capitalism.

Conversely, *socialism* is defined as "any of various economic and political theories advocating collective or governmental ownership and administration of the means of production and distribution of goods, or a system of society or group living in which there is no private property."[3] Socialists focus on equality. Socialism's protagonist supports a happy utopia of everyone embracing the same standard of living, and assumes a preexisting and unending amount of government wealth. The antagonist envisions a world of lazy people milking the system amid a few suckers working hard for no reason, assuming zero incentives equals zero work.

In short, a purely capitalist economy would believe in zero taxation and eternal individual property rights. A socialist one would believe in 100 percent taxation and the sharing of every creation and accumulation. The capitalist yearns for a level playing field whereas the socialist wants level results.

These two economic disciplines can serve as a societal guide but often produce contradictory results. For example, Russia has historically leaned socialist, but has witnessed a long-standing wealth gap between the concentration of money among oligarchs versus the rest of the populace. The 500 richest Russians hold over 40 percent of the country's wealth, three times the global average distribution of wealth.[4] This suggests either a façade of socialism masking true capitalism of which the Russian elite outcompeted their peers, or a socialist society grossly abused by a corrupt few.

On the other side, America has been considered the capitalist capital of the world. However, the by-products of the country's capitalism have always been geared toward the masses. R. H. Macy, the founder of Macy's department stores, sold "goods suitable for the millionaire at prices in reach of the millions." Henry Ford's Model T was a "car of the common man." Amadeo Giannini, founder of Bank of America, swore to bring banking to "the little guy." Jeff Bezos, the richest man in history, created a product equally accessible to over 200 million subscribers.

One could argue that the ultimate purpose of globalized capitalism is to make unaffordable items affordable everywhere. However, the process in accomplishing this feat is an economic catch-22. Before capitalism becomes beneficial to the working class, it is initially most harmful to the same working class. For example, thousands of blue-collar workers lost their jobs in Detroit's auto factories before they could buy improved and cheaper cars by way of Japan. The bane of capitalism's existence is in creating some new losers before creating lots of new winners.

Removing any preconceived biases or emotional attachments to either school of thought could be worth the price of this book by itself. Unfortunately, it has become incumbent upon any leader or elected official to pledge allegiance to either side and then request undying loyalty. When comparing societies and nations, the labeling of *capitalist* or *socialist* is casually tossed around, despite the reality that neither practicum can ever be fully realized.

The US Economy

The US Constitution, written in 1787 and ratified in 1788, established that America would be a unified common market free from taxes on interstate commerce and without internal tariffs. Federal income tax was not even made permanent until 1913. Prior to that time there were only temporary experiments in taxation used to finance war debts, such as President Lincoln's

Revenue Act of 1861 to fund the Civil War. Otherwise, a dollar earned was a dollar kept.

In respect to the other tenet of socialism—government control—the few publicly controlled aspects in early America were relegated to policing and public safety. That all changed on a dime in FDR's first 100 days in office when he proposed the Federal Deposit Insurance Corporation (FDIC), Securities Exchange Commission (SEC), Civilian Conservation Corps (CCC), Federal Emergency Relief Administration (FERA), Tennessee Valley Authority (TVA), National Recovery Administration (NRA), and Public Works Administration (PWA), just to name a few acronyms that rewrote America's playbook. FDR officially put the lid on the laissez-faire capitalism that the robber barons enjoyed at the turn of the nineteenth century with the passage of the National Industrial Recovery Act. This shifted power from the boss to the worker, causing trade-union membership to skyrocket. By 1945, nearly one in three nonagricultural workers belonged to a union.[5]

Historians and economists alike still debate whether the New Deal saved America from the Great Depression or not. No one will ever know for sure as the alternative approaches are pure speculation, but the immediate economic indicators did not favor FDR. Much of the business world felt that FDR had declared war on the same economic machinery that the United States needed to mount a comeback. According to the League of Nations, in 1929 America had the lowest unemployment rate in the world at 1 percent, versus a 5.4 percent international average. By 1932, in the depths of the Depression, US unemployment was 24.9 percent versus the global average of 21.1 percent. By 1938, after the New Deal, American unemployment lingered at 19.8 percent, well above the 11.4 percent international average.[6] (See Figure 4.1.)

Many people often forget that one of the worst market downturns in history happened shortly after the Great Depression. From 1929 to 1932 the Dow infamously plummeted 89 percent from its peak. This cast a long shadow over the stock market's performance. But after passing the New Deal, during FDR's second term, the 1937–1938 crash caused the Dow to drop almost 50 percent.[7] The ultimate cure for America's darkest days will be discussed in a later chapter.

As the twentieth century unfolded, the give and take between America's government and its citizens continually shifted. In 1913 the top tax bracket was 7 percent on all income over $500,000, by 1944 the top rate peaked at 94 percent on taxable income over $200,000, then from the 1950s to the 1970s, the top federal tax rate never dipped below 70 percent.

The trend toward bigger government continued uninterrupted for almost four decades. It was not until American dominance began to waver during the stagflation of the 1970s that change came from an unlikely source. The influence of unions peaked as laborers overpowered employers, striking for more pay and less work. At the same time, globalization supercharged foreign economies and linchpin American industries fled overseas to new hubs of innovation like Japan and Germany. President Jimmy Carter, a Democrat, displayed his aggravation in his second State of the Union in 1979 saying, "Government cannot solve our problems. It cannot eliminate poverty or provide a bountiful economy, or reduce inflation, or save our cities, or cure illiteracy, or provide energy." While socially liberal and a proud supporter of civil rights, Carter was surprisingly fiscally conservative and quick to deregulate America.

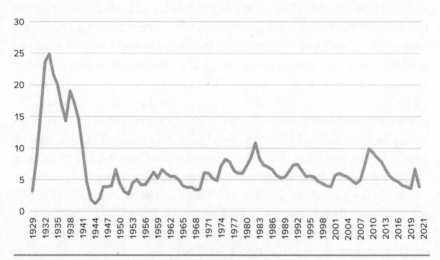

Figure 4.1   US unemployment rate, 1929–2021[8]

To complete the back-to-back ironies, capitalism finally came back in vogue by way of Hollywood. In his first year in office, President Ronald Reagan passed the Economic Recovery Tax Act of 1981, bringing the top marginal tax rate from 70 percent down to 50 percent. Defending his argument for smaller government, Reagan blamed politicians for ending America's postwar boom. "Government's view of the economy could be summed up in a few short phrases," he declared. "If it moves, tax it. If it keeps moving, regulate it. And if it stops moving, subsidize it."

However, the Great Communicator began a trend of conservative contradictions that needs to be analyzed by time frame, as it seemingly yields great economic results in the near term, with potentially hidden traps in the long term. Reaganomics became famous for cutting taxes, *not* for cutting spending. During his tenure, public expenditures increased significantly, particularly for the Department of Defense. Reagan created more national debt than all the presidents who preceded him combined. He found cutting taxes to be far easier than cutting spending. The process of cutting taxes while borrowing to uphold spending repeated itself in a similar fashion via the second George Bush and more recently by Donald Trump.

In 2022, the highest personal income tax rate was 37 percent. It is common to brand a nation as capitalist or socialist based on its rate of taxation. A country with little taxation, in which companies and productive givers don't have to give much to their government, is clearly capitalist. A country with very high taxation, taking many of the fruits of its best laborers to share the wealth, is obviously socialist. According to the metric of taxation, America has shifted its socialist and capitalist tendencies dramatically.

So was America more capitalist in 2022 than in 1944, a time when the highest income tax rate was more than twice as high? Many observers would say absolutely not, referencing the current number of government programs and spending that dwarf the entire economy of 1944. But the opposing side could cite the lower top marginal tax rate along with the richest companies in world history, such as Amazon and Apple, as proof of modern American capitalism.

In viewing national debt as a measure of state intervention, Democrats and Republicans are both present. The top five socialist-friendly administrations, in terms of leverage used for public good, would be FDR (national debt increase of 1,048 percent), Woodrow Wilson (723 percent), Ronald Reagan (186 percent), George W. Bush (101 percent), and Barack Obama (74 percent)[9].

According to the 2022 Economic Freedom of the World Index, the United States is the twenty-fifth most capitalist country on Earth (Singapore coming in first). America is defined as a mixed-market economy, parts capitalist and parts socialist. The capitalist parts include private ownership and for-profit businesses. The socialist aspects involve taxation, government regulation, subsidies, and some public control over healthcare, education, and infrastructure. It is these latter components that caused the United States to receive its lowest economic freedom ranking ever, as the report cited "excessive government spending, unsustainable levels of debt, and intrusive regulation of the health care and financial sectors."[10]

The Chinese Economy

The opposing superpower, and socialist counterpart, would be China. Despite its full name the "People's Republic of China," capitalist at face value, it is governed by the more aptly named Communist Party of China. China's history dates back thousands of years, led by various monarchies and dynasties, but it was not until 1971 that the United Nations formally recognized the People's Republic of China.

China's identity as a one-party state is why it is recognized as communist. Communism is a further iteration of socialism, exercising absolute control beyond the financial realm. It is "a theory advocating elimination of private property. A totalitarian system of government in which a single authoritarian party controls state-owned means of production."[11] All communists are socialists, but not all socialists are communists. An example of China exercising total control, moving beyond economically socialist into being governmentally communist, is the fact that the most populated country in the world follows a single standard time offset of UTC+8:00, despite spanning five geographical time zones bordering 14 different countries.

Concentrating on the financial aspect, China actually has a progressive marginal tax system not all that different from the United States. As of this writing, the Chinese income tax brackets range from 3 percent to 45 percent.[12] However, its minimum social security contribution is relatively high, which creates a regressive effect by disproportionately hitting poor workers. According to the World Bank's 2017 "Doing Business" report, a report designed to enlighten policymakers, help countries make informed decisions, and measure economic and social improvements accurately, the estimated corporate tax rate on profits, from direct and indirect taxes, was a staggering 68 percent (the top US corporate tax rate was 21 percent in 2022). The majority of tax revenue comes from China's VAT (value-added tax), a type of tax that is assessed on the price of a product or service at each stage of production, distribution, and sale. Most Chinese companies remain either state-owned or effectively controlled by the government.

Despite China's high tax status, it offers a low level of public benefits, as most tax revenue is spent on military and infrastructure. The 2022 Chinese defense budget was $230 billion.[13] This is second only to the US defense budget of $770 billion in 2022.[14]

Despite their socialist reputation, China's economy has grown 36-fold over the past three decades. After the death of President Mao Zedong in 1976, Deng Xiaoping took control of the economy and implemented China's "Open Door Policy," embracing globalization and foreign trade and investment. These market-oriented reforms created an unforeseen private sector. According to the World Bank, China's GDP has averaged over 10 percent growth every year since 1978, fueled by manufacturing, exports, and low-paid labor. China's share of international exports increased from 1 percent in 1980 to 15 percent in 2020, the most in the world.[15] China is closing in on having twice as many billionaires as the United States does.

To compare the overall economic strength of the world's two premier competitors, the United States has a $21 trillion GDP versus China's $15 trillion (see Figure 4.2). However, in translating these statistics to what it means to the individual citizen, America's GDP per capita is $63,051, six times greater than China's $10,582.[16] (See Figure 4.3.) China has nearly 600 million citizens living in poverty, nearly double the population of America.[17] Like Russia and its oligarchs, this wealth disparity could be considered the antithesis of socialism.

However, over the past decade Chinese economic growth has tapered. Exporting dominance appears to be peaking as domestic demand increases, more educated youth enter the workforce, and increased automation offshores their foothold on manufacturing. While China's GDP growth has still been above average, it has slowed dramatically. It's annual GDP growth rate exceeded 14 percent in 2007, but since 2014 has been only half that and plummeted most recently to 2.3 percent during the 2020 coronavirus pandemic. Granted, the US annual GDP growth rate has not eclipsed 3 percent since 2005 and actually went negative in 2020 and 2022.[18] Both countries are rapidly running into an aging crisis that typically translates to more takers and fewer givers. By 2035, an estimated 20 percent of China's population, equal to roughly the entire US population, will be senior citizens.[19]

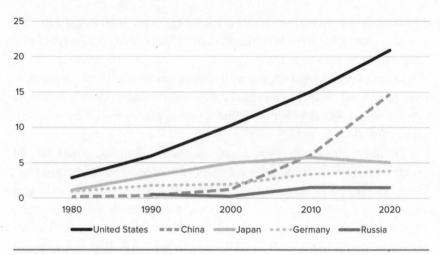

Figure 4.2   GDP (trillion USD)[20]

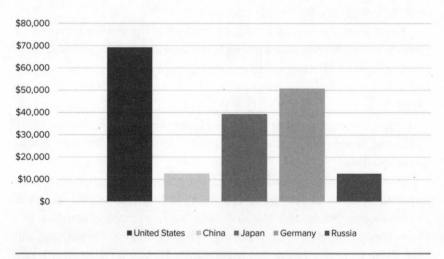

Figure 4.3   GDP per capita (USD, 2021)[21]

China is not ready to let go of its grasp on international exports, though. In 2013, President Xi Jinping pledged to start a modern version of the Silk Road, the ancient trade routes connecting the East and West, which he calls the Belt and Road Initiative. The first phase is the "Silk Road Economic Belt" and the second phase is the "21st Century Maritime Silk Road." The plans call for a network of roads, rails, and shipping ports that will connect China, Europe, Asia, and the Middle East, touching 65 percent of the global population and 40 percent of world GDP. With an estimated cost of $5 trillion, China sees the investment as an opportunity to monopolize its trade, tax member countries, limit dependence on the United States, internationalize the Chinese yuan, and possibly ban competitor nations from using its trade routes. As Sun Tzu, the legendary Chinese author of *The Art of War*, once said, "The line between disorder and order lies in logistics." However, China now has a Belt and Road 2.0 initiative after billions of dollars of its loans to developing nations have not been repaid.

The most recent growth in China has stemmed from a transition from manufacturing to real estate. Real estate and property services now make up an astounding 29 percent of China's GDP,[22] versus 16.9 percent in the United States.[23] China has adopted a strategy of building on credit to boost its GDP, which appears unsustainable as millions of properties sit vacant across the country.

This smells of the American building boom, excessive development propped up by subprime mortgages, that led up to the 2008 Great Recession. Perhaps China likens its speculative real estate development to the birth of the American stock market on the backs of nineteenth-century railroad tycoons. But even then, the approach of building ahead of demand led to many useless railways. In 1890, America west of the Mississippi had only 24 percent of the country's population but 43 percent of its railroads. This overbuilding led to the bankruptcy of over 700 railroad companies.[24] China appears to be breeding a similar debacle with real estate in modern times.

The China Evergrande Group, a property developer and one of China's largest companies, watched its stock price fall over 80 percent in 2021. As of this writing, the overleveraged company holds more than $300 billion of debt and is struggling to sell assets in a slowing real estate market. Lenders around the world, particularly within China, are left wondering if they will ever see repayment. The Chinese government will likely have one of its first go-rounds of "Too Big to Fail," a government bailout of systemically critical companies, like Americans witnessed in 2008.

China's relatively new experiment with state-run capitalism may encounter the human error inherent to economic freedom. Capitalism can supercharge an economy to the point of hubris. Hubris in finance easily leads to leverage. Bubbles are a part of any growing economy; most bubbles deflate, but leveraged bubbles can burst.

ECONOMIC INSIGHT

A prudent investor must consider the who, what, when, why, where, and how in every financial decision. "Where" has become a larger factor since globalization and the internet made the world a much smaller place. One hundred years ago, investing in companies in another state was out of reach for most Americans. Today, investing in an unheard-of company across the globe can be done by almost anyone with the click of a button.

Based on the past few pages, it would be fair to discern that enterprise wants capitalism. Companies relish in low taxes, low regulation, and high property rights. One might argue that this type of free competition inevitably leads to monopolies and the crushing of former industries. Shouldn't a nation pump the breaks in concern of caring for its losers? The truth is a purely capitalist government is like that win-at-all-costs coach who so easily shucks aside his legendary captain for a rising star in better shape. It may be unfortunate for the player, but the team is all about winning.

It behooves an investor to notice where a company calls home. Remember the discussion on population migration and its economic impact, particularly on real estate prices; political stance is as relevant between state lines as it is internationally. According to the 2022 Index of Economic Freedom, the top three economically freest countries are Singapore, Switzerland, and Ireland, respectively. In regard to the two superpowers, the United States ranks at 25 and China 158. The countries with the lowest scores belong to North Korea, Venezuela, Cuba, and Sudan, respectively.[25]

Does this suggest dumping all your investments in the United States for opportunities in Ireland? Of course not. Smaller, more nimble countries typically make up the ends of the spectrum as they have an easier path to extreme capitalism or extreme socialism. Megaeconomies like the United States or China will fall closer to the mean, as it requires a sea change to move them in either direction. As a side note, many investors are surprised to find so many Chinese companies within their emerging markets fund, asking how the second biggest economy on Earth is "emerging." This is because technically its GDP per capita is low enough to fit the category. What data on economic freedom can suggest are rising opportunities, like Ireland or Singapore, and obvious red flags—good luck investing in North Korea or Sudan.

Historically speaking, large-cap stocks, companies with a market capitalization over $10 billion, have been less volatile than small-cap stocks, typically regarded as those worth $300 million to $2 billion. That does not necessarily mean they are better or worse, though. In 1997 and 1998, Amazon was a small-cap stock. In 2010, Tesla was a small-cap stock. Now, they are both recognized as two of the largest companies in history. Conversely, Lehman Brothers had assets worth over $691 billion when it declared bankruptcy in 2008. So, will Ireland or Singapore become two of the biggest macroeconomies in history, performing like Amazon or Tesla? Can a United States or China go bankrupt like Lehman did? Probably not, as there are more layers to nations than corporations. The analogy displays areas for private investors and corporations alike to pursue newfound profits, with the pros and cons inherent to small-cap volatility.

The takeaway in analyzing and debating various economies is that absolute classification is unfair. This should provide two sources of comfort to humanity. First, if wars are waged on the basis of economic disagreement, the world's two superpowers are beginning to look more alike, and more important, its people want to look more like the other. America, particularly its youth, has welcomed socialist concepts with open arms, whereas Chinese business, especially its somewhat included city of Hong Kong, is scrambling for capitalism. The United States has undoubtedly become more socialist in recent memory, whereas China has grown more capitalist.

Second, if one school of thought is superior to the other, capitalism over socialism or vice versa, the shifting blend within these mixed economies should provide a relatively level playing field over time. Without completely putting on rose-colored glasses, this suggests that people from opposite sides of the globe with completely different upbringings share a desire for a somewhat similar balance of free enterprise and government support.

So who picks a country's posture toward capitalism or socialism? *The people!* A free democratic society is truly a reflection of its citizens. Entrepreneurs, unions, and corporate execs all ask the same "What should I do with my money?" question. The answers often involve politics.

A Painless Refresher of the US Political Pipeline

A quick refresher on how the American economy takes one step in either direction can help make sense of why the world's biggest economy is the way it is. As everyone's middle school social studies teacher explained, there are three branches of the US government—the executive, legislative, and judicial. There is one other major economic influencer, not directly tied to the government, in the Federal Reserve System (the Fed).

The three branches of government control what is known as "fiscal policy," the use of government spending and taxation. The chain of events for such decisions typically follows as such . . .

The president (executive branch), with help from relevant government agencies, the IRS, and various professionals, recommends new tax legislation or spending projects. These monumental proposals are usually the follow-through on prior campaign promises championing capitalism and less taxes and regulation, or socialism and taxing the rich to provide more public benefits. The Treasury then fine-tunes the draft.

Next, the president formally submits this draft to Congress (legislative branch). The president can propose legislation anytime, but taxation is usually discussed in the annual Economic Report of the President every January. According to Article 1 Section 8 of the Constitution, the so-called Taxing and Spending Clause, Congress has the power to "lay and collect taxes" to "provide for the common defense and general welfare." Tax legislation originates in the House of Representatives (the congressmen and congresswomen), specifically with the House Ways and Means Committee.

If the bill passes through the House, it moves on to the Senate (US senators making up the other side of the legislative branch), specifically to the Senate Finance Committee. Rarely does the Senate immediately agree with the House and send the bill back to the president; rather they create a new, amended version of the House's bill. The House usually disagrees with the Senate's bill, and then both bills get sent to a Conference Committee. The Conference Committee then sends its compromise back to the House and Senate for vote. Much of this back-and-forth is guided by "special interest groups" lobbying for their cause with war chests full of cash, while reminding their elected representatives and senators where their votes and campaign financing come from.

If the bill is adopted, it is then sent back to the White House for the president to either veto or sign into law. The president can choose to follow through on those prior campaign promises, adapt and do what he thinks is best at the time, or jump on the bandwagon by following what the current ever-changing polls of the American people show. He, maybe someday she, must analyze what they want to do, need to do, and can do.

While the judicial branch is not directly involved in such tax and spending decisions, it does have the ability to challenge these laws as unconstitutional. The Supreme Court, comprising justices serving lifetime terms at the appointment of the president, can render an ultimate decision.

Aside from this lengthy process, the president does hold the power of executive orders. Executive orders are not law, they do not require approval by Congress, and they can only be overturned by the sitting president. Their purpose is to guide operations of the federal government.

Monetary Policy

While politicians and their fiscal policy play a huge role in America's financial well-being, equal, if not more impactful, tools are granted to the Fed to control "monetary policy." The Federal Reserve System, founded in 1913, is the central banking system of America. The Fed serves a dual mandate to maintain low unemployment and control inflation. The Fed is able to add or subtract money in the economy, stabilize the financial system, keep banks safe, and keep consumers safe from fraud and predatory institutions.

The Federal Open Market Committee (FOMC) consists of seven members of the Board of Governors of the Federal Reserve System and five Federal Reserve bank presidents. Its main controls include raising or lowering the federal funds rate, the interest rate that financial institutions charge each other for loans in the overnight market for reserves. Banks must keep a minimum reserve level in proportion to their customer deposits on hand. If a bank has excess reserves at the end of the day, it may lend them at interest to a bank that is in a deficit. A lower rate, or "accommodative rate," means it costs less for the bank to acquire an overnight loan, a benefit passed on to American consumers through "cheap" lending, leading to more money flowing through the economy and spurring inflation. A higher rate, or "restrictive rate," can accomplish the opposite outcome through relatively costlier loans. The Fed also can adjust short-term interest rates, the discount rate banks pay on loans from the Fed, and similarly increase or decrease the money supply.

The Fed also governs the reserve requirements of banks, how much cash they must keep on hand or in reserve bank accounts. After climbing out of the 2007–2008 financial crisis, the Fed dramatically increased reserve requirements. During the 2020 coronavirus pandemic, the Federal Reserve reduced reserve requirement percentages for all depository institutions to zero, essentially asking banks to flood the economy with their cash on hand.

Last, the Fed, particularly the Federal Reserve Bank of New York, can conduct what are known as "open-market operations" by buying and selling US government securities, such as treasuries. The US Treasury issues new debt, treasuries backed by the full faith and credit of the US government, which go up for auction to banks and other financial institutions. The Fed buys these bonds from banks, instantly crediting their accounts to increase bank reserves and foster more lending. This is what critics refer to as "the Fed printing money out of thin air." Technically speaking, the US Treasury prints actual dollars, but the Fed is the one instantly creating electronic dollars at name-brand banks such as Wells Fargo, Bank of America, and so on. This exercise has led the Fed's assets to grow from less than $1 trillion in 2008 to nearly $9 trillion in 2021.[26] In 2022, the Fed reversed its quantitative easing by letting assets roll off its balance sheet to reduce inflation.

While the Fed is considered independent, it is overseen by a board of governors appointed by the president, called the Federal Reserve Board. The chairman of the Fed also reports to Congress twice a year.

The Fed is not directly responsible for any preference toward capitalism or socialism. However, it is an indirect participant in the conversation as a reactionary mechanism to the effects of government spending. An administration undertakes capitalist or socialist initiatives, and the resulting financial flaws can be lessened or enhanced by the Fed's toolbox. They are the cleanup crew on Aisle Five.

The difficulty, which is also a strength, in a free society like the United States of America is that not everyone is on the same page, nor will they ever be. Presidents are elected to a maximum of two four-year terms. Fed chairs serve four-year terms nominated by the president. Senators serve for six years at a time and congressmen and congresswomen are elected for two-year terms; however, both can serve an unlimited number of terms.

These public servants must constantly reflect the pulse of 330 million Americans. Some voters might be worried about centuries of American solvency, whereas others might just need a stimulus check to pay this month's rent. Some voters might be recalling a family history of eight generations of voting, while others just immigrated to America this year. Either way, each and every single vote carries the same exact weight. Therein lies the perpetual change of a democracy's goals.

ECONOMIC INSIGHT

"Don't fight the Fed." The mantra, referring to investing in line with Fed policy by being aggressive amid lowering rates and conservative when they raise rates, is famous in finance and for good reason. Traditionally, when the Fed cuts interest rates and pumps liquidity into the economy, the stock market goes up, at least in the near term. Conversely, when the Fed raises interest rates, it usually has a negative effect on the stock market. The bond market is directly impacted too. Bonds perform like a seesaw, in that as interest rates rise, the value of existing bonds issued at previously lower rates will go down. When rates go up quickly, like in 2022, bond funds can take especially hard hits, leaving fixed income investors wondering what was so fixed after all.

Fed rate adjustments can take time to actually impact the economy; some estimates assume 12 months. For instance, if the

Fed raises interest rates by 50 basis points (0.50 percent), there can be a small lag before banks pass the effect on to their customers. Assume banks then adjust their interest rates upward on a 30-year fixed-rate mortgage and alter loan underwriting to their liking. There may be another lag before consumers across the country adjust how much they would be willing to pay for a new house because of the higher interest cost on their mortgage. Eventually, enough buyers will feel the pain of higher interest rates and lower their offers, depressing the real estate market. The family home is not bought and sold throughout the week with clicks of a button, but stocks are. This is one reason why the stock market is viewed as a leading indicator. It only takes a rumor of the Fed adjusting rates for investors to exchange trillions of dollars in minutes.

MICRO

"Dude! USA, Switzerland, United Kingdom, Taiwan, Germany. Need I say more?" The young man touts some of the nations widely regarded as economically free, champions of capitalism. "GDP, just look at it," he holds up a chart with USA highlighted at the top. "Wealth per capita, c'mon, man. How's life in Cuba, North Korea, or Venezuela?" He holds up a list of the least economically free nations and concludes his debate triumphantly.

"You're just being general. Stereotyping." The young woman ignores being called "dude" and "man"; it's just how he talks. They're close friends. His frat and her sorority have mixers every month together. "You know all those wealthy nations you brag about are really mixed economies, so stop just shouting 'capitalism.' Prior generations would laugh at all of their modern welfare programs being called anything but socialist."

"Not a bad opening, both of you," the professor compliments the two students as they remain behind their podiums. "Now, enough opinions, tell the class what hypotheses you came up with to support your analysis."

The young man starts with a renewed sense of energy, relieved to be presenting to the class and done debating his sharp-witted friend. "For macroeconomic conjecture, nations can be graded based on their taking and giving. Since capitalism is based on zero taxation, or zero government 'taking,' and socialism on 100 percent taxation and taking, nations or states could be judged by overall tax revenue as a percentage of GDP." The professor is already intrigued. He continues, "This could offer a fair glimpse of how much of a country's production is recaptured by its own government. For instance, in 2020 the United States had a tax-to-GDP ratio of 25.5 percent and China's was 20.1 percent, I guess making China appear more capitalist by this metric. (See Figure 4.4.) The average for the 38 member countries in the OECD was 33.5 percent. Opposite of the capitalist countries was France's tax-to-GDP ratio of 45.4 percent.[27] This is one context in which debaters could define a society as capitalist or socialist, perhaps using the OECD average as the crossing point." The young woman suddenly sees him as more than a frat boy, impressed that he traded in "dudes" and "c'mon, mans" for hard-core statistics.

He resumes, "Then the next factor in classifying a society as capitalist or socialist would be its support or entitlements provided to the masses, the 'giving' side. A good measure in this regard would be a similar ratio of government spending as a percentage of GDP, as government spending is always for the people. In 2020, US government spending was 44 percent of total GDP and China's was 36.53 percent." (See Figure 4.5.)

"Wait, so is the United States more socialist than China?" The young woman is unable to resist the obvious corroboration of her opening rebuttal. The professor shoots her a look for interrupting.

"Well," he stumbles for a moment, "there are countries further away from the mean like India spending just 17.6 percent of GDP versus France spending 62.1 percent of GDP.[28] Using these factors to help classify societies as socialist or capitalist can provide a fair frame of reference. When analysts examine a particular topic (education, social security, small business growth, etc.), they may then review its progress in connection to its government's relative stance on giving and taking."

"Very good job," the professor says with authenticity. "You get an A+ for these two grading systems and your time researching is obvious. However, can you see how your research does support your opponent's argument?" The student looks down at the podium, having come to the same realization moments ago as he reported his statistics. The professor continues, "Your analysis of 'giving' and 'taking' reaffirms how most societies are indeed mixed. USA appears capitalist in its relatively low tax revenue, but socialist in its excessive government spending."

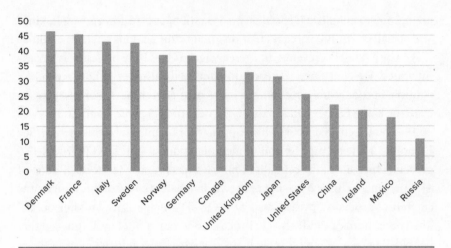

Figure 4.4 Tax revenue as a percentage of GDP[29]

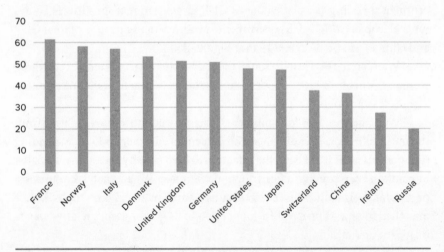

Figure 4.5 Government spending as a percentage of GDP[30]

This Econ 101 class is about using financial and empirical evidence to lead the way. The professor begins each class asking her students to avoid the emotional associations mistakenly attached to capitalism and social- ism, imploring them to disconnect fiscal and social agendas. She's overheard the member of the LGBTQ+ club called out by her friends for shopping on Amazon and told to go join the greedy monopolists in the Entrepreneurship club. She sees fans of socialism across campus successfully branding it as the righteous choice with posters affixing socialism to the core principles taught in kindergarten—sharing is caring—and other signs depicting capitalism as materialistic and nefarious.

Impressionable youth can feel compelled to choose sides, form an identity, and then defend it without compromise. Libertarianism may sound feasible, a chance at finding happy middle ground, but that's only until election season nears and society demands a binary choice. For this professor's Gen Z students and the millennials before them, adopting socially liberal ideals of embracing all people from all walks of life is an easy choice; it does not take a PhD in economics to support "support." But she begs them to realize the endless economic consequences of a possibly permanent tax designed for a corresponding, possibly temporary, initiative. Many taxes began as a way to fund a specific project or special interest, but linger far after that original bill was paid.

The professor is tired of seeing colleges and universities being ranked as "more liberal" or "more conservative." She's on a crusade to stop prospective students from diving deeper into preconceived notions, missing out on meeting different thinkers, just like her friends who watch only the news channel that agrees with their existing biases. It hinders future leaders at the most susceptible stage of life. She's tried to broach the subject at board meetings, about how academia is making every effort to be more diverse and inclusive, routinely asking questions in regard to ethnicity, gender, religion, sexual orientation, and financial background. However, political diversity is not a motive in class makeup. Colleges could foster more open debate and innovation by recognizing their student body and faculty's political orientation and aim for equal representation.

A fanatic for data, she sees that the misunderstanding of capitalist and socialist doctrine is more than anecdotal. As she's often told her students, according to America's Small Business Development Center's (SBDC) white paper on generational studies, 61 percent of millennials say there is more security in owning your own business than working for someone else, and 62 percent have a business in mind they want to start.[31] With almost eight million people regularly tuning in to *Shark Tank,* millennials have fallen in love with the idea of striking out on their own. But nationwide studies show that 50 percent of millennials now have a positive view of socialism,[32] and 70 percent say they would be comfortable voting for a socialist.[33] It appears millennials want the core of capitalism—entrepreneurship—while championing its main opposition.

How can these numbers coexist? The professor feels as if her department is failing their students. It is as if one poll says 60 percent of respondents rank cheeseburgers as their favorite food, yet 70 percent of them identify as vegan.

The next speaker trades spots with the "dude, c'mon, man" debater and takes the podium. He wears a curly mop-top cut, flannel shirt, and matching Vans sneakers. His opponent conveniently missed class, a victim of Thirsty Thursday, so a monologue it will have to be. He musters up his oratory skills and loudly begins, "Economics is essentially the financial practice of one's mentality."

"A regular Aristotle, huh?" the prior debater jokes to his friend.

"Long before children are even exposed to the ideas of wealth and economics, they are taught the importance of recognizing people's differences while treating everyone equally. Socialist views can accidentally warp this worthy doctrine. Seekers of equality ignore the first part, that everyone is different. In an attempt to eliminate disparity, they elevate the lesser and suppress the greater by redistribution. In short, they aim for fairness by being unfair."

Some of the known members of the Young Democrats begin to roll their eyes and look at each other. The professor motions for him to go on, hoping this one's not too one-sided.

"My hypothesis examines the youth psyche. The push for high self-esteem during youth is welcomed by all, but some of the approved methods stir controversy. It would be preposterous to say such psychological initiatives have any direct economic intent," he looks to the Young Democrats hoping this might appease them, "but they can subconsciously underpin the pros of socialism and cons of capitalism.

"Every recreational sport now touts its own form of a 'participation trophy'; at the same time, many do away with keeping score or team records. Opponents feel the movement is delaying life's inevitable rites of passage, leaving youth ill-prepared for bouts of failure on the path to success." He looks back to the Young Dems. "But proponents argue that the fragility of a child's mental health must come first and participation awards reinforce just that, continued participation in competition." The students in defense of socialism nod in agreement.

The boy in flannel continues, "These proponents are able to cite count-less mental health issues that cannot be overlooked in good conscience. Prior to Harry Truman passing the National Mental Health Act in 1946, mental health was largely relegated to the most severe disorders that required psychiatric hospitalization. It was not until the late 1980s that fluoxetine revolutionized depression therapy and turned antidepressants mainstream. Today an estimated 44 million Americans suffer from one or more of the over 200 classified mental illnesses. According to the CDC, 1 in 10 American adults currently take an antidepressant. Usage is highest among whites, more than twice any other race, and particularly among white women, one out of every five. In a reversal of almost every measured benefit of higher education, treated depression becomes more prevalent with each degree of education."[34]

The professor finds these statistics very interesting, but wonders where he's headed.

"Similarly, for generations a distracted child could be fairly or sometimes unfairly disciplined. It was not until 1980 when the American Psychiatric Association began labeling struggling kids with attention deficit disorder (ADD), later renamed attention deficit hyperactive disorder (ADHD) so that it could be further broken down to inattentive, hyperactive, and mixed types. The ever-growing number of labels must be addressed to ensure proper mental hygiene, but carefully enough so as not to deter removal of those labels."

He gently holds his hand up, motioning for his class's patience as his point is coming. "One can see the delicate risk between an unearned participation trophy spawning a lazy loser versus a dominant winner injuring an opponent's ambition and pride. The United States needs more innovators and entrepreneurs, and innovation and enterprise need kids who get back up after being knocked down. The debates between capitalists and socialists may occur on different fields, but the stigmas attached to each are in the same park." He walks back to his seat as his fellow students absorb the analogy.

The last presenter of the day stands up. As the closer, her hypothesis is meant to address the harsh realities that hamper both capitalist and socialist progress. She dons baggy sweatpants with their school logo and her boyfriend's even baggier hoody.

"Corruption," she announces. "Capitalism and socialism both look like utter failures in the face of corruption. Every year, Transparency International ranks over 180 countries in their Corruption Perceptions Index. In 2020, the United States ranked at 25, whereas China ranked 78 and Russia

129.[35] Granted, this is a measure of perception, not necessarily actual corrupt activities.

"Corruption can be defined in more than one way. Most Americans would associate corruption with heinous activities such as bribery, extortion, money laundering, and the like. These forms of corruption are more prevalent in less-developed countries. Corruption in America may not appear as egregious as a mafia movie, but many would argue that the subtle business of lobbying can be just as nefarious."

The class perks up at the mention of the mob, crime, and innuendo of lobbying in the smoke-filled rooms of power brokers. "As railways sprawled across America in the mid-1800s," she says, "stories of men like Cornelius Vanderbilt and Jay Gould hiring judges and bribing legislatures were commonplace. As a result, on February 4, 1887, the Interstate Commerce Act was passed to oversee the railroad industry. The attempt to clean up the industry essentially created a target for the robber barons' war chests, as they began to *legally* lobby federal regulators and state and local politicians. President Rutherford B. Hayes said, and I quote, 'this is a government of the people, by the people, and for the people no longer. It is government by the corporations, of the corporations, and for the corporations.'

"Ever since the government sought an end to laissez-faire capitalism, regulators have been imposed on every industry. Major companies now use teams of lobbyists whose sole purpose is to influence legislation, regulation, and other government decisions that can offer them preferential treatment.

"Studies show that the pharmaceutical and healthcare industries are the most focused on lobbying. From 2000 to 2021, the industry has spent nearly $5 billion on lobbying. Of the roughly 1,600 healthcare lobbyists in the United States, 59 percent are former government employees. The insurance industry comes in second, with over $3 billion spent in the past two decades. Some of the other top spenders should come as no surprise—the tech industry, utilities, and oil and gas.[36] Facebook, which has spent time testifying before Congress for its use of customer information as well as facing antitrust lawsuits, spent nearly $20 million in lobbying in 2020, nearly three times that of Google."

Even the professor seems surprised by these revelations.

The young woman in sweats continues, "Where pharma and tech have their lobbying battalions, the trades still largely have union representation in certain areas of the country. The original unions described earlier mainly served to protect their workers from the extreme dangers of working in a coal mine or steel factory. In the modern era its purpose is to protect its members' jobs and increase their pay and benefits. In 2009, construction of arguably the most modern and exquisite stadium, AT&T Stadium, was completed. Seating over 100,000 people, the home of the Dallas Cowboys is the largest stadium in the NFL. Also known as Jerry World, an homage to the team's owner, Jerry Jones, it took four years to construct with a price tag of $1.3 billion. John Hutchings, principal of HKS Architects, who designed the stadium, credited cheap labor as to why AT&T Stadium was 'such a bargain.'

"One year later, the most expensive stadium, and often worst-ranked from a fan experience perspective, New Jersey's MetLife Stadium was completed in 2010. The home of the Giants and Jets cost a reported $1.6 billion to complete. Kent McLaughlin of 360 Architecture, which partnered on the design of MetLife Stadium, blamed union labor for the high cost. 'Dealing with three or four union trades definitely has an impact. You need somebody to make it, somebody to drive it, somebody to unload it off the truck, somebody else to erect it.'[37] The permits, approvals, required consultants, and fees for each step of the project add to the inefficiencies of dealing with a major metropolitan area."

She caught everyone's attention with the sports reference and quickly switches gears. "Mixed into the realm of lobbying lies the relatively new world of Super PACs (Political Action Committees)." The professor cringes at the introduction of politics, but knew it was coming. "In July 2010, the federal court decision *SpeechNow.org v. Federal Election Committee* gave rise to this new type of committee, technically known as independent expenditure-only committees. They are allowed to raise unlimited sums of money from corporations, unions, associations, and individuals and then spend unlimited amounts of money against or for particular political candidates. There are 2,276 groups organized as Super PACs, which raised nearly $3.5 billion in the 2019–2020 election cycle.[38] Between 2010 and 2020, 47 percent of all Super PAC donations came from just 10 individuals."

"And I bet those 10 are your classic beneficiaries of American capitalism," a classmate whispers loud enough for everyone to hear.

The speaker proceeds, "And in 2020 alone, over $16 billion was spent on federal, state, and local elections. On the federal level, Republicans spent $3.8 billion for President Trump and their congressional contests. Democrats spent nearly twice as much, $6.9 billion, for President Biden and other

Democratic candidates, helped by billionaires Tom Steyer and Michael Bloomberg.[39] Beyond outright financial influence, there are other methods of garnering power. Amazon founder Jeff Bezos paid $250 million in 2013 to buy the *Washington Post*. The *Post* has long been regarded as the nation's top resource for politics and policy.

"Humans have forever tried to manipulate fellow power brokers to further their own self-interests. This is not necessarily an evil thing, as a justified end can justify its means. If it takes lobbying, networking, and marketing to cut the red tape in front of the righteous leader of a righteous company, then so be it. But when corruption, whether visible or invisible, distorts right from wrong and fact from fiction, then a system requires a fix."

"Well, guys," the professor resumes her place in front of the class, "you all killed it today. Very good job on your research and way to use empirical evidence. What I would like to wrap up with is a quick discussion on politics. You all know how I hate bringing politics into the fray, but as you can see, when exploring economics, it is often inevitable.

"I want you all to understand your incredible worth in guiding the economy. Rather than just talk with your friends or bash the other side, I want you to continue to stay informed and get involved. No matter what side it's on. Submitting to be another cog in the machine eliminates the need for knowledge in the first place. Don't forget that the entire ideal of the USA arose from economic suppression, ultimately a tax on tea! Remember that when someone tells you your vote doesn't matter.

"I can see the passion politics invokes in many of you. I can see how many of you would love to serve, but never dare campaign. Unfortunately, there are many politicians who seem not to truly serve, but love to campaign," she says reluctantly, "but that's not you guys!

"You and your generation must hold politicians accountable. We all know elected officials need to get reelected and might lose their roots to appeal to new public opinion. Aside from the Twenty-Second Amendment enacting presidential term limits after FDR's four terms in the White House, there has been little change. On the flip side, lifetime appointees such as Supreme Court justices, or congressmen and women who are ordained by their jurisdiction's political machine, may never adapt to the needs of our evolving country. Do you think term limits are a good thing or a bad thing?"

She always likes to end on a note like this. No specific solution. No do this or do that instruction. Just a quick, open-ended thought to keep them thinking. She likes to hear about the ensuing nightlong argument among roommates, starting over economics and what needs to be fixed in the world. Whether to start paying their student loans now or defer until graduation, delve into crypto or stay on the sidelines, to save or spend. These debates may be the most effective moments of higher education. Her students pass her class able to use economic philosophy as a tool to justify the costs in every argument.

WHAT SHOULD I DO WITH MY MONEY?

Economic philosophy guides money decisions, considering their potential impacts and the impacts of those impacts. While it is convenient to study history and select a format that has generated the most widely accepted success, there are bound to be opponents in that society who felt slighted. There will always be trade-offs. Someone fearful of uncertainty and do-it-yourself attitudes will naturally gravitate toward a structured system: guaranteed pensions, Social Security, group benefits, and other entitlements afforded by the government or corporation. While that does not mean this employee is in any way a socialist, it would befit them to find a corporation, municipality, state, and even country that shares such a supportive mindset. Conversely, someone who possesses an ideology built on independence, is not willing to compromise their earnings for someone else, and has the ego to be the boss would benefit from a capitalistic type of culture. Thinking this way affects everything from where to live, what school to send your children to, and which companies to work for, to how much you might personally need to save in one scenario versus another.

Economic philosophy affects both the macro and the micro. When a borrower can't repay the bank a $1 million loan, the borrower is in trouble. When a borrower can't repay the bank a $100 million loan, the bank is in trouble. The same goes for any union, company, state, or nation that upsets an individual who then eventually becomes a very large group of individuals. Just as companies can use money (M) to push social agendas and support an economic philosophy, so too can investors vote with their dollars by studying which companies make up their portfolio. Realizing that one can become many is all the evidence you need to know that your financial decisions can control not only your own economics, but also the economics of many.

ENVIRONMENT

The environment is a story about the natural world we live in. It is about the source. The genesis. Economics studies givers and takers of things, but as previously noted, everything comes from something and nothing comes from nothing. The earth is why economics exists. Earth is the gift that keeps on giving, until maybe, one day it cannot. Humans may argue right and wrong and debate the costs attached to every decision, but Earth will have the final say.

The strongest witness is the vast population of the Earth to which we are a burden and she scarcely can provide for our needs.
—Tertullian (AD 160–AD 220)

B orn in Genoa, Italy, in 1451 to a family of wool weavers, the boy dreams of sailing the open sea. The crashing blue waves and salty mist hold a certain allure.

There must be more out there!

Curiosity mixed with youthful ambition and ignorance of what could go wrong give rise to his first real venture as a young man. He moves to the port city of Lisbon, Portugal, and hops aboard any seafaring job he can find.

Ships matriculate through the bustling harbor, each carrying goods of great value. These are not trips of leisure, rather each voyage transfers sustenance of all kinds, pumping the lifeblood of progress for each country and town across Europe. The expeditions teach him invaluable lessons on supply and demand. The more demands his trips can fulfill, the more money he makes and the more prosperous his homeland becomes.

Rumors spread among the sailors about a foreign land of plenty. The far east is believed to be a treasure trove of silk and spices. If his crew could only sail west and find a quicker route to India and China, the fortunes would be theirs. The young explorer convinces King Ferdinand and Queen Isabella of Spain to finance his journey.

He sets sail with a crew of 90 men working across three ships—the *Niña*, the *Pinta*, and the *Santa Maria*. After 10 weeks at sea, they land in the Bahamas and claim the island for Spain, despite its already being populated by who they call "Indians," thinking they have found the Indies.

He has risen to become a daring captain, reaching destinations once considered to be unreachable. He is crowned Admiral of the Ocean Sea and Governor of the Indies. His name is Cristoforo Colombo. Though he never learns the place he's discovered is not the Indies and that what he calls "Japan" is actually Cuba, he accidentally discovers something far greater—the New World.

Over the next few centuries, millions of Europeans travel to the Americas in hopes of taking advantage of its natural riches and flourishing economy. Corn and tobacco are as plentiful as salt in the sea. In due time these resources will be overtaken by something even more valuable to the thriving textile business—cotton.

* * *

Almost four centuries later, the growing United States entices another young, high-reaching trailblazer. The adolescent spends his days running from machine to machine, frantically changing spools of thread. A tough job it is, but one he's grateful to have as a new immigrant. He is determined to outrun his father's failures. The undersized boy pushes up his sweaty sleeves, so they don't get caught again in the spinning device. At 12 years old, the life of a bobbin boy in a cotton factory can be a precarious job. But for $1.20 a week, it will have to do.

"Hurry up, boy!"

"Outta the way, next one!"

Shouts pierce through the hum of whirring gears, shuffling feet, and voices echoing off the stone walls.

I will find my way out of here. On the up-and-up. He reassures himself.

The Scottish lad escapes the factory and networks from one post to another, transitioning from telegraph operator to eventually becoming the superintendent of the Pennsylvania Railroad in 1859. It is here that valuable lessons are learned. "Rich" people get other people to do their dirty work and make them money. "Wealthy" people get their money to make even more money.

He notices his mentors' mentors make their fortunes not from toil, but from investing. Furthermore, he notices every new investment has one thing in common—they revolve around coveted and finite natural resources, those earthly minerals and fuels that a country has naturally. He discovers the value of what Columbus discovered so long ago—the opportunity to convert natural environments into economic environments.

At first, he tries iron. The same iron that lays thousands of miles of railroad connecting east to west. Then it is oil. The same oil that is converted into kerosene and lights up almost every home and office in America. It is a race to seize every resource fueling the Industrial Revolution. Finally, it all leads to steel. The same steel that allows him to sell his company to J.P. Morgan for $480 million in 1901 (almost $17 billion today).

Andrew Carnegie is just one of the many rags-to-riches stories of the nineteenth century. America lives up to its mythology of being the land of opportunity. Its ports are open, and its grounds are rife with crops and treasures. More and more immigrants will continue to chase the same dreams. But since the annexation of Hawaii in 1958, the US territories no longer grow in size. The country's nonrenewable resources, by definition, are diminished year by year.

MACRO

From water and oil to stone and wood, the speed at which natural resources are used is commensurate with the exponential growth of population. Humanity sips and nibbles from the earth every day, always has, and always will. These daily actions, these choices, microscopic in the scheme of things, are what make environmental initiatives so complex. Joseph Stalin, dictator of the Soviet Union from 1929 to 1953, once said, "The death of one man is a tragedy. The death of millions is a statistic." The loss of a family's home to a wildfire is a tragedy, but the loss of 100 billion tons of ice in the arctic is a statistic.

The statistics of the environment can be analyzed from two angles, let's call them the normal-macro and the super-macro. The normal-macro addresses the economic advantages and disadvantages inherent to a nation because of its natural resources, or lack thereof. Super-macro, while not a technical term, is reserved for that rare domain that impacts everything, literally all eight billion people. Since Earth is the only universally shared platform for humanity, as the sun's rays shine on rich and poor alike, the environment might be the only super-macro study. Both views of environmental economics are easily ignored in everyday life, but as mentioned earlier, ignorance is bliss, until it shows up on your doorstep.

Normal-Macro

In dealing with natural resources, value can be defined as the worth or usefulness of a commodity and the availability of that commodity. Before exploring national treasures, note that commodities' worth and usefulness do not always have to be directly correlated. For instance, until gold started being used as a noncorroding conductor inside electronics and computers, it was used almost exclusively for jewelry making or financial backing (the United States came off the gold standard in 1971). Many commodities have not served well as long-term assets like real estate or equities, though, as illustrated by gold trading at $2,581 per ounce in 1980 and $442 per ounce in 2001 (adjusted for CPI).[1]

Thanks to global markets, commodity prices are quotable and understandable. Costs and lost opportunity costs may tell the whole story, but at least pricing presents a starting point for discussion. The status of a country in the global economy is most often measured by its monetary wealth. This is typically ranked by national GDP, average salary, or similar benchmarks. The connection between monetary wealth and a country's finite natural resources is unmistakable.

Since the kerosene lamp was popularized in the late 1800s, and then the automobile in the early 1900s, oil has been one of the most valuable of all commodities. The Kingdom of Saudi Arabia clearly illustrates the correlation between finite natural resources and wealth. For millennia, the kingdom survived as a subsistence economy, restricted to herding and agriculture. Then in March of 1938, oil was struck in the Dammam oilfield. After signing an oil concession agreement with Standard Oil Company of California, drilling overtook the country's terrain, instantly making it one of the wealthiest nations on Earth. A very useful resource, suddenly very plentiful in one spot of the globe, equaled tremendous value.

Any object of value offers the beholder or exporter, in this case Saudi Arabia, leverage over the beholden or importer, the rest of the developed world. In 1973, America supported Israel in its fight against Egypt and Syria in the Yom Kippur War. Throughout the Cold War, America believed stabilizing Israel was critical to stalling the Soviet Union's influence over the Middle East. In response to America's backing of Israel, the Organization of Arab Petroleum Exporting Countries (OAPEC) imposed an oil embargo against America and other nations supporting Israel. An embargo may be the most severe display of manipulating supply and demand. The 1973 oil embargo hit the United States particularly hard, compounding an already economic rough patch as American oil fields ran dry. The price of oil quadrupled from $2.90 a barrel to $11.65 a barrel within months.[2] The balance of power shifted toward Arab countries ready to wield their oil weapon.

Saudi Arabia's reliance on oil as liquid gold offers up a lesson on diversification just as applicable to a rookie investor's brokerage account. The scarcity of oil eventually became less scarce and former importers found other avenues to obtain oil. As of 2022, the United States has the most oil in the world with an estimated 264 billion barrels of recoverable oil reserves, followed by Russia, Saudi Arabia, Canada, and Iran, respectively.[3] The Trump administration sought energy independence by rolling back several climate regulations, which boosted domestic oil production to record highs in 2018 and led to lower gas prices and less dependence on foreign oil.

Nearly 2,000 years ago, Emperor Marcus Aurelius instructed the world in *Meditations*, "To live as nature requires." Macroeconomies that choose to hitch their wealth to a commodity, such as the OAPEC members, can face two potential risks in ignoring nature's signals. The first is competition, like importers who find other suppliers, whether motivated by financial or socioeconomic reasons. The second is when valuable goods go the way of the dinosaur, usually provoked by subtle microeconomic changes that go viral. Oil may once have been great for kerosene lamps and since then fuel for cars, but electricity is trying to steal its value. The private sectors in developed nations, particularly America, are concurrently trending green and shunning fossil fuels wherever possible. Tesla, under Elon Musk's leadership, revolutionized the landscape with practical electric vehicles. The combination of government policy and corporate innovation has redefined the worth and usefulness part of the value equation.

Saudi Arabia has responded to a drastic decrease in oil income, caused by the prevalence of oil in other countries and fuel-efficient technologies, by seeking foreign investors. From 2016 to 2018 the kingdom sold over $60 billion of bonds, becoming one of the most indebted countries in the emerging market space. In 2019, foreign business licenses increased by over 70 percent year-over-year, led by Britain and China.[4] Just as it's best to cash in on real estate before the neighborhood goes bust, Saudi Arabia is leveraging its wealth in oil in case someday oil becomes like the coal that once moved locomotives.

Saudi Arabia is scrambling to find new ventures to stimulate its GDP, such as real estate development and travel and tourism. Geopolitical issues can interrupt nature's course, for better or worse. The 2022 international embargoes against Russian oil, in light of Russia's invasion of Ukraine, helped send the price of oil soaring. While Saudi Arabia has many reasons to dislike Russia, such as Putin's support of Iran, with whom Saudi Arabia severed diplomatic ties in 2016 and considers the biggest threat to stability in the Middle East, and Saudi Arabia's supporting Ukraine's territorial integrity, the kingdom certainly appreciates how increased oil prices have taken pressure off its budget.

Other oil-dependent nations, whether friend or foe, have been given more time to think because of not just Russia's actions, but also those of the United States. Upon entering the White House, the Biden administration reversed many of Trump's energy independence initiatives. President Biden immediately signed executive orders to stop drilling on federal land and blocked drilling on 23 million acres leased to energy companies, causing an immediate boost in gas prices. Oil traders look at crude inventories to project production and consumption trends and exchange futures contracts based on their assumptions. However, in July of 2022, under pressure from rising gas prices and Russia's oil dominance, President Biden reversed course by issuing onshore leases of 120,000 acres for oil and gas development, mostly in Wyoming, and released a proposal for offshore drilling in the Gulf of Mexico and Alaska's Cook Inlet.[5] The oil industry complained the Biden administration has not done enough, while environmentalists immediately filed several lawsuits against the administration for breaking campaign promises. How quickly money (M) can regain the MICE.

The manipulation of oil displays the collision of microeconomies, macroeconomies, and the super-macro. Normal citizens not being able to afford the price of gas, the United States and Europe shopping in Saudi Arabia and Venezuela for alternatives to Russian oil, and oil wells around the world being opened and closed illustrate the continuum of commodities. It is an exchange of wealth based upon something Earth has contained for thousands of years.

ECONOMIC INSIGHT

Strike while the iron is hot. Most optimal decisions have a relatively small window of time before they become bad ones. Just as the blacksmith hammers a glowing red iron to form his masterpiece, so must a country, business, or individual seize their chances of fortune.

When a company wants to raise capital by going public (sell shares of the company on a public stock exchange), or acquire venture capital or financing, it is best to do so through a position of power. A position of power for a company could be defined as one in which the company has good cash flow, a loyal customer base, high reserves and low debt, a strong management structure, substantial market share, unique competitive advantages, and is still in the early stages of growth. Once competitors enter the market and the company's product or service is devalued, raising capital becomes more difficult.

Similarly, an ideal time for an individual to obtain capital is when they are in a position of power. This might be after a great year at work yielding an impressive tax return, when the bank accounts are flush and debt is low, and their credit score is superb. This prime financial profile can allow the individual to get mortgages, auto loans, and other financing at prime interest rates and terms.

Unfortunately, good microeconomic circumstances don't always cross paths with good macroeconomic circumstances. A young couple that just landed two great jobs and finally paid off their credit cards might be ready to apply for their first mortgage, but if prevailing rates at the time are 10 percent on a 30-year fixed-rate mortgage, they can feel disadvantaged. This is why consumers should always be on the lookout for "deals" the macro world provides, while doing their best to create their own luck through maintaining sound financials.

A country and its government are no different from the microeconomies of normal families. The best time to issue debt is when interest rates are low and your credit rating is high. Saudi Arabia struck, and is continuing to strike, while oil is still coveted around the world. It is a rational example of using today's strength to plan for the future before it disappears. An irrational example, because of its hostile nature, was Russia's invasion of Ukraine. Knowing it was Europe's primary, almost sole supplier of oil and that the other power of the Western world, the United States, was emasculating its oil by writing off fossil fuels, surely influenced Russia's timing.

Environmentally Rich and Poor Nations

Since monetary wealth is so closely connected to *natural* wealth, it is worth noting the top five countries with the most natural resources. According to the World Atlas, they are China, Saudi Arabia, Canada, India, and Russia. Russia has significant oil reserves and the biggest mining industry in the world, being the largest producer of aluminum, copper, silicon, limestone, and magnesium, just to name a few. It has the largest gold mine on Earth in Polyus too. India is known for its large coal reserves, oil, natural gas, and thorium, as well as being the leading producer of manganese ore. Canada is the world's main supplier of natural gas and phosphate, and the third largest exporter of timber. Saudi Arabia continues its reign as the world's largest oil exporter. China has the most natural resources and rare earth metals of any country.[6]

The United States is close to the top five, but more important, America has a seemingly perfect combination of resources. The United States is the third-largest country by land mass (following Russia and Canada). According to the World Bank, an estimated 17.2 percent of US soil is arable, thanks in large part to the Great Plains. The United States is flanked on the East and West Coast by ocean, providing countless trade routes. The country has a variety of climates to accommodate different resources, and an abundant fresh-water source throughout the land. Last, America enjoys vast coal, timber, and oil reserves that have carried the country from the colonial times to the modern era.

It is not a coincidence that the aforementioned countries that are rich in natural resources are also relatively rich in the bank. Just as being in the right place at the right time made Carnegie and Columbus household names, so too did natural resources spur the golden age of empires.

This begs the question, what about parts of the world void of such raw finite materials? Are they eternally condemned to poverty? The least resource-rich country on earth, technically speaking, is Vatican City, home of the Catholic Church. This provides poor analysis as it is also the smallest country on Earth and completely subsidized by tourism and international tithing. The richest country, by GDP per capita, is Monaco. This is another tough example as the beautiful French Riviera principality primarily serves merely as a tax haven for the ultra-rich by not imposing any income tax or capital gains tax.

Some appropriate examples include Costa Rica, which thrives on tourism and the export of *renewable* resources such as coffee, bananas, and other tropical fruits. Switzerland also has very limited nonrenewable resources—salt is its only mined resource—but has the seventh-highest GDP per capita in the world.[7] It has taken advantage of a wet environment and range of elevations ideal for generating hydroelectric power. In addition, its service sector makes up 74 percent of GDP. Switzerland also has a manufacturing sector based on specialization, particularly engines, turbines, and the exportation of more watches than any other country in the world.

Then there are Japan, Taiwan, Hong Kong, and Singapore, all seemingly poor in natural resources, but rapidly growing in financial standing. Each of these countries relies heavily on imports for energy, agriculture, nonrenewables, even water. In return, they are successful in manufacturing, service sectors, and exports ranging from automobiles to advanced technology. These countries may not possess the independent wealth to ever consider isolationism that a nation blessed with derivatives and services might consider, (e.g., United States, China, or Russia), but have found economic success through trade and capitalistic structure.

The availability of nonrenewable raw materials is a distinct advantage, but not a prerequisite, to prosperity. Furthermore, the correlation between resources and economic power is present, but not guaranteed. Countries such as Liberia and Sierra Leone possess the former, but not the latter, due to a variety of reasons stemming from poor governance. Venezuela has more oil reserves than any country on Earth, including Saudi Arabia, but is also poorly governed and lacks the ability to extract oil from its very deep and mostly offshore reserves. (See Figure 5.1.)

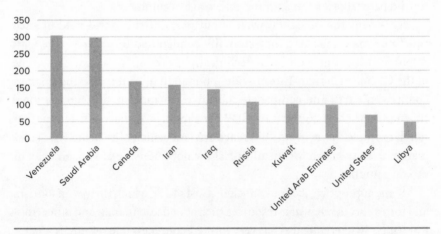

Figure 5.1   Oil reserves (in billion barrels)[8]

Mankind will continue to uncover new resources and new uses for old resources, making yesterday's trash today's treasure. The necessity of adaptation is bound to redefine what is valuable versus what is not, proclaiming in with the new and out with the old. While the extraction and utilization of each of Earth's precious resources has led to a better world and way of life, unintended consequences have muddied the waters.

Super-Macro

In 1824, Joseph Fourier hypothesized that a planet the size of Earth with the same distance from the sun should have a temperature much colder. He suggested something in the atmosphere must be acting like an insulating blanket. In 1856, Eunice Foote revisited the idea and discovered the source of that "blanket" by illustrating how infrared radiation bouncing off of Earth's surface was trapped by carbon dioxide (CO_2) and water vapor in Earth's atmosphere, a phenomenon eventually referred to as the Greenhouse Effect.

Whether or not global warming is real, if it's happening quickly or slowly, the reality is that a polluted environment harms everyone. Pollution, while concentrated in certain areas, a ghetto more than a farm, a dorm room more than a cabin, is by itself unprejudiced. The environment is economic because caring for it has costs, and not caring for it also has costs. Because it's economic, it has value that can be leveraged one way or the other by those who care and those who do not.

Much of the aversion to global warming stems from the politicizing of the subject. In the United States, the Democratic Party has successfully aligned itself as the green side, while tagging Republicans as oblivious to the issue. This has led to many people identifying global warming and all the conversations surrounding it as fact or fiction without any basis, other than adopting political doctrine.

SEP Risk Assessment

Even when someone fears global warming, new scientific claims can be downplayed and left as someone else's responsibility. This is often a result of people's natural inclination to use a SEP risk assessment when evaluating problems. *SEP* stands for *severity*, *exposure*, and *probability*.

If severity equates to the end of the world, with probability determined to be 100 percent on the current course, one would expect a global
panic. But if the exposure in our lifetime of the end of the world is near
zero percent, then our risk assessment is nil. Or if exposure to strong UV
rays is 100 percent, probability is 100 percent from walking outside each
day, but the severity is a bad sunburn (at least in the near term), then the
risk assessment is still negligible. Therefore, if a parent's mind is wrapped
around getting kids back into school post-Covid while keeping their
job and paying this month's rent, is it realistic for them to prioritize the
potential impacts of an increase of 0.5 degrees Celsius in the Arctic circle's on Earth 100 years from now?

The other hurdle every hypothesis must face, beyond relatability, is
provability. Many of global warming's reference points date back thousands, even millions, of years. It is fair to question the validity of data
from a time before man chiseled symbols onto rocks with other rocks.

Know how food in the freezer can maintain its integrity for a really long
time? Ice is not much different. In Antarctica and Greenland, drills dig over
two miles deep into enormous glaciers and extract cylinders of ice that may
have never changed since the beginning of mankind. Layers of ice represent
years and seasons that grow older the deeper they drill, similar to the rings
in a tree trunk. Then scientists from the National Science Foundation's Ice
Core Facility gather atmospheric samples from the cylinders that act as time
capsules.

According to findings, CO_2 levels never eclipsed 300 parts per million,
in the history of Earth, until 1950. Since 1950, measurements have increased
over 30 percent to more than 400 parts per million.[9] The main culprits of
elevated carbon dioxide are deforestation, burning fossil fuels, methane
(produced by landfills), rice cultivation, manure management, cement production, and fertilizers. China has experienced the largest increase in modern
history. (See Figure 5.2.)

NASA states that since the mid-twentieth century, "It is undeniable that
human activities have warmed the atmosphere, ocean, and land and that
widespread and rapid changes in the atmosphere, ocean, cryosphere, and bio-
sphere have occurred."

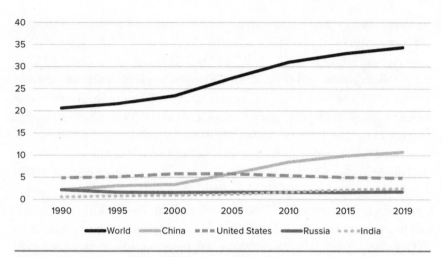

Figure 5.2 CO_2 emissions (kiloton, millions)[10]

Earth's average surface temperature has risen by roughly 2.212 degrees Fahrenheit since the late 1800s. Warming has accelerated the most since the 1980s, and the years 2016 and 2020 are tied as the warmest years on record. NASA's Gravity Recovery and Climate Experiment show Greenland lost an average of 279 billion tons of ice per year between 1993 and 2019, while Antarctica lost about 148 billion tons per year. As a result, the global sea level rose about 8 inches over the past 100 years, but mostly within the past two decades.

Rather than immediately blame mankind, it is sensible to hypothesize if the sun has gotten warmer. Since 1978, satellite instruments have measured the energy output of the sun directly.[11] The findings actually show a slight decrease in solar irradiance over this time.

The ultimate results of global warming are still largely untold. The majority of near-term effects are expected to be weather related, in particular, increased heavy rains, severe heat waves and draughts, and more common and intense hurricane seasons. Again, opponents can call out the validity in matching up weather events and their causes when comparing old data with new data.

The National Centers for Environmental Information points out that from 1980 to 2021 there were 308 weather and climate disasters in America, which caused over $2 trillion worth of damage.[12] The costliest events are in recent history: Hurricane Katrina in 2005 cost $178.8 billion, Hurricane Harvey in 2017—$138.8 billion, Hurricane Maria in 2017—$99.9 billion, Superstorm Sandy in 2012—$78.7 billion, followed by Hurricane Ida in 2021—$64.5 billion.[13] Of the costliest US tropical cyclones, only one occurred before 1940 (the New England hurricane of 1938, nicknamed "The Long Island Express"). This Category 3 hurricane caused $5.9 billion of damage (adjusted to 2021 CPI), a far cry from Hurricane Katrina's $178.8 billion.

These figures nicely fit the narrative of increasingly common severe natural disasters. But what if they are a by-product of a developed country with a much richer population and infrastructure than in generations past? Simply put, a minor flood in modern New York City would cause much greater financial harm than a string of F-5 tornadoes rolling through the untouched plains of Oklahoma in the early 1900s. It should come as no surprise that since 1970 the top six costliest natural disasters in the world all occurred within the United States. Does this imply that the United States is somehow more susceptible to the negative effects of climate change, or that the states just have more to lose?

In respect to the frequency of reported natural disasters, the naysayer will immediately repeat the key word, "reported." The International Disaster Database is the largest disaster data depository in the world, but was created only in 1973 under the Centre for Research on the Epidemiology of Disasters (CRED) and became part of the World Health Organization (WHO) in 1980. The frequency of reported climate disasters increased in step with the dawn of the internet, naturally implying that smaller disasters today are automatically reported whereas they may have gone unnoticed a generation ago.

The reporting of death totals does have a longer running history and is less pliable than economic statistics. Since 1970, not one of the top 10 deadliest natural disasters occurred in the developed world (unless including the extreme heat wave of 2010 in the Russian Federation).[14] In the first decade of the 1900s, there were 153,678 deaths from natural catastrophes. The worst decade on record is the 1920s, in which 540,329 people died from natural disasters. In the second half of the twentieth century, international deaths dropped precipitously, despite the explosion in population growth and apparent rise in global temperature. In the first decade of the 2000s, 78,086 people died and in the most recent data as of this writing, 2020, global natural disasters were responsible for 8,200 fatalities.[15, 16]

The causes and effects of global warming can be interpreted or misinterpreted based upon the lens one is looking through. The data show that climate-related events have become far more painful from an economic standpoint, but fortunately, far less harmful from a loss of life perspective.

Hopefully, much of the harm and fear surrounding climate change is overblown. Whether it is or not, it is universally agreeable that several pollutants are a part of everyday life that did not exist for most of mankind's history, and there are far more people using these pollutants than have ever walked Earth before. The extent to which pollution is bad is debatable, but that it is bad is indisputable. This at least provides common ground from which to work. But even when opposing sides come together for a good cause, the best intentions do not guarantee the best results.

MICRO

Smoke drifts through the crowded upper room of a swanky Manhattan lounge. Men clad in suits and ties unwind from a long day at the office. It is a popular watering hole for the elite.

"Scotch, on the rocks," Thomas, a middle-aged banker, shouts across to the bartender.

"What'll it be, nine ball?" His friend asks.

"Rack 'em!" Tom replies with a freshly poured scotch in hand.

He unlocks a tall wooden case against the wall and pulls out his favorite cue. It is made entirely of ivory with his name embossed in gold lettering at the bottom. This one likely comes from a subtropical region in Asia.

Billiards are the thing-to-do in cities across the globe. These pool cues are not only a practical enjoyment, but a showpiece of the rich and famous. The ivory necessary to make each stick is becoming harder to find. The evil deed of slaughtering elephants and cutting their tusks to feed another hobby is not sustainable.

The year is 1869, and John Wesley Hyatt decides to respond to a New York firm's offer awarding $10,000 to anyone who can create a substitute for ivory. He discovers that by treating the cellulose from cotton fiber with camphor, he can create a substance similar to that of a turtle shell, horn, or ivory.

Hyatt does far more than create a new brand of pool cue, he revolution-izes the entire manufacturing industry. The world can offer only so much wood, metal, stone, and elephant tusks, but now the limits of nature are cast aside. A nonrenewable resource has not just been replaced, but upgraded. The new material is inexpensive and invincible, bound to not only save wildlife, but save Earth itself. It will be used in lifesaving medical devices, make space travel possible, lighten cars and jets to reduce fuel consumption, and improve helmets, incubators, and water purification equipment, the benefits are end-less. It is . . . plastic.

* * *

Halfway between Chile and New Zealand lies an uninhabited atoll called Henderson Island. It is a tiny speck of land in the South Pacific Ocean, visi-ble only on the most magnified of maps. It is thought to be the most isolated island on Earth, perhaps never inhabited by man. Henderson Island is in the middle of nowhere.

In June of 2015, Dr. Alex Bond, senior curator of birds at the Natural His-tory Museum, led an expedition to Henderson Island. What he found was shocking . . . an estimated 38 million pieces of plastic. "The density of debris was the highest recorded anywhere in the world, suggesting that remote islands close to oceanic plastic accumulation zones act as important sinks for some of the waste in these areas," he wrote in 2017 in the Proceedings of the National Academy of Sciences. Plastic items strewn about its shores came from Russia, Japan, China, and the United States They were carried there by a circular ocean current known as the South Pacific gyre.[17]

If plastic found on the remotest lands on Earth was not enough, later in 2017, photos from the Deep-Sea Debris Database revealed plastic in the remotest seas on Earth. Over 36,000 feet down in the Mariana Trench, plastic was found to be the most prevalent form of debris, plastic bags to be precise. The most sobering finding was that 92 percent of plastics identified were single-use products, those used once and thrown away, such as plastic bottles and disposable utensils.[18]

In the 1800s environmentalists debated coal, in the 1900s it was largely oil, and now the 2000s are shaping up to be a dilemma of plastics. Plastic is not new, but it is more abundant now than at any point in history. No one can escape its grasp on society. From the beeping smartphone that wakes us up, to the toothbrush and bottle of toothpaste, the car to work, the pen beside the laptop, the bag of frozen veggies at lunch and box of forks in the break room, it is everywhere.

Discovering a substitute for dwindling natural resources ought to be an automatic panacea, especially if it can be more durable and cheaper to produce, but plastic proves otherwise. The production of plastics increased from 2.3 million tons in 1950 to 448 million tons in 2015. Half of all the plastics ever manufactured have been made in the past 15 years.[19]

The developed world is making tremendous progress in the replacing of limited raw materials through the innovations of renewable resources. But along the macroeconomic trend line of progress lies eight billion microeconomic daily decisions. Governments can rally together through various acts and accords to create rules protecting the environment, but rules are only as valuable as they are followed. Unfortunately, countries struggling for sustainability will struggle to prioritize global sustainability, the same way individuals living in poverty will opt for a car barely passing emissions standards over an unaffordable electric vehicle. If money were not a concern, conservation would be a matter of convenience. But money is a concern.

WHAT SHOULD I DO WITH MY MONEY?

Where does a cleaner planet fit into your financial plan? The answer always comes back to your MICE. But let's be real, the available options will be better or worse depending on the financial status of your microeconomy. For an average earner trying to take care of their family and one day retire, if a brown investment (environmentally unfriendly) were guaranteed to yield better returns than a green investment (environmentally friendly), the incentive to pick the former is high. That same investor might also settle for a slew of items packaged in plastic from Dollar General rather than the eco-friendly products lining the pricier shelves of Whole Foods.

Just like the SEP risk assessment model pointed out earlier, the severity component of pollution appears to be so distant that it can be easily ignored. *If I use one more plastic straw, is it really going to change the world, let alone my life?* This feeling of being unattached, combined with so many variables in cleaning up the planet, can make the issue seem insurmountable. However, these are the same excuses nonvoters make during each election.

Once it is understood that the choices of each individual actually do count, just like each vote does, then solutions can become attainable. Every human being is guilty of pollution to some extent. Improvements in technology, quality of life, and overall population growth are all contributing factors to pollution, but ones most people would never want to reverse.

The keys to a healthy planet lie first in identifying polluters. Polluters can be grouped into two categories that initiatives can target: those who do not care and those who cannot care.

Those Who Don't Care

Fortunately, people who choose not to care represent the minority. The solution to converting this group into green advocates is education and inspiration. As alluded to earlier, someone with this unclean mentality is likely to bypass a piece of trash on the curb because it won't stop an ice cap from melting thousands of miles away.

The greatest gains for this segment can come from good old peer pressure. Municipalities across the country can make littering illegal, but how many people know someone sitting in jail for leaving a plastic bottle on a picnic table? The real progress is in making good cool and bad uncool. Look no further than the stigma surrounding cigarette smoking. A deluge of formal education combined with Hollywood erasing cigarettes from the big screen raised a generation mocking those who still pick up cancer sticks.

Where microeconomies, households, may litter due to ignorance, macroeconomies, nations and large corporations, may do so for financial gain. Manufacturing, traveling, and simply living in a cleaner fashion can come with significant financial costs, at least in the short term. Therefore, nations, like the offshore manufacturing hubs of Mexico and China, and the companies that outsource to such environmentally lax countries, have a distinct competitive advantage in ignoring the high costs of compliance.

The interconnectedness of global economies can make possible the same peer pressures from a macro standpoint. Passing resolutions to achieve carbon neutrality is in vogue across the world. Political campaigns trade the limelight by one-upping each other with loftier goals—carbon neutral by 2050, by 2045, or by 2030! While such proclamations grab headlines and sound noble, most of the men and women staking these claims cannot be held to any accountability decades past their time in office. They are politically risk-free slogans, often ridiculed as "feel good, do nothing" moments.

The Paris Agreement signed in 2015 by 196 parties is a nice formal promise to limit global warming, which pledged to limit the increase in global temperatures by 1.5 degrees Celsius above preindustrial levels. However, it lacks the power to "force" a party to act a certain way, like not being able to punish the lazy child leaving a plastic bottle on the curb. Educated groups of people within free-speech countries can leverage social media and voting power to share unlimited opinion on going green, not unlike responsible friends egging on the litterer to pick up their trash.

For economies able to care, but not willing to, political and corporate leaders can make the acts of disobedience more costly than the alternative. China, the second richest country in the world, has felt the peer pressure against their manufacturing economy. The international community is pressing for "deglobalization" with China due to their social and environmental concerns. Tariffs on Chinese imports (also provoked by Chinese currency manipulation and intellectual property theft) have led to factories again moving overseas, many back to Mexico. This could be seen as shifting the smog around the world.

Those Who Can't Care

The harder group to reach, which likely represents the majority of carbon culprits, are those who cannot care. Due to their life circumstances, or the country's economic and technological situation, there are priorities that take precedence over recycling or revamping a country's outdated infrastructure. This is where leaders are investing entirely new sections of government budgets to empower rather than punish.

While the United States may be portrayed by Congresswoman Alexandria Ocasio-Cortez (AOC) and her Green Deal entourage as a gas-guzzling country overtaken by monster trucks, the reality is America has made great environmental strides over the past 40 years that had nothing to do with going green. In 1953, one out of every three American workers was employed by manufacturing, and manufacturing accounted for over one quarter of GDP. Since then, the United States moved away from making things to thinking things. In 2021, manufacturing made up only 11 percent of GDP, less than one-sixth of the services industry, and accounted for 11 percent of US jobs.[20] Factories gushing pollution into the air have largely been replaced by office parks, and big machines by tiny laptops.

The snag is that these manufacturing plants were not eliminated. Americans still want to drive cars and hold things; they were simply moved. Manufacturing initially migrated to Mexico (and is starting to return there), but now takes place mostly in China. The wealthiest country in the world is left asking other countries to clean up their act, while the world continues to ask for the same goods at the same low price.

According to the WHO, the 10 most polluted countries in the world in order of the worst are Bangladesh, Pakistan, Mongolia, Afghanistan, India, Indonesia, Bahrain, Nepal, Uzbekistan, and Iraq. Bangladesh blames its huge brick-making industry, followed by the rest pointing primarily to vehicle emissions, coal, and factories. One can quickly garner that most of these countries are also poor, needing to make economic decisions before environmental ones.

However, the wealth-to-pollution ratio, even the initiative-to-pollution ratio, is not always consistent. On a more micro level, California is the wealthiest state in America, with by far the highest GDP of over $3 trillion in 2020. It is also recognized as the home of the most liberal green initiatives. Nevertheless, 7 of the 10 most polluted cities in America are in California. Los Angeles remains the city with the worst ozone pollution in the nation, as it has for all but 1 of the 22 years tracked by the American Lung Association's "State of the Air" report.[21]

Fortunately, economics has a way of instigating positive change. In China, the trend toward state-run capitalism, perhaps mixed with the impact of recent tariffs,has spurred economic benefits that are beginning to deter manufacturing. China's ability to evolve past purely manufacturing reinforces the ideal that building the economy must come first, and then going green can become a reality. Once financial security and personal freedom are available, each nation and individual can choose to go green. Intergovernmental tariffs, sanctions, and policies can follow as a supplement against bad actors, but not until the polluted party can get out of its own way.

Green Initiatives

The Conference of Parties (COP26) of 2021 in Glasgow, Scotland, centered around four common initiatives that will affect financial decisions across the world.

1. Net Zero Carbon Emissions

The most popular goal was to achieve net zero carbon emissions. The United States has pledged to cut emissions by 50 percent by 2030 (relative to 2005); Europe pledged 55 percent reduction by 2030 (relative to 1990); China, the largest emitter, intends to peak in 2030 and eventually reach net zero in 2060; followed last by India's goal of net zero in 2070. All the leaders in attendance vowed to stop deforestation by 2030. The rhetoric and actual results continue to differ in an international climate, no pun intended, that appreciates global concern, but favors national interests.

2. Financial Aid

The second talking point involved fiscal efforts, carrots for companies and microeconomies to get onboard with going green. The European Union earmarked 30 percent of their 750-billion-euro Recovery Fund for climate benefits. The Biden administration's $1.2 trillion Infrastructure Investment and Jobs Act passed in November of 2021 with a major emphasis on updating the US grid and shifting toward emissions-free electricity. This will be accomplished through new power lines, building transmission lines with higher voltage capacities, electrifying public transportation, building more electric car chargers, and cleaning up soil and groundwater in old mines and gas fields. The Congressional Budget Office (CBO) predicts this will add $256 billion to the US budget deficit. The administration followed up in 2022 with the "Climate Bill" (somehow formally called the "Inflation Reduction Act"), which included $369 billion in climate and energy provisions.

3. Climate Financing

This iteration of financial aid calls for greater public-private partnership to stimulate green initiatives. This is often done through no-interest loans, forgivable loans, grants, and similar forms of financing that encourage private companies to go green, but with more skin in the game than pure subsidies.

4. Carbon Pricing

In 2021, carbon pricing through carbon tax or emmissions trading schemes covered 22 percent of global greenhouse gas emissions.[22] Carbon taxes resemble the longstanding sin taxes used in the US—taxes levied on harmful goods like tobacco and alcohol.

Once those who do not care are motivated to care and those who cannot care are afforded the ability to care, then households can assume responsibility for a greener future. So long as certain economies are slaves to their money and not masters of it, curbing global warming and reducing dependence on plastic will be seen only as an inconvenient good deed.

The individual choices to stymy global warming are elementary to the point of condescension, but critical enough to be broadcast by the United Nations. The UN's *Act Now* steps include reduce heating and cooling at home, use new energy-efficient appliances, bicycle when possible, eat more produce and less meat, train ride instead of plane ride, recycle, buy an electric vehicle, and reduce water consumption.

Environmental Innovations

Scientists have only the 118 elements within the periodic table to work with. Elements are the problem and the solution. As global warming becomes harder to curtail amid a growing population, scientists will continue to look for faster solutions. This is the happy place where economically driven innovation can run parallel to conservation. Progress was apparent before going green was even in fashion. For example, the proportion of total US land dedicated to farming rose from 16 percent in 1850 to 39 percent in 1910 as bison were wiped out across the West and forests uprooted. Thanks to improvements in agricultural and mechanical science, the usage of land has not changed from 1910 through today, despite incredible population growth.[23]

Inventors will continue to think of the unthinkable, unleashing new fields of study such as "climate engineering" or "geoengineering." Outrageous ideas such as injecting reflective particles into Earth's upper atmosphere to scatter and reflect sunlight back into space and reduce heat penetration, or seeding the ocean with iron to stimulate phytoplankton blooms, diminishing carbon dioxide through photosynthesis, may someday be as normal as solar panels and wind turbines.

The automobile is one of the most common culprits of pollution. For nearly all of history, such machines never existed. It was only in 1914, in Cleveland, Ohio, that cars became prominent enough to necessitate the first traffic light being installed. About one century later, there are over 238 million drivers traversing America's roads.[24]

Fortunately, mankind always finds a way to right its wrongs. Like in 2008, when Tesla Motors released its first car, the completely electric Roadster. As of 2022, Tesla is selling over 300,000 electric vehicles per quarter.[25] Almost every other major car brand has followed suit with their own electric models. However, as the world has witnessed the difficulty in recycling its favorite product, plastic, there will inevitably be difficulties around recycling the hazardous chemicals of more and more lithium-ion batteries. Currently an estimated 5 percent of lithium-ion EV batteries get recycled, versus 95 percent of traditional lead-acid batteries.[26]

ECONOMIC INSIGHT

Tesla launched its initial public offering (IPO) on the NASDAQ stock exchange on June 29, 2010. They issued 13.3 million shares of common stock for the public at a price of $17.00 per share. Exactly 10 years later, shares of Tesla closed at $1,009.35, marking a 4,125 percent increase since its IPO.[27]

If everyone bought Apple, Amazon, and Tesla when they say they should have, I wouldn't have to write this book. The reason it's hard to find a diamond in the rough is because there's a lot of rough. Are you familiar with Molycorp, HiSoft, Qlik, JinkoSolar, or Amyris? They're just a few of the other highly anticipated 152 companies that went public in 2010 alongside Tesla.[28]

The field of climate change is gaining momentum and is backed by the largest bank accounts in the world . . . international governments. Nations are prepared to mobilize trillions of dollars to reach their environmental goals. This will retire old industries while giving rise to new ones, new ones that are prime for investors.

Perhaps the last trend to garner as much attention as environmentally conscious investing was the internet boom. The late 1990s turned the stock market into the Wild Wild West of dot-coms. The fanaticism around making quick money on the internet prompted investors from average-Joe's up to prominent venture capitalists and hedge funds to buy up any company ending in dot-com. Just like when the football team wins states and the following year sees a huge turnout at tryouts, they might not all be players. Revolutions can change the world for the better, but that does not condone anointing everyone who claims to lead the team.

Regarding wind and solar, aside from looking at big silver panels on roofs and hoping seagulls don't fly into turbines along the shore, the costs and time needed to scale these technologies are immense. Initiatives in this realm face three glaring hurdles. First, financing such projects through usual subsidies and tax credits will inevitably require taking from other programs, increasing taxes, and/or adding to public debt. Second, the physical footprint of these technologies is obvious, and in a world growing more crowded, someone has to give up their land or sea to fit them. Third, traditional forms of brown energy represent a multitrillion-dollar industry that employs millions around the world. Any government-backed action opposing these companies and their workers is guaranteed to face extreme lobbying.

ECONOMIC INSIGHT

The point about aggravating an established industry is a tough pill to swallow, but one that routinely heals humanity. It is creative destruction. Joseph Schumpeter, finance minister of German-Austria in 1919 and later an economics professor at Harvard University, said in *Capitalism, Socialism, and Democracy* (1942), "The process of creative destruction is the essential fact about capitalism . . . It is what capitalism consists in and what every capitalist concern has got to live by."

This ultimate form of constructive criticism is what drives innovation and progress. Naturally, these benefits, which every society adores, are the product of change. The great paradox of innovation is that it temporarily hinders capital in many forms—jobs, money, companies, even industries, in order to provide far greater long-term capital. As such, change is bound to upset the status quo, transforming those unwilling to change into victims. Any innovator, in this case environmental saviors, is sure to find staunch enemies in all those who benefit from the old way and only moderate friends in those who might benefit from the new way. Microeconomies, such as companies revamping their product line, can make this transition more comfortable and acceptable through new job training and bonuses or promotions for those willing to make the jump.

Another proposed solution wrangled in flak is nuclear power. During World War II, the United States realized the huge advantage of using submarines, but were hamstrung by their short battery life. Diesel electric submarines had to surface every 12 to 24 hours to recharge and refuel. The original subs were essentially ships that could temporarily submerge, as opposed to submerged vessels that would temporarily surface. In 1951, Admiral Hyman Rickover put on full display the future of nuclear energy with his submarine, the *Nautilus*. Propelled by the Submarine Thermal Reactor, a pressurized water reactor, nuclear subs could run for about 20 years without needing to refuel.[29]

Since Rickover revolutionized the Navy, nuclear technology has expanded far beyond submarines. According to the US Department of Energy, it would take three million solar panels or more than 400 wind turbines to provide the same power as a one-gigawatt reactor.[30] NASA climatologist James Hansen, Kerry Emanuel of the Massachusetts Institute of Technology, Tom Wigley of the University of Adelaide in Australia, and Ken Caldeira of the Carnegie Institution together stated that, "there is no credible path to climate stabilization that does not include a substantial role for nuclear power." A recent case study is available in Europe; Germany's carbon emissions are 10 times greater than those of France, which gets 70 percent of its electricity from nuclear power.[31]

What Is Nuclear Energy?

Since fear and confusion are major reasons why the economically and environmentally advantageous approach keeps stalling, it may be worth a quick sidebar on what nuclear energy actually is. Nuclear power plants do not emit greenhouse gases while generating electricity. They produce power by boiling water to create steam that spins a turbine. The water is heated by a process called fission, which makes heat by splitting apart uranium atoms inside a nuclear reactor core. In current reactors, nuclear fuel is made up of metal fuel rods that contain small ceramic pellets of enriched uranium oxide. The fuel rods are combined into tall assemblies that are then placed into the reactor. After use, the fuel rods are first moved into steel-lined temporary storage pools that are about 40 feet deep. After at least three years of wet storage, they are then sealed inside welded steel-reinforced concrete containers.

Spent fuel is safely and securely stored at more than 100 reactor and storage sites across the US. The fuel is either enclosed in storage pools or dry casks as mentioned earlier. On-site storage at nuclear power plants is not intended to be permanent. The US Department of Energy is requesting funds to restart its application process for a permanent repository site and to initiate a robust interim storage program. Framatome, GE's Global Nuclear Fuel and Westinghouse are currently testing their accident-tolerant fuels. With support from the government and national labs, these companies hope to commercialize their fuels and deploy them to commercial reactors by 2025.[32]

Americans have been averse to the conversation of nuclear energy, often because of the inherent fears surrounding the word *nuclear*. However, the United States already is and has been the world's largest producer of nuclear power. Thirty states have commercial nuclear reactors, providing one-fifth of US energy. Commercial nuclear power plants have supplied around 20 percent of the nation's electricity each year since 1990. As of 2017, the breakdown of what qualifies as US emissions-free electricity is 1 percent geothermal, 4 percent solar, 18 percent wind, 21 percent hydro, and 56 percent nuclear.

Nuclear energy is also extremely efficient. Nuclear power plants are designed to run 24/7/365, requiring little maintenance and refueling. They operate at full capacity more than 92 percent of the time, making it nearly twice as reliable as coal-sourced energy, which works at 54 percent capacity. Furthermore, the physical space requirement of these dangerous chemicals is eye-opening compared to the acreage needed by solar and wind farms. One pellet of uranium, the element used in nuclear reactors, is equal to one ton of coal or 120 gallons of gasoline.

The Democratic Party and most environmental groups have long opposed the use of nuclear energy. In 2005, almost 300 environmental groups—including Greenpeace, Sierra Club, and Public Citizen—signed a manifesto that said, "We flatly reject the argument that increased investment in nuclear capacity is an acceptable or necessary solution . . . Nuclear power should not be a part of any solution to address global warming."[33] However, President Biden's infrastructure bill is a big bipartisan step toward the proven green energy. It allocated $6 billion to enhance existing reactors and an additional $2.6 billion for advanced nuclear development through the Department of Energy's Advanced Reactor Demonstration Program (ARDP).

* * *

Regarding the plastics problem, the solutions are again simple, but not easy. The final destination for most plastics is the ocean, at which point it is near impossible to stop where they flow. Therefore, the best solution is prevention in the first place. A piece of plastic left on the curb might as well be considered washed away into the ocean's worldwide stream.

In August of 2014, California became the first state to ban the use of single-use plastic bags at large retail stores. Why did it take decades of millions of bags floating around before a change was made? How come as of this writing, in 2022, 40 states still permit these plastic bags? The world is not waiting for a complicated innovation subject to approval and countless safety standards and tests to be a replacement. It's just a matter of shoppers packing up their items in their own bags. Simple, maybe not easy?

As the planet continues to get more crowded, pollution will continue to be inevitable. Thankfully, developed economies are slowing the trend, possibly even reversing it, by making a cleaner lifestyle more possible every year. Just as investors spent much of the Industrial Revolution searching for companies that could bring people closer together, and now look for tech companies that can allow people to be further apart (see Chapter 1, Population), investors will now target companies that can maintain modern living in a greener fashion. Cleaning up the planet is yet another want that may someday become a need. There may be no greater example of tiny choices making huge impacts than in the field of climate change.

TECH

Technology is a story about organic assistance. *Tech* and *organic* in the same sentence might seem an oxymoron. Technology is arguably the purest form of help; it is completely man-made and confined by earthly elements. From the wooden wheel to satellites orbiting the sky, every step of technological progress represents a human innovation, a new pathway to wealth. Tech always has been, and always will be, big business.

It has become appallingly obvious that our technology has exceeded our humanity.

—Albert Einstein

"**C**'mon, Titled Towers! You go! GO . . . NOOOO!" Jimmy's voice screams.

One more time and I swear, Dad thinks to himself. He looks to the ceiling of his sweltering garage-turned-office. *Exhale first. Push all of the old, stale air out of the diaphragm, then inhale through the nose and fill the belly, not the chest.* Refreshed, he returns his gaze to his laptop and begins searching for the Zoom login code.

"FRICK! I can't believe you grabbed a pistol when the SMG was right there!"

Thin walls are all that separate the living room and world of Fortnite from his world of business. Competing technologies. Dad ignores the beads of sweat dripping down his forehead. His new ring light flickers at him from across his desk, taunting him, not compatible with MacBook's USB-C port. More innovations, more business. The webinar begins with a grainy image of his forehead.

"Allll right, how's everybody doing today?" Dad says while adjusting the laptop to fit his face on screen. "Can you guys hear me?" he asks. Several black boxes pop up. He waits for the one brave soul who might unmute and chime in, or perhaps even click the video button to present a fellow live human being.

"NOO! Whyyyyy?" The familiar crash of Jimmy's Xbox controller from the next room.

"Sorry if you guys can hear my dog," Dad jokingly disguises the noise to his attendees.

It has been one month, give or take, since the novel coronavirus took the world by storm, but thanks to technology, the show goes on.

"Unprecedented."

"Cautiously optimistic."

"It's like the flu."

"Put on your mask and wash your hands."

It is a year of sayings no one will ever forget. The global landscape changes, never to be the same again. Technology, so easily labeled an enemy and a savior, is called on more now than ever before.

Jimmy has had enough Fortnite for one homeschooled morning. He heads up to his bedroom and picks up his iPhone. Three videos flash by, almost too quick for the brain to recognize what his eyes are capturing. Hip-hop music morphs into a fun dance-along followed by a girl screaming profanities. Millennials touting the latest cryptocurrency one second, then Gen Z-ers doing backflips off benches the next. The last clip manages to get a full 30-second watch; he clicks the like button.

The app launched in 2016 in China and quickly became the world's fastest-growing social network, billions of downloads and hundreds of millions of users. TikTok may be seen as an annoyance to parents of teens, as the app cycles through videos quicker than Grandpa changes channels on the outdated television. However, the algorithm driving its "For You" page is more than the latest addicting fad. Luring in the average user for 21.5 hours per month,[1] it is advanced enough to be named a "breakthrough technology" by the Massachusetts Institute of Technology.

Messenger RNA vaccines defeating a global pandemic, lithium batteries carrying electric vehicles farther, green hydrogen, GPS with ground-based augmentation offering millimeter-level accuracy, sure, these are all impressive achievements, but capturing the eyes, ears, thumbs, and minds of an entire generation, that is brilliance.

MACRO

The prior chapters spoke of each nation's global standing in terms of human capital, test scores, GDP, and natural resources. All these values share two commonalities: they can be quickly quantified but are slowly developed. Technology flips the equation upside-down. It is difficult to quantify each technological advancement, but when they arrive, they can explode onto the scene and change the course of humanity in an instant. Technology is driven by one goal, and that is speed. Satisfy every want and need faster. Communicate faster. Make money faster. Travel faster. Check off every task faster. Even meditate faster.

Consider the way people used to shop. In 1873 Charles Montgomery Barnes opened a secondhand book business for fans of literature in Wheaton, Illinois. In 1917, his son expanded upon the idea by investing in an educational bookstore, Noble & Noble. He renamed the store Barnes & Noble. One hundred twenty years after its inception, Barnes & Noble raked in a record $1.62 billion in total revenues in 1994.[2] In that same year, Jeff Bezos created a company called Cadabra with the unique idea of selling books online. His attorney mispronounced the company name as "cadaver," which led Bezos to change the name to Amazon. In 2021, just 27 years after its creation,

Amazon generated $470 billion in revenues.[3] Where storefronts once spent generations to acquire thousands of customers, online platforms now spend years to acquire hundreds of millions of customers; proving it takes hard work to make millions, but it takes tech to make billions.

Technology can be defined as the practical application of scientific knowledge. Its aim is to empower and optimize human abilities. Technology is as natural an ambition as finding food and shelter. So while sciences can include nearly any field of study, be it cooking, traveling, or manufacturing, *tech* can be considered that cutting-edge by-product of the latest engineering and gadgetry.

Tech is omnipresent. It encapsulates MICE. It hovers over every decision of money (M), while teasing one's thoughts about ideology (I), compromise (C), and ego (E). Its speed is demonstrated by the fact that at the turn of the millennium, only a few of the Nasdaq 100 (recognized as the preeminent tech index) companies made the S&P 500 (recognized as the largest companies in the world), whereas now they almost all belong to the elite index. The wreck of the dot-com bubble in 2000 looks in the rearview mirror more like a sticky piece of gum run over by a steamrolling sector. Its influence on ICE is evidenced by a vacation industry dominated by slogans such as "unplugged" and "off-the-grid," in which the wealthy happily pay to escape the grasp of tech.

The economics of supply and demand have officially merged with the economics of convenience, speed, and scale. Innovators fueled by the capitalistic bug of doing better, quicker, and cheaper to appease the almighty customer are literally redesigning maps. Wall Street power brokers in suits have taken a back seat to millennials in flip-flops from Silicon Valley and Austin, Texas. Rockefeller and Carnegie have been replaced by a Gilded Age 2.0, featuring tech titans like Bill Gates, Jeff Bezos, and the PayPal Mafia. The power of tech cannot be overestimated. However, as Edmund Burke once said, "The greater the power, the more dangerous the abuse."

Tech can be characterized by four applications that target MICE. These applications are unique abilities that microeconomies can use to alter macroeconomies with devastating efficiency. The first application shall be identified as mind persuasion. The second is computer mind manipulation. The third is anonymity. The fourth is tech parts, those rare materials inside every device you own. Each application offers both strengths and weaknesses, opportunities and threats. Tech brings immense value to users, but of course, not without its costs.

Mind Persuasion

On mind persuasion, genius is no longer a man able to answer every Jeopardy question; any kid with Siri can do that. Genius is not just knowledge, but the thoughts surrounding knowledge. Tech enables people of power to impress their thoughts on more people, faster, continually reeducating people on what to do with their money. Influencers capitalize on these thoughts by giving users what they want first, and then what they need, or at least what the influencer wants them to think they need. This tech-assisted persuasion is employed everywhere from Fortune 500 companies to presidential campaigns to moms soliciting a PTA vote.

Mind persuasion is nothing novel. Advertisers were playing on consumer emotion long before the first dress shop ever displayed a pretty mannequin. The old marketing rule of seven used by advertisers in the 1930s suggests that people must see an advertisement at least seven times before they are motivated enough to consider buying the product or service. The difference between then and now is that the majority of influences an individual used to absorb were irrelevant (e.g., a school-bus full of middle schoolers passing by a billboard for workmen's boots). Therefore, reaching a buyer or voter seven times in a short time frame proved difficult. Now, the target market can not only be reached seven-plus times in quick fashion, but through revolutionary methods customized to each potential buyer.

The secret potion in tech's mind persuasion is algorithmic-guided marketing. It is based on one critical asset—data. Data collection is improving exponentially each second, primarily led by the social media giants. Data allows any person or company looking to wield influence the ability to enhance the rule of seven by exercising the *illusory truth effect*, a term made popular by a 1977 study from Villanova University and Temple University that hypothesized a tendency to believe false information as truth through repeated exposure. Algorithms can overwhelm users' minds with a perceived positive message and turn fiction into nonfiction, a want into a need. The key word is "perceived"; after all, perception is reality.

In the 1930s the consumer goods powerhouse Procter and Gamble spent such a fortune buying commercials on addicting radio programs that the shows became known as "soap operas." Today's soap operas can be found unfolding every day across the internet. With the median age of cable television viewers being over 60 for each major network, Chapter 1's population trends clearly indicate even more advertising dollars to head toward the internet.[4] Social media has become an advertiser's dream come true by providing a far more addicting platform with deep emotional impact. Tech has allowed marketers to enhance their budget by clearly connecting the price and return of each advertisement.

However, the costs to society of tech-assisted mind persuasion are impossible to calculate. When Beatles legend John Lennon said, "The more I see, the less I know for sure," he likely could not have imagined the bombardment of the internet, particularly its ability to perplex youth. According to a 10-year study by Brigham Young University, 13-year-old girls using social media for at least two hours daily show a significantly higher clinical risk for suicide as emerging adults in their early twenties.[5]

If mind persuasion, and the data that serves as its foundation, is considered an asset of a country, then China is growing its portfolio quickly. One of China's largest companies, Tencent Holdings Ltd., is a major shareholder of Epic Games, which owns the ultra-popular game Fortnite and completely owns Riot Games. ByteDance is another Chinese multinational internet technology company, which owns TikTok, the fastest-growing app used by Generation Z. Over 37 million Americans between the ages of 9 and 24 have a TikTok account, more than Instagram and quickly catching up to Snapchat.[6]

Computer Mind Manipulation

The second application, computer mind manipulation, is known as artificial intelligence (AI). The persuasion of human beings is being led by the persuasion of robots. It is another step toward getting more done faster. AI is adept at replacing minor human errors or acts of laziness, like spellchecking an email before the sender has even finished their thought. However, where AI struggles is in that which is unfamiliar.

AI can process nearly unlimited subsets of yes or no and this or that, but it cannot quite think or feel. It still struggles with issues such as common sense, emotional perception, and sensory recognition. AI can help a robo-advisor automate an investment portfolio based on a generic questionnaire, but it may not advise an investor how to coordinate assets to help their special-needs son or affluent daughter amid a divorce. It can steer a car, but may not slow at an intersection with a stop sign covered in overgrown foliage. AI's emotional shortcomings have opened the door to the field of science known as artificial general intelligence (AGI), the practice of giving computers human thought. The idea of computers thinking on their own still remains somewhat sci-fi; however, robots have an almost unlimited memory and 24/7/365 workload accelerating their compounding advancement.

There is another form of AI called deep learning that is commonly associated with "deepfakes." Deepfakes are synthetic media that use an existing image, video, or audio sample replaced with someone else's likeness. It allows the user to swap a face and voice onto another person. Deepfakes are usually created by what is called a generative adversarial network, or Gan. Gan pits two algorithms against each other to continually modify a clone countless times until it generates an appearance almost completely realistic to its target. The confusion this can present in citing visual or audio proof of any statement is inconceivable.

As if AI in the wrong hands is not enough to worry about, the other difficulty with machine learning models is that they can become "black boxes," meaning they can reach results, but often through paths of calculations even the engineer cannot comprehend. It is not unlike the amateur golfer who finally hits the perfect drive and has no idea how that swing was different from the prior 20 hooks and slices.

Anonymity

The third application of anonymity is another paradox. Privacy is a luxury in a crowded world. Unfortunately, it is getting harder for normal people to stay private at the same time it is becoming easier for evil actors to hide in the shadows. "The greatest threat today is cyber," said Fed chairman Jerome Powell on *60 Minutes* in 2021. It may sound a bit unorthodox for perhaps the most important financial leader in the world to be geeking out, but his comments underscore the incredible economic power of an interconnected cybercommunity.

Hidden, anonymous criminals present problems for security forces that Sherlock Holmes never had to deal with. The world knew who Hitler was, America knew who attacked Pearl Harbor, the CIA tracked down Osama bin Laden across the world, but a hacker may never be known. Aside from gradual mind persuasion and its steroid, AI, tech offers a playground for invisible nefarious actors seeking instant harm. American victims reported $6.9 billion in losses due to cybercrime to the FBI in 2021, a 50 percent increase from 2020[7].The FBI's Internet Crime Center averages over 2,000 complaints per day, almost half of which are phishing complaints (fraudulent email scams that induce individuals to reveal private information). It is worth noting that these statistics represent what was "reported," as many businesses and individuals quietly eat the loss for fear of losing the trust and confidence of their communities.

Cryptocrime

A common theme in cybercrime is a financial trail of cryptocurrency. Cryptocurrency is a type of digital currency that generally exists only electronically. Bitcoin was the first crypto, created in 2009. Cryptocurrency is stored in a digital wallet, which can be online, on a computer, or on an external hard drive. The digital wallet has an address, which is usually a long string of numbers and letters.

Bitcoin and other nonfungible tokens (NFTs) certainly provide benefits as a global currency with potential to help citizens of countries like Venezuela who might otherwise lose the value of their currency amid national turmoil. But without major governments formally adopting cryptocurrency, there exists a cloudy realm of finance for criminals to operate in. Crypto is not backed by a government. If the company holding your digital wallet were to go bankrupt or be hacked, the government has no obligation to help retrieve lost funds, like the FDIC would do for US dollars in a bank account.

From January 2021 through March 2022, more than 46,000 people reported losing over $1 billion in crypto to scams. More than half of these scams originated on social media, and the hardest hit demographic was people in their thirties.[8] There is no bank or centralized authority to monitor or stop suspicious and fraudulent actions. The lure for scammers has been the belief that crypto transfers can't be reversed and can't be traced; once the money is sent, there's no getting it back. However, the recovery by the US Department of Justice of $2.3 million in cryptocurrency ransom paid by Colonial Pipeline in 2021, approximately 85 percent of the total ransom paid, showed the possible traceability of crypto through blockchain analysis. Security experts have said the more ransomware criminals use crypto, the more opportunity they will have to disrupt the ransomware supply chain due to the information that can be pulled from blockchain records.

China was one of the first countries to embrace cryptocurrency, creating an exchange known as BTC China in 2011. However, one decade later, in November of 2021, China issued an absolute ban on cryptocurrency.[9] This was not meant to end crypto in China, but rather open the door for a government-backed digital currency. The People's Bank of China issued a working paper describing the development of e-CNY (China's digital yuan) in 2017 and began piloting it in 2022.[10] The digital currency is meant to provide anonymity to users, but remain available to law enforcement and security agencies.

In the United States, the Securities and Exchange Commission (SEC) created a Crypto Assets and Cyber Unit in 2017 (formerly known as the Cyber Unit) to address the growing concern.[11] Gary Gensler, SEC chair, said the crypto industry is "rife with fraud, scams, and abuse." Regulation is still being debated between federal and state agencies as to who should ultimately oversee crypto, whether it belongs to the SEC or the Commodity Futures Trading Commission.

Aside from the risks of cryptocrime, cryptocurrencies are also highly volatile because they are based entirely on supply and demand. In November of 2021, total cryptocurrencies reached a $2.9 trillion market cap. By June of 2022, their combined value fell below $1 trillion. Governments are getting serious about increased oversight, hoping not only to deter criminal activity, but also to legitimize a new financial sector.

Business email compromise (BEC) continues to be the costliest scheme, responsible for over $2.4 billion in losses in 2021.[12] BEC is a popular method in which a criminal enters a legitimate email account through hacking or social engineering and then requests a wire transfer from an unsuspecting victim. Some of the latest scams include obtaining an ID from an unsuspecting victim, then establishing a bank account with their information to receive stolen funds, which is then commonly converted to cryptocurrency.

Ransomware is another infamous form of cyberattack. Hackers lock up computer systems with malware and demand a payment from victims before its release, again usually through Bitcoin or cryptocurrency payments. In just the first six months of 2021, over $590 million was paid out by victims of ransomware attacks.[13] Targets have trended away from data-rich companies to key providers of public needs, such as hospitals and mass transit. The majority of these attacks appear to come from Russia and eastern Europe, where the line between private hackers and state-backed initiatives is unclear.

Tech Parts

The fourth application of tech on economics, both micro and macro, is the actual parts that make up tech. Before coronavirus, only the nerdiest of tech junkies fully understood the inner workings of robots and computers. The rest of the world happily synced up their smartphones to iPlay and FaceTimed their friends while driving down the highway on cruise-control, all thanks to some difficult-to-explain magic.

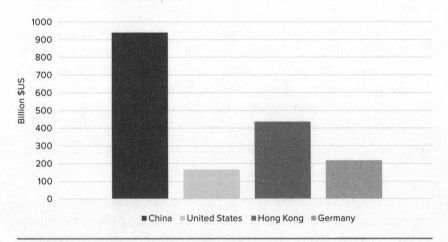

Figure 6.1 High-technology exports*[14]

---

* Products with high R&D intensity, such as in aerospace, computers, pharmaceuticals, scientific instruments, and electrical machinery.

ECONOMIC INSIGHT

Athletes are fond of saying speed kills, but it's true in pretty much every competition. While tech can make seemingly everything happen faster, the people behind tech (i.e., investors, engineers, tech executives, and government think tanks) are in their own race. Tech, perhaps more than any sector before it, has a way of rushing into and out of existence. This reality makes it very difficult to stay ahead of the pack, like sprinters relaying through a marathon.

Companies and nations, just like private investors, can sustain volatility through diversification. As the last chapter showed the risk the Middle East runs by tying its economy to the global oil market, so the United States and China do by depending so heavily on Taiwan for semiconductors (as of 2022, Taiwan produces 90 percent of the world's advanced chips[15]). Like an investor with all their eggs in one basket, a company with a single product line or a country dependent on one revenue or supply source is not in a position of power. When the stars align, the old way of doing things may appear to be the right way of doing things, but it is only a matter of time before the world catches on to something new. In the face of tech, that time can be very short. Having more players on the bench may be the only difference between forfeiting and staying in the game when the competition heats up.

MICRO

Mrs. Ivana Car walks through the car dealership lot, slowly giving up hope on a good deal. *Nissan, Chevy, Toyota, Tesla. American-made or not, electric or gas, I don't care anymore. I need something to drive!*

Despite the discount ads peppering her Facebook newsfeed, the prices of certified preowned cars continue to rise quicker than she can test-drive the latest online special. From 2021 to 2022, new-car prices rise 12.2 percent and used-car prices jump 40.5 percent.[16]

As Covid-19 engulfs the world, people immediately stop traveling. Auto manufacturers stop building and cancel orders for new parts. Nissan cuts its 2021 production by 500,000 vehicles and other manufacturers follow suit.[17] But soon the world gets back on the streets, and flush with savings and stimulus money. But there's one very tiny problem.

The most valuable car parts are no longer tires and brake pads, but rather computer chips. Chip manufacturers do not miss a beat in the pandemic as the use of home office items like laptops and smartphones explodes. They simply refocus on other customers. In a race to play catchup as the world resumes driving, the auto industry slams into reverse and demands more of the microscopic technical marvels that host billions of transistors within them.

The world turns to Taiwan, the largest supplier of computer chips. Almost all this production comes through its premier company—Taiwan Semiconductor Manufacturing Company (TSMC). Samsung, a South Korean company, is the only other manufacturer of the most advanced 5-nanometer chips.

China finds itself just as strapped as America. Led by Semiconductor Manufacturing International Corporation (SMIC), China trails the United States in chip production and also depends heavily on Taiwan. China encounters even more difficulty advancing its technology since the Trump administration's blacklisting of SMIC. The most advanced chips depend on extreme ultraviolet lithography equipment, which is produced primarily by ASML, a Dutch company. The Trump administration pressured the Netherlands in 2019 into cancelling ASML's export license with China, which has yet to be renewed as of this writing.

Already stretched to the limit, the supply and demand of technology's lifeblood collides with Mother Nature. TSMC uses a self-reported 156,000 tons of water daily to produce its chips. At the most inconvenient time possible, Taiwan experiences its worst draught in decades. Not far away, Japan's largest chip producer, Renesas, watches one of its top factories burn to the ground after a plating tank catches fire. Meanwhile in America, a cold snap in Texas triggers domestic plant closures. The world begs them to move faster; in January of 2021, chip sales eclipse a record $40 billion in one month,[18] but producers are forced to go slower. Major car factories continue to sit idle as they wait their turn in line for these precious chips.

Mrs. Ivana Car can either wait a year or two for a hopefully fairer price, or she can pay a premium to get back to driving with a car possibly void of popular features such as climate control. She returns home and walks into a house full of children complaining that the release of their favorite PS5 game has been delayed, another victim of the microchip shortage. For now, they all resort to their iPhones, only wishing they could somehow transfer these parts into the rest of the tech machines they depend upon.

WHAT SHOULD I DO WITH MY MONEY?

Mankind is on a never-ending quest for more. In a way, it's a part of satisfying the natural desire for wealth, well-being. Fill the day with more work, more fun, more relaxation, more energy, more friends and family. Fill the accounts with more money to make it all possible. There's only so much time in life to fulfill.

Population has compounded more of everyone wanting more of everything. Entitlements have entitled more. Education has empowered more. Economic philosophy has enabled more. Environment has fueled more. Tech has sped up more. If speed of more fulfillment is what the people want, it would make sense to invest heavily in the tools that make this possible—technology. But as has been apparent throughout this writing, progress is a contradiction in a world with free will. Whether it be mind persuasion, AI, cybercommunication, or computer manufacturing, each domain holds equal threats to its opportunities.

What They Should Do with Their Money

In a free-market economy like the United States, there is a fine line to toe between allowing people and companies to operate however they see fit, versus creating new laws and regulations that force another line item onto their budgets. If the rational observer realizes the dangers of a see-no-evil approach to governance, they will realize there must be a set of rules to play by. What "they" can do with their money to help serve as a big brother, without actually becoming Big Brother, hints at what you should do with your money.

In respect to mind persuasion, it is imperative that youth are not only taught how to use technology, but how to maintain proper cyber hygiene.

Since many parents have to ask their kids how to even use the latest tech, "they" (governments and schools) may consider investing in the equivalent of social media guidance counselors who can educate students on the newest opportunities and threats exposed to teens.

The iPhone was created in 2007, meaning millennials were the last generation to traverse adolescence without a mobile addiction. Generation Z is the first cohort to be raised from birth in the presence of cell phones and social media. It can be hard for parents to compare, "When I was your age ___," against a social setting that did not exist yet. So, how can one know if they are living in the Matrix, if they were born in the Matrix? Just as microeconomies can vote with their dollars for a cleaner environment, so might they do for a safer internet.

Altruistic social media designers can easily use self-identification to prevent access to social media when it should not be allowed in the first place. The major players certainly have the technology to detect if a six-year-old has logged into their mother's TikTok account and is clicking through obviously non-Mom content.

Another controversial, but widely agreed upon, solution involves constraining social media use. China saw a major problem brewing with its young population's time in front of video games. The government took its second step to control video game usage in 2021, barring online gaming on school days and limiting to one hour per day on weekends and holiday evenings. The Chinese government requires all online game players to register under their real names and submit to monitoring by the government.[19] This is an easy directive to implement in a communist country as opposed to the United States, but should at least serve as a reminder of the severity of technology's impact during the developmental stage of life.

Most high school students in America are free to carry their cell phones throughout the day and check in on the universe at their leisure. School hallways full of teenagers bumping shoulders while looking down at their phones was the result of a slow progression. There was a time where not every student had a phone, and the ones who did could do nothing more than make an emergency phone call or possibly play a game of Snake. The evolution from a beeper to calling device, to texting, to full-blown computer in a pocket took time. Schools might benefit greatly by imposing stricter rules around cellphone use during school hours.

In looking at the "grown-up" consequences of mind persuasion, the key involves controlling the dissemination of disinformation. Herein lies an infinite gray space capable of rebranding a group's mentality, as clearly seen in the generational changes of economic philosophy in Chapter 4. The blessing and curse of taking 10 minutes to open a Twitter account is that the new user is truly a global entity, able to espouse ideas on audiences around the world. A local news station may have to staff a team of employees to help comply with various regulatory authorities and the Federal Communications Commission. Meanwhile, a creator of a new Twitter account in Moscow is welcome to spread outlandish international stories without any red tape or fear of penalty.

Social media companies have to comply with the laws of the country in which they operate. However, the fact that Facebook or YouTube is not the owner or creator of a person's comment releases them of most liability. Companies can do their best to police billions of people's comments, automatically banning violence, sexual content, and hate speech, but cannot be expected to catch everything of concern. Facebook employs roughly 15,000 moderators in addition to its use of AI. On the flip side, the sites are financially driven to attract and retain the most users possible and stimulate the most conversation and activity possible. The enormous lobbying industry described in Chapter 4 is paid to protect such profits.

"They" may someday need to recognize social media platforms as news sources, and apply the same standards to their content, regardless of creator, as would be applied to a CNN or Fox News. The Facebooks and Twitters of the world could then somehow divide their users, or at least their users' content, into categories such as "news" and "other." This would delineate one section for puppy pictures, gender reveal videos, and bashing Trump or Biden, and another section for verified objective news.

Artificial intelligence is in a race to outpace human thought. The challenges "they" will need to address can be divided into two categories—limit unintended consequences by the good guys and eliminate intentionally heinous activities by the bad guys.

A prime example of unintended consequences can be found in the quickly growing spaces of autonomous driving and radiology AI. AI has the potential to offer tremendous convenience and free up hours of commuting in the latest cars, but has already resulted in several fatalities due to computer error.

Similarly, radiology AI can help bring effective imaging to more patients while lowering the overall cost of healthcare, but as the Department of Health and Human Services' Patient Safety Network (PSNet) points out, discrepancies in the data used to train AI systems can lead to errors, and in the event of misdiagnosis, who would be held liable?[20] The only feasible protections for innovations that few outside of the innovators can understand are exorbitant amounts of testing and patience. While penalties and legal culpability might stifle the entrepreneurial spirit, the consequences to the innovator should be commensurate with that of a potential victim. This is similar to what pharmaceutical companies must go through with new medications.

Bad actors abusing AI to cause harm is a much harder problem to resolve. The most notable threat goes back to mass mind manipulation, such as tampering with news and political influence across social media platforms. The key here segues into the next characteristic of modern technology—anonymity.

How do "they" find out who's making harmful unintended errors versus those who are purposefully abusing tech for foul play? The ongoing debate over healthcare insurance offers a great parallel. One key to cybersecurity and identifying the bad guys may involve a private/public infrastructure that allows companies of all sizes to either self-protect or pay a premium to a government plan for comprehensive cybercoverage.

Government interference is impossible to avoid due to the ubiquity of cyber. A slip and fall in a store is an isolated liability issue. Stealing personal identity and financial info from a credit card hack on a gas station can lead to endless exposure for those customers and anyone else the hackers penetrate while infiltrating data further down the line. Every app and website must be able to offer the same secure parking garage that a venue might offer to a visitor.

Unfortunately, according to the Federal Cybersecurity Risk Determination Report and Action Plan, the Office of Management and Budget (OMB), in conjunction with the Department of Homeland Security (DHS), determined that 71 of 96 government agencies (74 percent) are either "at risk" or "high risk" of cyberattack. OMB and DHS also found that federal agencies are not equipped to determine how threat actors seek to gain access to their information.[21]

The Biden administration mandated that all federal agencies patch over 200 security flaws identified between 2017 and 2020, and an additional 90 discovered in 2021. The Cybersecurity and Infrastructure Security Agency (CISA) said these flaws pose "significant risk." This may be a case of playing catchup, locking the doors after the robbers have already made their way through the neighborhood.

Last, "they" must address the creation and distribution of tech parts. This poses perhaps the greatest competitive advantage, or threat, to international affairs. Politicians have long touted the importance of domestic manufacturing in the healthcare industry and other sectors for their economic benefit. Reshoring can bring about new jobs, add more tax revenue, strengthen communities, and proudly stamp "Made in the USA" on its goods. But when it comes to technology, the benefits are not just financial, but include national security.

Governments may benefit from investing in education not just of safe tech use, but in the creation and development of tech, particularly STEM subjects (science, technology, engineering, and mathematics). American high schoolers learn a broad curriculum of subjects from biology to geometry, with a class schedule that may not look too different from their grandparents'. Adding a course in the basics of computer coding would be a good launchpad for homegrown techies.

A nation forced to rely on nonallies for tech runs the same risks as the issues previously discussed in energy dependence. The storylines will continue to play out as world superpowers jockey for position in the quest for technological independence. Until then, China and the United States will court Taiwan and its latest riches, just as the world once did for Saudi Arabia and its oilfields.

Back to What I Should Do

The tech space obviously offers many opportunities for financial gain, whether it be through investing in tech or using tech for business operations. However, each of the paradoxes discussed in this chapter have to be observed.

Security and convenience may be on opposite sides of the spectrum, but you can still lock your doors. Professional recommendations include simple steps like using different passwords for different accounts, enabling two-factor authentication wherever possible, and insuring against risk. The cybersecurity insurance market was valued at $7.36 billion in 2020 and is expected to reach over $27 billion by 2026, registering a compound annual growth rate of 24.30 percent over the forecast period (2021–2026).[22] Businesses, especially in data sensitive industries such as healthcare, will continue to focus heavily on this coverage. Individuals can also take advantage of the many identity-theft protection programs now available.

Finally, you can take advantage of the bits and pieces that make up the construction of tech—by thinking of them in similar terms as other consumer products. Just as oil makes gas that fuels your car, so do rare earth metals and elements that make semiconductors that power your computer. The entire continuum is investable, from commodities like copper to microchip manufacturers up to Apple and Microsoft.

ECONOMIC INSIGHT

There's a parable on observation that Warren Buffett, the investing legend and CEO of Berkshire Hathaway, likes to share about his investment in American Express. During the early 1960s, Amex shares dropped precipitously on rumors of a scandal. To see how bad the problem was, Buffett asked to spend an evening with the cashier at Ross's Steak House in Omaha, Nebraska, to see if guests still paid with credit card. Sure enough, bills were paid all night long on Amex cards. With his concerns put at ease, Buffett purchased a 5 percent stake in the company for $13 million and happily watched his profits accumulate.

Tech can be a confusing investment. Most people are not software engineers, so it's understandable to not be able to fully explain the latest advances for such companies. Coupling this aura of mystique with the fact that tech companies often trade at very high valuations, commonly as growth stocks with high price-to-earnings (P/E) ratios, can create a certain level of speculation.

A recent example of this is cryptocurrency. From about 2019 to 2021, younger clients shared hundreds of investment form 1099s with me, probably more than I've ever seen from Gen X or baby boomers with exponentially more money. From Robinhood, Acorn, Coinbase, and other new "free" online platforms, I saw countless short-term gains and losses of crypto, sometimes as small as a few dollars per trade.

My first question was typically, "OK, why do you like to invest in _____ (pick a popular crypto)? Can you tell me a little bit about how it works?" I don't believe I ever received a response beyond, "It's like digital money." I'd reply, "OK, sounds interesting. Tell me, how often do you use it? Do you buy a lot of normal items with it?" To this follow-up, I never heard anyone report being a user.

This is certainly not to disparage the future of cryptocurrency, but rather to illustrate the violation of investing in what you know. One of the greatest investors of all time, Buffett, practiced the simple exercise of seeing if people liked the company's product to help him determine its value. Technology might be clouded in terms and gadgetry you've never heard of, perhaps this is part of the allure, but simply going back to observing its usability and public acceptance can go a long way. When too many people buy too much of what they don't understand, a bubble (e.g., the dot-com bubble) often follows.

WAR

War is a story about the end and the beginning. The end as it is the carnal result when all else fails. The beginning as life can never be the same after it. War defines economies, and economies define wars. It always, without exception, involves MICE. War unfolds when compromise (C), a respect for diplomacy, is finally discarded.

This is a war to end all wars.

—President Woodrow Wilson, 1917

They pack their equipment and set off for another adventure. Shovels, pickaxes, notepads, magnifying glasses, all the usual utensils—and Bibles. It is the mid-1800s, and the world's best archaeologists are traveling to the Middle East, looking to prove or disprove biblical correlations. The Bible makes mention of cities like Babylon and Nineveh, and so they begin their task in the surrounding region of Mesopotamia (now southern Iraq). As fate would have it, they stumble upon a previously unheard-of city, Sumer, and its treasure trove of relics.

Archaeologists have discovered ancient artifacts suggesting war before. Stone pictographs of clashing armies. Mass grave sites ranging from northern Mesopotamia to Egypt with skeletons clearly the victims of violent deaths. Objects dating back to 10,000 BC illustrating the use of bow and arrow in conflict.[1] But what lies here in Sumer is the oldest recorded war known to man . . .

It is the land of civilized kings. Here, time shall be divided into day and night by two 12-hour periods, hours made up of 60 minutes, and minutes of 60 seconds. Their people stake claim to the first schools, irrigation systems, wheeled vehicles, monumental architecture, and government bureaucracies.

In the Uruk Period (4000 BC to 3100 BC), at the core of Sumer's villages are households. These households are not simply a mother, father, and their kids, but a collection of families and neighbors held together by a common belief in their god or king. They represent the entire chain of economics, from production to consumption. Households multitask their way through the grind of farming, building, and raising children while fending off raiders and slavers. The leaders of the households are warrior-poets.

The exhaustion caused by isolationism spurs these growing households to look past the horizon. They merge into villages and morph into cities. These blossoming metropolises magically give way to all the advantages of division of labor. Larger populations free up artisans, merchants, metalworkers, and philosophers from the drudgery of daily survival so that they may specialize in their industries. Warrior-poets can choose to become warriors *or* poets.

Not all households are so quick to join the crowds with their different ideologies and gods. But there is one necessity that forces even the proudest households to embrace collaboration—water. Irrigation is a complicated process involving the constant digging and repairing of canals, and then an equitable distribution of water across land. Equitable distribution. This is what prompts the need for governance and gives rise to a united Sumer, a macroeconomy.

In 2700 BC, Enmebaragesi is the king of Kish, one of 12 city-states in Sumer. He is determined to grow his empire. He sets his sights on Elam, a region named for Elam, son of Shem, son of Noah (the same Noah from Noah's Ark).[2] Enmebaragesi leads the Sumerians into battle against the Elamites. To the victor go the spoils. In the *King List*, an ancient record of the rulers of Sumer, Enmebaragesi is noted as having "carried away as spoil the weapons of Elam."

Why did the Sumerians lay siege to Elam? Was it just to steal another army's weapons? To acquire more land? Seek revenge? Find gold or new trade routes? What were King Enmebaragesi's MICE?

MACRO

For millennia, all wars had one thing in common—proximity. It was not until the eighteenth century that the dangers associated with advanced transportation and intercontinental trade were laid bare. Places way over there, separated by oceans, suddenly became worth fighting for. The French and Indian War, and later the Revolutionary War, made the world too close for comfort.

America's Early Wars

How does a nonexistent country find the money to fight a war against one of the world's superpowers? After the Sons of Liberty cried, "No taxation without representation!" and while dressed as Mohawk Indians, dumped 342 chests of tea into Boston Harbor in protest against the Parliament, the colonists needed cash. The Continental Congress couldn't possibly levy taxes on a people who just declared war over being taxed. So they found the funds necessary to wage war via loans from France, mostly negotiated by Benjamin Franklin. Smaller loans were also obtained from the Spanish government and private Dutch investors.

After the Revolutionary War, under the guidance of the first secretary of the Treasury, Alexander Hamilton, taxes became inevitable and helped acquire new favorable loans to repay old loans. By 1795, the United States had paid off its debts to the French government and prevented diplomatic embarrassment. With improved credit on European capital markets, the

United States was able to acquire low-interest loans for the Louisiana Purchase in 1803.[3]

Once the United States claimed its independence from Great Britain, the country turned toward building a country. The economy north of the Mason-Dixon line transitioned away from one of agriculture and into one of industry. Urbanization took hold and cities like Chicago, Cleveland, and Detroit boomed. In the mid-1800s, roughly 88 percent of European immigrants chose to settle in the free North. As a result, the Union (Maine, New York, New Hampshire, Vermont, Massachusetts, Connecticut, Rhode Island, Pennsylvania, New Jersey, Ohio, Indiana, Illinois, Kansas, Michigan, Minnesota, Iowa, California, Nevada, and Oregon) soon had a population over 23 million, versus the Confederacy (Texas, Arkansas, Louisiana, Tennessee, Mississippi, Alabama, Georgia, Florida, South Carolina, North Carolina, and Virginia) of 9 million.

The fear of overseas wars was silenced as the Industrial Revolution of the late nineteenth century launched the American economy. However, the United States had unofficially become two separate economies—"free market" and "slave labor." By 1860, the financial value of slaves in the United States exceeded the total investment in all of the nation's railroads, factories, and banks combined. In 1861, cotton prices hit an all-time high. For all the innovation of the free North, the South was confident that the importance of cotton on the world market, particularly in England and France, would sustain its existing economy.

It was at the conclusion of the Industrial Revolution, without outside interference, that America experienced its bloodiest war ever—the Civil War. (See Figure 7.1.) Estimates show roughly 750,000 Americans died, more than every subsequent war.[4] The economic cost was staggering as government debt exploded over 4,000 percent in less than five years. Worst of all, this leverage was used solely to destroy America's own land, soldiers, and economy.[5]

On paper, the victor of the Civil War should never have been in question. The North was an educated economy led by the new industries of steel, railway, banking, and oil. The North possessed over 70 percent of the country's wealth (not counting the monetary value attached to slaves) and 80 percent of its banks.[6] By virtue of the disparity in population, the North had 3.5 times as many males of fighting age than the South. Amid all the wonderful advances of its manufacturing economy, the Union also ushered in the devastation made possible by machines. Unreliable muskets carrying one metal ball at a time were replaced by the invention of repeating rifles capable of carrying cartridges and more accurate from even five times farther away.[7] Meanwhile, the much smaller South was married to one business—slavery.

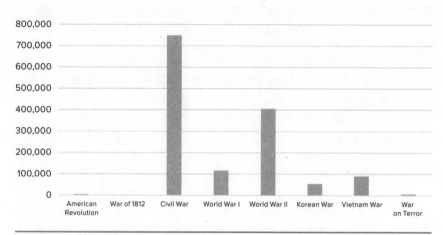

Figure 7.1 Deadliest American wars (American lives lost)[41]

Both sides financed most of the war through fiat currency (a currency not backed by a commodity like gold or silver). The Union printed over $500 million in greenbacks. The National Bank Act created a national banking system and formalized a single federal currency. The Internal Revenue Act eased the inflation caused by the war by placing excise taxes on luxury goods like tobacco and jewelry. The United States also enacted its first income tax in July 1861, at 3 percent of incomes over $800 and up to 10 percent over $100,000. The South's currency, the Confederate dollar, ended up being completely worthless, leaving the region woefully behind its northern neighbors.[8]

Since General Robert E. Lee surrendered his Confederate troops to the Union's Ulysses S. Grant at Appomattox Court House in Virginia, the United States trudged through the Reconstruction Era of 1865–1877 and grew stronger. The second industrial revolution, or technological revolution, followed and brought about the American entrepreneur. Carnegie, Rockefeller, and other business icons thrived in the Gilded Age.

The newly formed United States of America enjoyed relative peace and prosperity. The world's conflicts remained other countries' affairs, separated by the oceans. Bystanders to a war could stay bystanders and be free of collateral damage from fights across the globe. This mindset changed for good in 1914.

ECONOMIC INSIGHT

Debt, a state of owing money, typically carries a negative connotation. However, when used responsibly and with great purpose, debt can be seen as one of the most powerful tools in finance. From acquiring a college diploma to buying a house, to empowering the forefathers of the United States of America to declare independence, debt can put what otherwise would be out of reach into reach.

Debt can also benefit both sides of the transaction. Alexander Hamilton's primary goal as secretary of the Treasury was to build America's international standing, to make it creditworthy. Without the credit to acquire new debt, he knew the United States would not be able to pay old debt and then would be blocked from financing American expansion. The ultimate payoff of America's debts to France came by the help of James Swan, an American banker. In 1795, Swan privately assumed the remaining French debts at a slightly higher interest rate. He then resold these debts on the domestic US markets in the form of bonds. In short, the United States repaid France and gained the faith of international financial markets, Swan profited from selling bonds to American citizens and companies, and those new bondholders enjoyed receiving a higher interest rate, which the US government was only too happy to repay.[9]

Ever since Hamilton guided the creation of America's financial system, the US federal government has never defaulted on its debt (not counting a few technicalities in which the government refused to redeem bonds for silver or gold as originally planned, having instead repaid with dollars). This has led to US federal debt, Treasurys, holding the highest credit rating possible from all major credit-rating agencies, except for when Standard & Poor's downgraded the United States from AAA to AA+ in 2011 due to budget deficits.

A World at War

Following the first Balkan War in 1912, Serbia and Austria-Hungary both left the negotiation table disgruntled with what each side felt was an unequal arrangement of territories. On June 28, 1914, in the city of Sarajevo, a young Serbian patriot by the name of Gavrilo Princip shot and killed Archduke Franz Ferdinand, heir to the Austro-Hungarian Empire. In prior history, this assassination could have gone relatively unnoticed in the annals of time, a "lone-wolf attack" by a disturbed youth. But by the early 1900s, nations were finished minding their own business. An attack on one had become an attack on many.

Count Theobald von Bethmann Hollweg, chancellor of Germany at the turn of the twentieth century, believed that "the old saying still holds good that the weak will be the prey of the strong." Germany, fearful of the east and west, signed an agreement with Austria-Hungary to protect one another. Russia and France signed a similar agreement. Countries had figured out a key to protecting their wealth, resources, and land. Militarism gave way to a new concept—international alliances.

Within a month of the archduke's murder, Austria invaded Serbia. Behind the scenes Serbia appealed to Russia for assistance, and within one week Russia, Belgium, France, Great Britain, and Serbia (the original Allies) had lined up against Austria-Hungary and Germany. Three years later, on April 6, 1917, President Woodrow Wilson could no longer ignore the fact that US merchant ships were being sunk around the British Isles at the hands of the German navy. He stated that war would "make the world safe for democracy" and Congress declared war on Germany. The Great War became everyone's war, the first world war.

It is hard to contemplate finances when discussing a war that caused over 37 million casualties,[10] but economics does not shy away from any moment in history. World War I (July 1914–November 1918) was the first time the global economic path took a detour. What sprung from ongoing disputes over land, quickly led to either financial progress or catastrophe for each of its participants.

The United Kingdom's economy (in terms of GDP) grew about 7 percent from 1914 to 1918, despite the absence of so many men in the services. In contrast, the German economy shrank 27 percent. By 1916, Britain was financing almost the entire war for the Allies, covering all of Italy's costs and almost two-thirds for France and Russia. Eventually, Britain ran out of money and was forced to take a $4 billion loan. That loan came from the US Treasury.[11] During the war, America pumped two-thirds of the world's oil, and directly supplied 85 percent of Britain's oil.[12]

Germany did not have as strong a balance sheet as Great Britain heading into the war. Total spending by its national government reached 170 billion marks during the war, of which tax revenues covered only 8 percent; the remainder was borrowed from German banks and citizens. National debt exploded from 5 billion marks in 1914 to 156 billion in 1918. By 1923, billions of bonds were worthless due to hyperinflation.[13]

Economically speaking, America was the greatest beneficiary of World War I. At the outset of the war, the United States was in the middle of a recession. Being late to join the war was a tremendous advantage. Before the war, Great Britain was both the largest importer and exporter in the world. But during the war, the United States produced and exported most of the munitions, oil, and food to its allies in Europe. From 1914 to 1918, American unemployment dropped from 7.9 percent to 1.4 percent as more manufacturing jobs were created overnight and over 3.5 million people were added to the military and government. Adjusted for inflation in today's dollars, the estimated $334 billion cost of war was paid for by 22 percent taxes, 58 percent borrowing, and 20 percent money creation. As a result of the war, New York bypassed London as the world's premier financial center.[14]

There were negative economic consequences to the war that hurt victors and losers alike. Perhaps the worst outcome involved the flow of goods and people. Up until World War I, trade was universally unrestricted. Globalization was taking off like a sprinter with fresh legs. Following the war, restrictions, embargoes, and tariffs became the norm. It took until 1979 for trade as a percentage of the global economy to reach its prior peak in 1913.[15] The same trend occurred in migration.

The success of America's inflated government and centralized policies during the war, on everything from food supply to ship manufacturing, inspired government control and programs for generations to come. One might say it was the final straw that broke the laissez-faire camel's back. In 1913, America's highest income tax rate was 7 percent; by the end of World War I it was 27 percent. Estate taxes rose to 25 percent. These newfound revenue sources were here to stay. Several federal agencies were created to steer the economy, such as the Food Administration, Fuel Administration, and the War Industries Board. Even the Sedition Act was passed in 1918, criminalizing any expression of opinion that used "disloyal, profane, scurrilous or abusive language" about America. In 1914, the national debt was a paltry $2.9 billion, but by the end of World War I in 1918 it ballooned to over $25 billion.[16]

Five years to the day after the Archduke was shot, on June 28, 1919, Germany signed the Treaty of Versailles, a peace treaty to end the war between Germany and the Allies. The already devastated economy was forced to relinquish 10 percent of its territory, hand over its foreign financial holdings and merchant carrier fleet, and pay for war reparations in excess of $30 billion ($269 billion today) over the next 92 years.[17] John Maynard Keynes, an English economist, quickly prophesied in his famous work published the same year, *The Economic Consequences of the Peace*, "If we aim at the impoverishment of Central Europe, vengeance, I dare say, will not limp. Nothing can then delay for very long the forces of Reaction and the despairing convulsions of Revolution, before which the horrors of the later German war will fade into nothing, and which will destroy, whoever is victor, the civilisation and the progress of our generation."

Keynes's predictions certainly did not "limp" into reality. Hyperinflation ravaged Germany, and the country fell hopelessly behind on its reparation payments. By the time the stock market crashed in 1929, Adolph Hitler took control of the Nazi party and rallied around the German people's hatred of the Treaty of Versailles to overturn Germany's government.

Around the same time Hitler came to power, America entered the Great Depression. Despite rumors of Nazi atrocities and Japan's expansionist efforts, the American people largely wanted to stay out of any war confined to Europe and Asia, preferring to focus on fixing the economy on the home front. Polls showed that in January of 1940, 88 percent of Americans opposed declaring war on the Axis powers. Even as late as June of 1940, only 35 percent of Americans felt the government should join Britain's war effort as Hitler swept through Europe.[18] One year into what was to become World War II, Japan and Italy joined Germany in the Tripartite Pact on September 27, 1940.

After defeating France, the German Luftwaffe pounded London and the cities of Great Britain with nightly bombing campaigns. Meanwhile, Japan was fighting China and taking European holdings in the Far East. Two countries thought to be crippled by the economic layout after World War I, Germany and Japan, appeared to be taking over the world. Prime Minister Winston Churchill fought single-handedly to preserve the western way of life.

While pleading to FDR for help, Churchill continued to instill confidence in his countrymen: "Upon this battle depends the survival of Christian civilization. Upon it depends our own British life, and the long continuity of our institutions and our Empire. The whole fury and might of the enemy must very soon be turned on us. Hitler knows that he will have to break us in this island or lose the war. If we can stand up to him, all Europe may be free and the life of the world may move forward into broad, sunlit uplands." Describing the horrific possibility of losing he continued, "But if we fail, then the whole world, including the United States, including all that we have known and cared for, will sink into the abyss of a new Dark Age made more sinister, and perhaps more protracted, by the lights of perverted science. Let us therefore brace ourselves to our duties, and so bear ourselves that if the British Empire and its Commonwealth last for a thousand years, men will still say, 'This was their Finest Hour.' "

The United States took a step away from isolationism and participated indirectly in World War II with the passage of the Lend-Lease Act on October 23, 1941, in which America extended over $49 billion of aid to nearly 40 nations, primarily to Britain.[19] Britain did not have the cash to buy military assets from the United States, but the new program allowed them to acquire such weaponry while deferring the cost. This allowed America to indirectly help defeat Nazism while becoming the preeminent economic power of the world. Then in what changed the course of humanity forever, Japan awoke a sleeping giant on December 7, 1941, in Pearl Harbor. Churchill finally had his fully committed ally in the United States.

The financial burden of World War II on America dwarfed that of World War I. Granted, America fought in World War I for just one year versus four years in World War II. But World War II had a way of jolting economic progress. The New Deal's impact on the Great Depression was still up for debate, but history shows that the more likely economic hero of the time was actually America's costliest war.

Prewar, America's unemployment rate hovered around 25 percent. After Pearl Harbor, American factories were retooled to produce goods and weaponry, young men went off to war, women took over their jobs for the first time in history, and unemployment plummeted to 10 percent.[20] Trade unions that spent the 1930s flexing their muscle instead pledged to not strike during the war. The federal government gave up fighting the rich and doled out business to the country's biggest companies. Under the guidance of icons like Henry

Ford and Henry Kaiser, the private sector churned out jeeps and military equipment at breakneck speed. Over 17 million new civilian jobs were created and industrial productivity increased 96 percent.[21] In 1941, privates in the service made $21 monthly, on average. The following year, their pay increased to $50 per month, more than what most civilians were making.[22]

In 1943 and 1944, more than 40 percent of US GDP was devoted to national defense. During the war years of 1940 to 1945, America spent over $5 trillion in today's dollars.[23] This helped send America's GDP growth sky-rocketing to 17 percent in 1942.[24] War bonds were again used to finance the bill, and taxes spiked to an all-time high of 94 percent for the top bracket in 1945.[25] There was such an overwhelming commitment to American victory that the US Mint stopped making its 1943 pennies out of copper, which was used in weaponry, and produced the only silver-colored pennies in history. Even Academy Award statuettes, normally coated in 24-carat gold, were plaster painted gold for three years.

Following the war, America deployed its historically high tax revenue toward reparations to damaged countries, but also to those who fought in the war. FDR was determined not to let American heroes fall back into another depression. Troops returning home benefited from the Servicemen's Readjustment Act of 1944, or "GI Bill." Over 9 million veterans received low-interest mortgages and college tuition stipends from 1944 to 1949.[26]

While the toll on American heroes was steep—over 400,000 American troops died in World War II—the damage to American soil was almost non-existent, save for Pearl Harbor. The European and Asian theaters were not so fortunate. Over 36.5 million Europeans died in the war, and those lucky enough to escape alive returned to find their homes and businesses in piles of rubble.[27]

In Great Britain, over 30 percent of homes were destroyed and more than 70,000 buildings demolished. Great Britain was nearly bankrupted from its second, long world war. Its gold reserves had fallen from 864 million pounds sterling to 3 million. On July 15, 1946, America made the Anglo-American Loan Agreement for $3.75 billion to the United Kingdom at 2 percent interest. This loan would not be paid off until 2006.[28] In 1948, the Marshall Plan, an American initiative of $114 billion of aid to western Europe, of which 26 percent went to the United Kingdom, helped Britain recover.

Germany's economy lay in shambles, yet again, after the war. Over 20 percent of housing was destroyed and the country was starving from strict food rations and price controls enacted by Hitler and Hermann Goering, violations of which were punishable by death.[29]

Despite the conditions, President Roosevelt said at the conclusion of the war, "Too many people here and in England hold the view that the German people as a whole are not responsible for what has taken place—that only a few Nazis are responsible. That unfortunately is not based on fact. The German people must have it driven home to them that the whole nation has been engaged in a lawless conspiracy against the decencies of modern civilization."

The Potsdam Agreement was signed on August 1, 1945, by the United States, United Kingdom, and Soviet Union and addressed the occupation and reconstruction of Germany and the rest of the European theater. Germany was divided into four distinct occupation zones—France, Britain, and the United States occupying the west and the Soviet Union covering most of the east. The overall tone of the agreement was one of belittling Germany, following the guidance of Joint Chiefs of Staff Directive 1067 (JCS 1067) in which the US military in Germany was ordered to "take no steps looking toward the economic rehabilitation of Germany [or] designed to maintain or strengthen the German economy." Beyond the almost impossible task of Germany physically rebuilding itself, there was an incredible amount of intellectual confiscation. The Allies sought all patents, technological innovation, and scientific know-how from the Germans. This spurred Operation Paperclip, a secret US intelligence program in which 1,600 of Germany's best scientists and engineers were moved to the United States to work directly for the American government.[30] The Soviet Union was even more harsh in its treatment of the Germans, confiscating most German land and forcing them into a communist "coalition" controlled by Moscow.

The tough stance against Germany was not without its opponents. Lewis Douglas, chief advisor to General Lucius Clay, US High Commissioner, denounced JCS 1067, saying, "This thing was assembled by economic idiots. It makes no sense to forbid the most skilled workers in Europe from producing as much as they can in a continent that is desperately short of everything."[31] In July of 1947, President Harry Truman rescinded JCS 1067. Fearing a repeat of the outcome Keynes had accurately predicted at the end of World War I, Truman sought a compromise, declaring, "The whole economy of Europe is interlinked with the German economy through the exchange of raw materials and manufactured goods. The productivity of Europe cannot be restored

without the restoration of Germany as a contributor to that productivity."
France, Britain, and the United States merged their three zones to create
West Germany and allocated 11 percent of the Marshall Plan funds to their
new ally.

Within West Germany, economist Walter Eucken helped further a
"social free market" based on capitalism. On June 21, 1948, under the guidance of the director of Economic Council for Western Germany, Ludwig
Erhard, a student of Eucken's, the government removed all price controls and
started a new currency. The deutsche mark replaced the former reichsmark,
made worthless by hyperinflation, and instilled confidence in the German
money supply. Meanwhile, the communistic East Germany was used by the
Soviets as a threatening "iron curtain" to the Western world.

Nearly five decades after World War II, the Treaty on the Final Settlement
with Respect to Germany was signed on September 12, 1990, in Moscow by
West and East Germany, as well as France, the Soviet Union, United Kingdom, and United States. This created one sovereign Germany.

Reparations

History is written by winners. The world can hope the good guys always
win, and that after victory, they remain forever righteous. But history is
not a neatly crafted poem; rather, it is a never-ending story with changing characters and evolving scenes. So when atonement is warranted, the
question becomes, to whom and from whom is it owed, and how much
is it?

The aftermath of both world wars underscored the difficulty in reparations. The emotion attached to completely destroying the enemy in
the darkest hours of war directly conflicts with the financial sequel of
helping the losers. The motivation to help up an opponent after knocking
them down, as if it were as simple as two boxers hugging after a bloody
bout, comes from two sources of hope. The first is that evil loses and then
has a change of heart in its moment of defeat. However, most rational
diplomats would agree that a Hitler or Stalin does not change. The second
motivation for financial reparations goes back to the changing characters
and evolving scenes within the story. Help the future because hopefully it
is better than the past.

The world wars showed that atonement across borders is important, but provides a margin for error. Where reparations fall short, a problem over there is their problem. However, atonement within borders is exponentially harder. A problem right here is our problem.

The Indians of eighteenth-century North America were certainly harmed on the lands of modern-day United States; however, history knows the offenders were mostly colonists from the United Kingdom. If America is the child of the United Kingdom, should children be blamed for the sins of the father? Slavery in the South is possibly the ugliest stain on the fabric of America. But in 1861 the Civil War began, a war between two separate and distinct entities based solely on their stance on slavery. It is necessary to emphasize "separate and distinct" when discussing the North and South. The Confederate States of America was a self-proclaimed nation, with its own president (Jefferson Davis) and its own capital (Richmond, Virginia). Of course, the North won, and the Thirteenth Amendment was passed, abolishing slavery across a united country. A new republic was born, the United States of America. Furthermore, the characters of this new republic changed as rapidly as the geographical scenery spread west. By 1890, 80 percent of New York's citizens were immigrants or children of immigrants, as were 87 percent of Chicago's. In other words, the vast majority of America's population entering the twentieth century never knew a slave and certainly never took land from a Native American. Nevertheless, reparations were warranted for these marginalized groups (see Chapters 2 and 3). A debt is obviously owed, but do the payers still exist, and if so, who are they?

ECONOMIC INSIGHT

In World War I, three million Germans were killed, reducing its male population by 15 percent. The nation's currency was literally worthless, its economy and infrastructure ruined, and it was on the hook for crushing reparations to its enemies.

One of the quiet mysteries of history is how then did Germany produce the most powerful military machine in the world in just over a decade? Sometimes money can run in circles. Germany quickly defaulted on its payments from World War I and by January 1923, France and Belgium occupied the Ruhr region, Germany's industrial hub, to try to force payment. Across the Atlantic, the United States was not concerned about receiving German reparations, as the American homeland had been untouched by the Nazis. But the United States did want to recoup the over $10 billion it loaned to 17 of its ally countries.

Charles G. Dawes, an American banker and soon-to-be vice president to Calvin Coolidge, headed up the Reparation Commission. In 1924, he designed a plan that reduced Germany's reparation payments with the ability to be increased as their economy improved. France and Belgium were ordered to leave the Ruhr, a new German currency was formed in the reichsmark, and foreign banks were to lend Germany $200 million to help rebuild its economy. None other than J.P. Morgan drafted a loan to be financed by American investors. These loans to Germany were used to repay reparations to France, the United Kingdom, and other affected countries, who then used these same reparations to repay their debt to the United States. Dawes received the Nobel Peace Prize for his plan.

Not long after, Owen D. Young, head of General Electric, created the Young Plan in 1929. In this, Germany's reparations were reduced again, more loans were floated on international markets, and occupying troops were ordered to vacate Germany. But by 1932, in the depths of the Great Depression, as there was simply no money to go around, Germany's reparations were cancelled. The United States felt the pain too as every European debtor except for Finland defaulted on its American loans.[32]

Meanwhile, Adolf Hitler amassed most of his personal wealth through sales of his book *Mein Kampf* (*My Struggle*), which he wrote while in prison, following his arrest for treason in a failed attempt at overthrowing the government in the Beer Hall Putsch. Once he came to power in 1933, copies of his book were gifted to newly married couples on their wedding day. As Germany struggled to rebuild its economy, many wealthy sympathizers to Hitler and the Nazi Party made lavish donations. Much of this private money was from abroad, reputedly including Henry Ford, a known anti-Semite. Much of this Nazi money was used for Hitler's own benefit, though, including his private mountain retreat, the Eagle's Nest.

When the Nazis started World War II they were no longer burdened by debt, but they were still effectively broke from World War I and the Great Depression. They utilized a strategy of autarky, economic self-sufficiency through cutting trade, rationing consumer goods, demanding longer work hours (including slave labor in concentration camps), and reinvesting any government funds into the military. One of the Nazis' first successful missions upon invading Austria was raiding its central bank, yielding Germany an estimated 105 tons of gold. The Nazis used this gold to purchase a reliable currency in the Swiss francs, which they then used to buy war supplies, often produced by US manufacturers. With each country the Nazis conquered, they sought first and foremost to capture the country's central bank's gold supply. Without gold, the world likely would not know the name Adolf Hitler.[33]

This harkens back to Chapter 5, Environment, and the everlasting importance of commodities, particularly when currencies crumble. In recent times, the terrorist organization ISIS (Islamic State of Iraq and Syria) seemingly came out of nowhere. Through brutal tactics, ISIS captured oil wells in Syria and used their profits to buy advanced weaponry on the black market.

Diplomacy After the World Wars

While the world wars largely shaped the landscape of today, there have been several wars and conflicts waged since. The pendulum of intervention swung in 1947 with the Truman Doctrine, as America abandoned its isolationist proclivity in favor of keeping its finger on international affairs. President Harry S Truman vowed to provide political, military, and economic assistance to any democratic nation under the threat of authoritarian forces.

This new stance on foreign policy originated from Great Britain's financial inability, or simply war fatigue, that forced it to leave the Greek government on its own during a civil war against the Greek Communist Party. Truman asked Congress to provide $400 million worth of aid to Greece and Turkey in their battles against communism.[34]

On June 25, 1950, 75,000 soldiers from the North Korean People's Army, supported by the Soviet Union, crossed the 38th parallel and invaded the pro-Western Republic of Korea. Fearing a domino effect of Korea and then possibly Japan succumbing to communist parties, America physically intervened in the altercation. Thus, the Korean War officially started the Cold War and America's commitment to policing the world against communism.

One of President Dwight Eisenhower's greatest objectives was to stop, and hopefully reverse, nuclear proliferation. He used the founders of our MICE, the Central Intelligence Agency, as the preferred weapon in the Cold War. In 1954, the "Report on the Covert Activities of the Central Intelligence Agency" (The Doolittle Report), led by Lieutenant General James H. Doolittle, concluded about the Soviet Union, "It is now clear that we are facing an implacable enemy whose avowed objective is world domination by whatever means and at whatever cost. . . . There are no rules in such a game. Hitherto acceptable norms of human conduct do not apply. . . . We must learn to subvert, sabotage, and destroy our enemies by more clever, more sophisticated, and more effective methods than those used against us. If the United States is to survive, long standing concepts of 'fair play' must be reconsidered."[35] The report exemplified the difficulties in confronting an enemy to whom money (M) and compromise (C) did not matter, allowing them to act irrationally in the full context of MICE, led only by their ideology (I) and ego (E).

In the same year, Eisenhower faced another temptation in confronting China. The communist People's Republic of China attacked the tiny islands Quemoy and Matsu, threatening Formosa (now Taiwan). President Truman had previously vowed to defend Formosa, fearing that a communist occupation of the island would threaten the entire Pacific and the United States. Often called a "paper tiger," referring to America's nuclear arsenal not being a deterrent if the United States vowed to never use it, Eisenhower was under pressure. The great fear was that an attack on China would equate to declaring war on the Soviets. Eisenhower's strategy of deference could be summed up in realizing that unlimited war in the nuclear age was unimaginable, and limited war unwinnable. (The twenty-first century shares a similar parallel in reverse, with the United States and NATO avoiding retaliation against Russia's aggressive attacks on small countries with the fear that China could come to its aid.)

After a largely stalemated 1950s, President John F. Kennedy inherited an apparent capitalist versus communist world. In 1963, President John F. Kennedy sent 16,000 "military advisers" to help the South Vietnamese army stand up to the North Vietnamese led by communist Ho Chi Minh. The North Vietnamese attacked the US Navy in the Gulf of Tonkin, leading to a full-scale war. Ten years later, there were over half a million American troops fighting in Vietnam and the war was costing $77 billion per year.[36] When all was said and done, over 58,000 American troops were killed and the war cost $828 billion to America. The world's greatest superpower effectively lost to a much smaller, undeveloped nation that remains communist to this day.

Aside from the costs in lives and money, America felt a shock to public morale unlike ever before. Young men dodged the draft, often seeking college as a way out, and used campuses across the country to hold protests. At one point, in 1968, over 50 percent of Americans opposed the controversial war.[37] Most notably, Cassius Clay (later known as Muhammad Ali) went to prison after declaring himself a "conscientious objector," a sentence that was later overturned by the Supreme Court. Of the over nine million US military personnel who served in the Vietnam era (August 1964–May 1975), roughly 28 percent, who either dropped out of college or never went in the first place, ended up using the GI Bill to pursue two-year courses of study, which gave rise to community colleges in the 1970s.[38]

Economics played another vital role in America's shortest war—the Gulf War, also known as Desert Storm. Iraq refused to repay a debt to Kuwait following the Iran-Iraq War of the 1980s. Under the leadership of President Saddam Hussein, Iraq annexed its oil-rich neighbor. Forty countries banded together in the "Coalition of the Willing"[39] to quickly defeat Iraq in just 43 days.

In the twentieth century, America's economy became permanently tied to the bloodshed of war. (See Figure 7.2.) Despite each conflict's staggering costs, both in lives and dollars, America experienced an increase in GDP growth during each period. Common themes during war included extremely low unemployment, increased tax revenue, reduced consumption (often tied to government control of raw materials and resources toward the war efforts), and government stimulus.[40] The fallout has often included inflation, residual high tax rates, and lingering budget deficits.

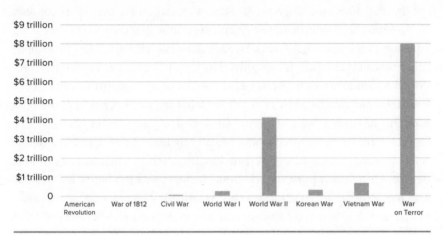

Figure 7.2   Costs of major US wars (trillions, present day)[42]

Can an Economy Thrive on Peace?

Would similar economic growth have been possible during a century of peace? Would the technological innovations, enlarged government, and newly created industries have ever occurred without the horrors of war?

The only feasible case study might be Sweden, a developed nation that has not participated in a war since 1814. Having pledged neutrality in both world wars, Sweden suffered no physical damage and was able to become an exporting powerhouse of raw materials following World War I.[43] Between 1850 and 1950 Sweden's tax-to-GDP ratio never exceeded 20 percent and income per capita increased eightfold.

This relatively good standing amid a lack of international competition allowed Sweden to pursue socialism and implement its welfare model named "Svenska Modellen." Public spending as a share of GDP almost doubled from 1960 to 1980, peaking at 67 percent in 1993. However, from 1974 to 1994 Sweden dropped from the fourth richest country to the thirteenth, burdened by its high entitlement expenses.[44] In 1976, Astrid Lindgren, creator of Pippi Longstocking, received a 102 percent tax bill due to her high income and self-employment fees. This event inspired her to author a sarcastic fairy tale about a writer named Pomperipossa, who quit writing books to live a carefree life, hence the economic term *Pomperipossa effect.*

In 1995, Sweden changed course and moved toward a capitalist economy by deregulating domestic industry, cutting public spending, and privatizing education and pension systems. Sweden does not have a minimum wage or inheritance tax. Sweden is recognized by the 2021 Index of Economic Freedom, an annual report by Heritage, as the 21st most capitalist country in the world. Ironically, the country many socialist fans still consider the model economy has nearly twice as many billionaires per capita as the US.

As of this writing, Sweden still has a fairly high tax wedge. A tax wedge refers to a market inefficiency created by tax, such as when taxes become a deterrent to a worker pursuing additional income and extra hours. Sweden has a 42.8 percent tax-to-GDP ratio versus America at 24.5 percent.[45] Its top individual tax rate is 57 percent and government spending is 48.5 percent of GDP.[46] For comparison's sake, America's government spending is 35.5 percent of GDP.

In response to the question previously posed, would the economic advances of the world be present today in a world without war?, the answer remains hypothetical. The world wars definitely affected Sweden's global standing and opened doors of opportunity, like the athlete on the sidelines who becomes far more valuable as starters get tired and injured. Sweden seems to have achieved the best of both worlds, peace and economic advancement, but it was not until it began capitalizing its economy.

It may not have been the violence of war that kick-started economies, but rather the rallying of a country's entire population focused on a united effort. Calamities, especially ones that threaten extinction, are rare motivators for an economy.

ECONOMIC INSIGHT

In President Eisenhower's Farewell Address on January 17, 1961, he warned the United States to "guard against the acquisition of unwarranted influence . . . by the military-industrial complex." The military-industrial complex referred to all the possible profiteers of war, including members of Congress from districts dependent on military industries, Department of Defense budgets, and privately owned military contractors. (See Figure 7.3.) Northern Virginia, with its direct business connections to Washington, DC, is a testament to Eisenhower's statement as it contains four of the top seven wealthiest counties in the country.[47]

President Biden's budget requested $773 billion for Department of Defense operations in fiscal year 2023.[48] This figure represents an almost untraceable web of buyers and suppliers spanning industries from healthcare to weapons manufacturers to climate-change scientists. The government sector is in constant competition with the private sector to attract and retain the most talented employees for national defense. Employees chart their careers motivated by their own MICE, networking back and forth between public and private opportunities. This back-and-forth was one of the reasons President Trump revoked many intelligence officials' security clearances after they left the government, to prevent profiteering through private contracts or through media commentary.

The military-industrial complex is not limited to America's borders. In a globalized world, companies quickly transact business near and far, driven by the need to satisfy shareholders, who are driven by watching their investments go up. Investors, from Gen Z-ers buying their first stocks up to multibillion-dollar pension funds, may unknowingly be weaponizing future enemies—whether it be through direct investments in American weapons or technology companies who operate abroad, or through funds and stocks of similar overseas companies. Even harder to track are investments in foreign, non-defense-related companies; buying 10 shares of an oil stock or social media company sounds innocent, but in a communist country those profits effectively belong to the government and its military apparatus. These personal investment decisions between money (M) and ideology (I) are similar to the 2022 American consumer boycotts of Russian vodka and Lukoil gas.

A globalized world is confusing enough, but the defense economy has literally gone to outer space. On February 4, 2022, Chinese President Xi Jinping met in person with Russian President Vladimir Putin and signed a joint statement that spoke of international space law and the UN Committee on the Peaceful Uses of Outer Space. The White House has its own manual, called the US Space Priorities Framework. Not all that different from the nuclear arms race of the twentieth century, nations will spend the future investing in education and innovation to control the cosmos. Patriotism can lead the way, but dividends, capital gains, and the highest bidders will always complicate matters.

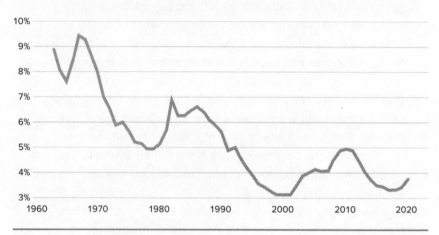

Figure 7.3   US military expenditure as percent of GDP: 1960–2020[49]

MICRO

Who attacked us? he asks himself. For this 22-year-old, the world seems to be coming into focus, but then there are these questions that lead to more questions.

He has been sitting alone in his dorm room, staring at a brochure with camouflaged warriors on the cover. An ROTC recruiter handed it to him in the student center. He tried to pass by and avoid eye contact, but felt guilty brushing off a serviceman clad in ribbons and medals. Plus, the pamphlet looks cooler than any handout a professor provided this semester.

"Give it a look. I'll be here all week if you want to talk it over," the soldier said.

His roommate is on a beer run; it's "Thirsty Thursday," and within a couple of hours their floor will be abuzz with evening activities. But tonight doesn't seem like one of those nights; he can't stop picking up the brochure.

Grandpa fought in World War II, don't know too much about what he did, but they're the Greatest Generation. My other grandfather was in Korea, know even less about that one. Then there's my uncle and Vietnam, I never even knew he was in the military until Dad told me. He tosses the brochure back on his desk and lays in bed staring at the popcorn ceiling.

He was just a little boy, but like everyone else, he can remember exactly where he was and what he was doing when the news broke. September 11, 2001, an attack that killed more people than Pearl Harbor did six decades before it. It seems to be the only "why" he can latch onto as he debates signing up. It's been two decades since 9/11 and the surge of American pride that followed it. The echoing chants of "USA" by hundreds of thousands of fans in football stadiums across the country are a distant memory, replaced by kneeling athletes.

"Bro, you could die, man," his roommate said earlier when he brought it up during an intense game of Madden.

He wonders if nights like this are what change history, at least his history. He feels like making a decision, right now. *Do I try to find an internship, some entry-level job, or maybe start a business?* Or, *Should I go talk to that army recruiter tomorrow?* Does graduating college mean it's time to pursue money (M), or does he have a patriotic ideology (I) bubbling to the surface? Perhaps his ego (E) is taunting him, prompting feelings of guilt one direction or the other. Before deciding on anything, he knows there needs to be a "why." He needs to know why they fight. . . .

The War on Terror

The initial goal of the War on Terror was to bring the 9/11 attackers to justice, particularly Osama Bin Laden and his terrorist organization, Al-Qaeda. Part and parcel to this was removing the Taliban from power in Afghanistan, as they harbored Al-Qaeda. The mission morphed over two decades to include hunting weapons of mass destruction in Iraq, defeating ISIS, and securing peace and democracy in the Middle East. Rather than fighting a country like in wars past, chasing terrorism, an ideology, proved beyond challenging. From the outset, there was no clear definition of success or failure.

The 20-year War on Terror has cost the American people over $2.26 trillion thus far, but the total cost is projected to exceed $8 trillion over time, when including veterans' benefits, Homeland Security prevention and response to terrorism, interest on debt tied to war, and other auxiliary costs.[50] Over 900,000 people have died because of the war, including 7,052 American servicemen and women.

Over $2.3 trillion of the larger projected figure was allocated directly to the Afghanistan/Pakistan war zone in an attempt to secure peace and democracy in this volatile region of the Middle East. Within one month of the August 2021 pullout from Afghanistan, the entire country fell under control of the Taliban, armed to the teeth with advanced American weaponry captured from an Afghan army unwilling to fight for their country.

Looking past political debates, the economist asks how the bill is paid. As mentioned previously, President Harry Truman raised the top income tax rate to 92 percent during the Korean War, President Lyndon Johnson did the same to 77 percent during Vietnam, but at the outset of the War on Terror, President George W. Bush cut taxes on America's top earners from 39.6 percent to 35 percent. Taxation as a percentage of war financing accounted for roughly 30 percent in World War I, 50 percent for World War II, and the Korean War was completely paid for by taxes.

The modern war has been paid for in a drastically different manner than the twentieth century's conflicts. An estimated $2 trillion of war costs in Iraq and Afghanistan have been borrowed, roughly 25 percent of which is from foreign investors.[51] The projected interest costs on this debt by 2050 totals $6.5 trillion.[52] Due to the extreme length of this war, spending has continued unabated through boom and bust economies, from the Great Recession through the longest bull market in history, to the coronavirus pandemic and ensuing government stimulus.

Since there is no free lunch in economics, and the costs of the War on Terror were not handled immediately, per se, but rather deferred via debt, its financial consequences are largely undetermined. Decades from now, the tragedies of this war will hopefully have lost their sting. However, the current affairs of future generations, whether it be student loan relief, taxes, or Social Security, will have to fit into a budget still dealing with the War on Terror. The war may have lasted 20 years, but its financial fallout is sure to drag much further.

WHAT SHOULD I DO WITH MY MONEY?

So how does war affect your money? Sadly, there are financial motives to waging war, whether through the military-industrial complex that Eisenhower mentioned, or one country stealing another country's commodities. All wars are waged for economic reasons, to gain more land and territory, acquire resources and wealth, or spread an economic ideology. This should provide some solace, as economics can be measured, addressed, and debated. Therefore, the lone key to stopping war is economic success on all fronts. If a man has all that he wants, why fight for anything else?

In the twenty-first century, the world's two superpowers are the United States and China. There is enough evidence, particularly through international trade, to show that both nations want and need each other to optimize their own economies. But if trade is perceived as a zero-sum game, it is in a country's best self-interests to achieve the winning side. This is where manipulation enters the equation and upsets the apple cart.

First start with what "they" should do with their money. The fact that both opposing sides must find ways to advance their position necessitates the skills to wage war and the skills to avoid war. Having the right set of skills forces the opposing side to rethink if its move is worth the potential penalty or lost benefits. Don't attack a pawn if it exposes your queen.

Historians widely agree that the Cold War stayed cold for four decades because of the MAD theory (mutually assured destruction). This military doctrine assumes that a full-scale nuclear war between two countries would result in total annihilation of both the attacker and defender. While a morbid thought, it is a severe deterrent toward war among superpowers. Most legitimate countries are not willing to put on a suicide vest. This leaves four realistic skills available to wage war.

How to Wage War

1. Economic Warfare

Economic attacks include sanctions, trade embargoes, tariffs, and currency manipulation. "The supreme art of war is to subdue the enemy without fighting," Sun Tzu said in the *Art of War*. However, using economic warfare comes at a cost. China has been devaluing the yuan for decades in order to make its goods cheaper to other countries and boost its exports. The Trump administration confronted China's currency manipulation and intellectual property theft by imposing tariffs on over $400 billion worth of imports.[53] This certainly caught President Xi Jinping's attention, but not without disrupting several American industries. In economics, added costs are passed on to the buyer. For instance, when tariffs on imported Chinese steel made building in the United States more expensive, costs were transferred to American companies and consumers, who essentially helped pay for China's penalty. The same occurred with worldwide oil embargoes against Russia. Who can hold out longer, the overpaying customer or the underselling dealer?

2. Cyberattacks

Chapter 6, Tech, touched on the damage associated with identity theft, ransomware attacks, phishing emails, and surveillance software. State-sponsored attacks have become a way to fight virtual battles without going to war. Russia is the country most prone to this activity, from meddling in the 2016 US election to constant cyberattacks on Ukraine since the Russian annexation of Crimea in 2014. According to Microsoft, Russia accounts for 58 percent of state-sponsored cyberattacks, with the United States, Ukraine, and Britain being the primary targets.[54]

In 2020, SolarWinds, a major US information technology firm, was the victim of a cyberattack that went unnoticed for months. Foreign actors, believed to be from Russia's Foreign Intelligence Service (SVR), added malicious code to the SolarWinds' software system, Orion. The system provides IT solutions to over 33,000 customers, including the Department of Homeland Security, the Treasury Department, and most Fortune 500 companies. The hackers were able to spy on a nearly unlimited amount of private information.[55] With data becoming a valuable commodity, such successful attacks can devastate an enemy.

The upper hand in any conflict has historically belonged to the more advanced side. Whether it was the musket in the Revolutionary War or the atomic bomb in World War II, technology tilts the playing field. If information technology is the newest threat, America has a lot to be worried about, but also a lot to be proud of. As of 2021, the five biggest tech companies in the world are Apple, Microsoft, Alphabet (aka Google), Amazon, and Meta (aka Facebook), respectively. They all share one thing in common: they call America home.

3. Biological Warfare

There is no evidence that the Chinese government had any intent behind the novel coronavirus escaping the Wuhan Institute of Virology, but the world has been put on alarm as to what could possibly occur if an evil actor was ever able to use gain-of-function research and weaponize a virus. Prior chapters discussed the economic pros and cons of domestic manufacturing versus offshoring, but if a crisis strikes and an enemy holds the antidote, even the strongest of the sick will bow down.

4. Proxy Wars

Proxy wars involve engaging in actual military battle by using other fighters and territories that act as surrogates in the conflict. Having other countries do the "dirty work" can be an effective strategy, but runs the risk of dragging the mothership into battle or possibly losing an ally that functions as a mercenary. This is one area where the United States has historically had a wide tactical advantage over any other superpower; it has a lot of friends around the neighborhood.

In the Far East, the United States participates in the Quadrilateral Security Dialogue (QSD), an alliance between the United States, India, Japan, and Australia. More recently, the United States and United Kingdom signed into the AUKUS trilateral pact, which will help Australia acquire nuclear-powered submarines and long-range strike capability, as well as collaboration on cybersecurity. In the Middle East, America's attempts have been lackluster. The United States has always been a steady ally to Israel, but has arguably failed in trying to build peaceful democracies out of countries like Iraq and Afghanistan. The majority of Europe is positively tied to the United States through NATO. The North Atlantic Treaty Organization was formed in 1949 and now has 30 member countries that pledge to protect the North Atlantic area.

How to Avoid War

The ways to avoid war are essentially the exact opposite of the threats of waging war. Rather than prepare to beat more enemies, a country can prepare to have more friends. Nations can find peace by offering trade, wealth, knowledge, and security.

Beyond the promises, handshakes, and contracts signed into by the world's leaders is the ultimate motivator—money (M). The US government provides more foreign aid to the rest of the world than any other country by a vast margin. In 2019, the United States provided over $47 billion in foreign aid, categorized as military aid or humanitarian aid. The largest recipients of such aid are in the Middle East, with Afghanistan, Israel, Jordan, and Egypt each receiving well over $1 billion annually.[56] None of these figures includes the enormous amounts of private philanthropic giving Americans donate to the rest of the globe. According to Giving USA, Americans donated a record $471 billion to charity in 2020, of which nearly $26 billion was allocated specifically toward international affairs.[57] Nations can be altruistic, but there is always a subtle reminder of accumulating debts disguised as favors. Countries have obvious financial incentive to invest and build infrastructures in lands that have something to offer; historically this has been commodities such as oil. A lot of foreign aid can be structured as grants or loans, which if unable to be repaid, can be restructured as repayments through commodities or leases that put the borrowing country in an even tougher position.

China, despite its enormous number of exports and its membership in the UN Security Council, looks far more isolationist in terms of foreign aid. In 2020, China provided an estimated $5.4 billion in foreign aid on a grant equivalent basis.[58] However, from 2000 to 2014, China gave $36.6 billion of aid to Russia, more than any other country. Much of this aid was to fund the infrastructure necessary to export oil from Russia to China.[59] China has said it advocates cooperation with all, but has only two formal allies in North Korea and Russia. In 1961, China and North Korea signed the Treaty of Friendship, Co-Operation, and Mutual Assistance, which still remains in force. In 2001, China signed the Sino-Russian Treaty of Friendship.

Despite governmental interference, currency manipulation, and countless other complaints by Chinese and American politicians, enterprise offers common ground for peace. China's number one trading partner is none other than the United States of America. According to the International Monetary Fund, in 2019 China exported over $481 billion worth of goods to the United States. Chinese companies love American consumers, and apparently American consumers love Chinese products. It is worth noting that the two "formal allies" of China hardly make a dent in its economy's bottom line—China exports $48 billion of goods to Russia and only $2 billion to North Korea. One might hypothesize that they like each other, but when push comes to shove, China does not have to care as much about the concerns of Russia and North Korea.

On the flip side, American companies and Chinese consumers share a similar love affair. China imported over $165 billion of goods from America in 2019, nearly three times what Russia provided.[60] General Motors sells more cars in China than in the United States, Mexico, and Canada combined. China has roughly twice the number of iPhone users as does the United States.[61] However, China is clearly looking to lessen its interdependence with America through the Silk Road 2.0 (see Chapter 4).

While shared business and foreign aid can be proactive, a large sum of aid is reactive, meant to fix the destruction of war. The Allies' goal in World War II was to destroy Nazism, but quickly realized the next goal was to help rebuild Germany and its war-torn neighbors. The relationship with the Middle East may be different than post–World War II Europe, but America has displayed the same mentality by helping repair Afghanistan and Iraq, and accepting its refugees when possible.

According to the US Department of Defense, America has already spent $130 billion on reconstruction projects in Afghanistan. Unfortunately, in a report to Congress from SIGAR (Special Inspector General for Afghanistan Reconstruction), an estimated $19 billion of this was lost to fraud. Furthermore, half of this $130 billion was allocated to the Afghan National Army and police forces, which fell to the Taliban within one month of the US military's departure.

Implosion

There is one unspoken element that has not been fairly addressed yet, and that is internal strife. Since cavemen roamed Earth, tribes, states, and nations have been able to conquer one another. True superpowers, however, usually write their own ending.

Many nations that are now relegated to history understood the need for their people to love their country above all else, but went about it by demanding their citizens do so. The United States shares the same eternal goal, but *asks* its patriots to stand for the flag. Once the pride of one's country disintegrates, so do any of the principles that make it a country. In 2008, when the incoming president's wife said, "For the first time in my adult life, I am really proud of my country," their followers were empowered to discard over 200 years of Americana, while enemies saw a potential new slate to write on.

America is in a state of political discourse and growing populism. The same populism that carried Trump into office with a rallying cry of the people to rock the establishment and "drain the swamp" is sure to come back. But amid all the bickering and finger-pointing, the American construct has never wavered. For nearly 250 years, the Constitution has offered a system of checks and balances, a three-branch government that grants states and citizens their rightful freedoms. From a civil war to an insurrection on the capitol, the United States has been able to maintain a peaceful transition of power from administration to administration and party to party. In speaking about preserving the Roman Empire, Marcus Aurelius said, "So long as the law is safe, so is the city—and the citizen." Once the faith in government is lost, there cannot be any government.

Russia and China both fully understand that achieving superiority over the superior (the United States) requires that the United States defeat itself first. It is a lengthy process of subversion toward implosion. Adversaries can fertilize discourse where it already exists. In the United States, Republicans and Democrats offer a lot to tamper with. Furthermore, both sides are made up of special-interest groups that are ready to oppose the system when it meets their agenda. Special interests are microeconomies that exist to amplify division. They preach a contradiction of inclusion through seclusion. Cohesion, peacefully belonging to one macroeconomy, would mean their demise. Just as any coach feels a jolt of confidence when the opposing team begins to yell and fight among themselves, so do American adversaries during riots and campaigns like "Defund the Police."

In 1984, Yuri Bezmenov, a KGB (Soviet Union's spy agency) defector, offered an inside look at these tactics in an interview with author and filmmaker G. Edward Griffin. Bezmenov described his four stages of brainwashing a nation:

1. **A 15-to-20-year process of "demoralization,"** which seeks to reeducate a generation of students. "What it basically means," Bezmenov said, "is to change the perception of reality of every American to such an extent that despite the abundance of information, no one is able to come to sensible conclusions in the interest of defending themselves, their families, their community, and their country." This propaganda was to be carried out through academia and the media.
2. **A two- to five-year process of "destabilization"** that targets essential structures such as the economy, education, foreign relations, and defense.
3. **Crisis.** The phase that ends in a violent change of power.
4. **Normalization.** The target nation adopts a new ideology.[62]

The catch-22 of a nation committed to protecting freedom of speech is that good and bad persuasions will always be allowed. Despite the constitutional promise, the presence of subverters has forced the United States to occasionally flirt with restraining the free flow of ideas. In 1938, the US government founded the House Un-American Activities Committee (HUAC), which was charged with investigating communist sympathizers and others sowing internal discord. The committee subpoenaed anyone of interest, particularly big shots in Hollywood. In 1975, the committee that too long resembled the same governmental controls exercised by the likes of China and the Soviet Union came to an end.

The Patriot Act, a landmark act by President George W. Bush, beefed up security efforts against terrorists through broad surveillance tools. Similar debates of government overreach returned about invasion of privacy violations.

While China has also tried similar tactics of subversion, it is trying to change the United States into what it has already failed at. China cannot stake the same claim as America as a 250-year-old country of solidarity. The Republic of China is just over 100 years old, having become a constitutional republic in 1912 after the Qing Dynasty. In 1928, Kuomintang (KMT or "Chinese Nationalist Party") became the governing body. In 1949 at the conclusion of a civil war, Mao Zedong, leader of the Chinese Communist

Party, defeated KMT and founded the People's Republic of China. He went on to lead a cultural revolution known as Maoism. Mao Zedong stomped out any forms of capitalism while killing over 40 million Chinese people in his two decades of reign, more than Stalin and Hitler. After Mao Zedong's death in 1976, China began its "Open Door" policy in 1978 and became a global economy, while also placing a two-term limit on its presidency. After three decades of rapid growth, current President Xi Jinping was elected to office in 2012. He has since sought consolidation of powers comparable to the Mao era and firmly disputes any claims by Taiwan or Hong Kong for independence. In 2018, Xi Jinping removed presidential term limits, allowing himself to effectively rule for life.

Speaking of open doors, over 51 million immigrants (including an estimated 11.5 illegal immigrants) call the United States home, making up roughly 15 percent of the population.[63] This can be considered not only an influx of knowledge and talent, but a growing connection to every corner of the globe. The top country of origin for recent immigrants to the United States is China. As of 2018, only India and Mexico represent a larger portion of America's immigrant population.[64] Conversely, there are just over 500,000 immigrants in China, or less than 0.04 percent of its population. It is estimated that Americans make up just 12 percent of China's migrant population.[65] This disparity suggests that America is continuing to show itself friendly to all parts of the world, while China becomes a less desirable destination.

Back to Your Money

In the face of war, an average investor might ask, how does my money matter, let alone what should I do with my money? It's critical to understand the first question before answering the second. Every war has some monetary motive, and carrying out a war takes lots of money. The ultimate payer for every conflict is always the people. People pay taxes, people buy war bonds, people invest in the military-industrial complex, people buy and use the commodities that sustain an economy. Your money is all that matters. What you choose to do with it is all that separates one fighter from being stronger than the other.

Reason assumes people are rational, and part of being rational is winning without fighting. The need to prevent war at all costs was summed up well generations ago by Otto von Bismarck, minister president of Prussia. "Woe unto the statesman who makes war without a reason that will still be valid when the war is over! After the war," he said, "you will all look differently at these questions. Will you then have the courage to turn to the peasant contemplating the ashes of his farm, to the man who has been crippled, to the father who has lost his children?" These words illustrate a reminder to the perils of resorting to conflict (Bismarck was actually a lover of war and used this speech as an act of deception to become prime minister and accomplish his true goal of destroying Austria, but the words still ring true.)

Current affairs offer a segue into what happens when economic freedom and repentance for collateral damage are not enough to preserve peace. The theme of this book is that economics pervades every decision, small or large. This hypothesis supports humanity's desire to explain everything and always realize patterns in life. However, reason can shy away in the face of beliefs. Fulfilling an ideology (I) is what can make a poor man feel rich and a billionaire feel poor. But it is also what can make someone do the unthinkable.

In the book of Genesis, "The Lord said to Himself, 'I will never again curse the ground on account of man, for man's heart is evil from his youth.'"[66] The unfortunate truth is evil does exist, and when tied to a belief, it can supersede any reason.

RELIGION

Humans need to exercise their money (M) and ability to compromise (C) to achieve whatever ends form their ego (E). Those ends are often a story about religion, one's guiding ideology (I), the answer to a pursuit of happiness. Every story follows a guiding light, a North Star. Even the stories that pledge not to, as believing in a belief or no belief is equally believing. Economies are grounded in agreeing and disagreeing beliefs.

When I do good, I feel good. When I do
bad, I feel bad. That's my religion.

—President Abraham Lincoln

P aul, like his five best friends, holds the right of free will. But as an orphan from birth, he's different, he is truly free. No mother, father, or guardian has ever encouraged a set of beliefs upon him. The orphanage he spent his childhood in believed in not discussing beliefs. The day after high school graduation, Paul sits down on the curb with a peanut butter and jelly sandwich beside his buddies. One is Jewish, another Catholic, another Muslim, another Hindu, and finally an atheist.

Paul thinks little of their physical differences. One friend wears a yamaka, the girl dresses in a black robe, another sings Christmas carols every winter, one boy has a gold cow sitting atop his dresser, and his atheist friend tags along with whichever seems cool. By his 18th birthday, Paul starts to realize that religion has a far bigger impact on the world than meets the eye.

Paul feels the pull of belonging to a community. Normal for a boy becoming a man. The old lady who ran his orphanage always taught him to be nice to everyone. The past four years have been spent bouncing around different foster homes in the city, thankfully never too far from his five best friends. Paul is heading off to college soon and he feels a little left out, but not sure why; it's confusing. He wants guidance; he needs understanding.

"Can you guys tell me why you are the way you are?" Paul asks his five friends as he peels the crust off of his sandwich.

They look at each other quizzically. "What are you talking about, man?" the Jewish boy responds with a small laugh.

"Well, why are you Jewish? Why do you wear that yamaka?"

"I'm Jewish because my parents are. I wear a yamaka because we have—"

"That's not what I mean." Paul cuts him off. "You never think about why you really are the way you are?"

"Deep, veryyy deep," the Muslim girl jokes.

"Look," Paul says, "I'm trying to be something too. I just don't know where to start. You guys have all been the way you are since the very first day I met you."

They can all see this has been on his mind for some time. It doesn't look like they'll be racing down the street to the city pool this afternoon. There's a moment of silence. The atheist loudly crumples up his brown bag, trying to signal it's time to get moving. He thinks they are all about to start talking crazy.

"Dude, we can go to the pool in like 10 minutes," Paul says looking at his friend with the brown bag. "You each have believed in this stuff for your entire life. Can't you just tell me really quick what's what? Help me out here."

The Jewish boy stands up and starts to summarize his religion, "So, it happened like this a long, long time ago . . .

"The Lord said to Moses, 'Come up to me on the mountain and stay here, and I will give you the tablets of stone with the law and commandments I have written for their instruction.' Then Moses sets out with his helper, Joshua, and they hike up to the mountain of God.[1]

"Up on this mountain," the boy continues, "the Ten Commandments set forth the foundation of Judaism. They are . . .

1. I am the LORD thy God.
2. Thou shalt have no other gods before me.
3. Thou shalt not take the name of the Lord thy God in vain.
4. Remember the sabbath day, to keep it holy.
5. Honor thy father and thy mother.
6. Thou shalt not murder.
7. Thou shalt not commit adultery.
8. Thou shalt not steal.
9. Thou shalt not bear false witness against thy neighbor.
10. Thou shalt not covet."

The Catholic kid jumps in, "And Christianity builds off of these same Ten Commandments with the teachings of Jesus Christ and his 12 disciples found in the New Testament of the Bible. Jesus reiterates many of those laws given to Moses and further commands his followers to forgive wrongdoers, beg for forgiveness to God, love enemies and neighbors as thyself, leave judgment of others to God alone, and reminds that God's kingdom belongs not to the rich and powerful, but the meek."

"OK," Paul acknowledges them both.

"And Islam follows Judaism and Christianity with very similar teachings," the Muslim girl says. "We worship one god and strive to be people of good virtue. There are 'five pillars of Islam' us Muslims seek to follow.

1. Shahada—There is no deity except Allah, and Muhammad is his prophet, his messenger.

2. Salat—Pray five times daily.
3. Sawm—Fast.
4. Zakat—Practice charity.
5. Hajj—Pilgrimage to Kaaba in Mecca."

"I never noticed, but I guess us Hindus are a little different than you three," the Indian boy follows up. "Hinduism combines many different ways of life and recognizes multiple gods and goddesses, but worships a single deity, known as Brahman. Our religion's overarching theme is that of karma—the universal law of cause and effect. Like if I steal your Doritos, you might finally beat me in a swim race," he teases Paul. "Karma posits that humans' actions and thoughts directly determine the path of their life and future lives. Through good conduct and morality, Hindus hope to achieve dharma—the fulfillment of our law."

"Enough already," their atheist friend says to them all. "You guys talk about stuff that supposedly happened thousands of years ago and about future lives we'll have that no one here has ever experienced before. What happened to, 'the wise speak only of what they know'? What I know is that we're not going to be able to get to the pool if you guys keep going on about all this."

Paul looks to each of his friends and sees the conversation has started to get a little tense. He thinks back to what the old lady who ran his orphanage used to say, the stuff about just being nice to everyone. He loves these five classmates; they've become his best friends. It seems that they have all found their own way to be nice to everyone.

MACRO

Where does faith fall into the conversation about what to do with your money? As Jesus said, "No one can serve two masters. Either you will hate the one and love the other, or you will be devoted to the one and despise the other. You cannot serve both God and money" (Matthew 6:24). This timeless advice illustrates the conflict between one's calling and the yearning for money.

School teaches that wealth, in the technical sense, is the abundance of valuable possessions or resources, including but not limited to land, currency, precious metals, and knowledge. But we now know that these are all just means to an end for wealth. To fully understand the transfer of wealth, one must go back to the genesis of trade and nationalization, while bearing in mind the goal has always been well-being.

Nation Building

The 193 sovereign countries recognized today are much younger than most people might think. The United States of America only dates back to July 4, 1776. China celebrates 221 BC as the date of its founding, but as mentioned in the previous chapter, it has drastically changed over time amid various ruling dynasties before becoming the Republic of China in 1949. The Russian Empire became the Soviet Union in 1917, or Union of Soviet Socialist Republics (USSR), but did not become the Russian Federation the world recognizes today until December 25, 1991.[2] Japan may be home to the five oldest companies in the world—Kongo Gumi, a construction company, being the oldest having existed since 578—but the country only adopted the Constitution of Japan in 1947.[3]

Before the formation of nations and elected officials, most regions were governed by empires. The Pandyan Empire in southern India was the longest-lasting empire in history, reportedly in power from 500 BC to AD 1350. Pandya was a stronghold of Shaivism, a branch of Hinduism that worships the god Shiva. However, the most glorious empire is widely believed to be the Roman Empire. Augustus Caesar proclaimed himself the first emperor of Rome in 31 BC, and the ensuing empire lasted until its fall in September AD 476 to the Germanic prince Odovacar.[4] Rome was a polytheistic civilization that worshipped many gods, most of which were iterations of ancient Greek gods. The Roman god Jupiter came from the Greek god Zeus, Venus from Aphrodite, Neptune from Poseidon, Pluto from Hades, and so on. Judaism and early Christianity were practiced in the Roman Empire, but they were frowned upon as emperors saw it as a threat to their throne. Many historians consider the beginning of the end for the Roman Empire to have been in AD 313 when Constantine the Great outlawed persecution of Christians, a monotheistic religion—a belief in one god—that directly contradicted Rome's polytheistic foundation. By the end of the fourth century, Christianity was adopted as the official state religion. The Roman Empire split into western Rome, which was Catholic, and eastern Rome, which was Eastern Orthodox, and the power and creditability of the emperor evaporated.

Despite the famous architecture, art, and legends that stemmed from ancient Rome, the values of its emperors are now viewed as philosophy and mythology. People still read their writings and teachings for both entertainment and advice, but they are hardly worshipped in modern times.

There is one dominion that has guided people's way of life long before and after the age of empires. It is theology. Faith-based beliefs have offered guiding principles on how to work, live, govern, and think about wealth to communities without borders since the beginning of time.

Timeline of Major Religions

Hinduism is the third-largest religion in the world with roughly 900 million followers. It is considered by many scholars as the world's oldest religion, as it comprises an overlap of developing religions in India since it was first inhabited. Vedas, Hinduism's primary sacred text, was composed around 1500 BC.[5]

The oldest monotheistic religion is Judaism. Greek records discuss Judaism during the Hellenistic period dating back to 323 BC. The first mention of Israel can be found on the ancient Egyptian document, Merneptah Stele, inscribed by Pharaoh Merneptah in 1208 BC. However, the story of Judaism reaches back to roughly 2100 BC with the birth of Abraham. Today there are approximately 14.7 million Jews.[6]

The Jewish faith eventually served as a starting point for Christianity. The teachings of Jesus Christ began to spread around the world in AD 46 with Paul the Apostle's first missionary journey.[7] It is now the largest religion in the world with 2.5 billion believers.[8]

Islam, also an Abrahamic religion, is the youngest of the world's major religions, but the second largest: 1.8 billion Muslims follow the lessons of Muhammad in the Quran. Scholars believe that in AD 610 the angel Gabriel spoke to Muhammad in Mecca, Saudi Arabia.[9]

Of course, not everyone believes in a higher being. One could say that atheism dates back indefinitely. From the outset of practicing religion, there have been naysayers of all deities. While atheists might share a common belief, in not believing, there is no central authority for their community.

Before delving further into the impact of theology on the global economy, it is important to examine the interplay between religion and governance. The United States of America was founded based on religious freedom, but undoubtedly followed the premises of Judeo-Christian principles. John Quincy Adams said, "The Declaration of Independence laid the cornerstone of human government upon the first precepts of Christianity." In 1800, Congress approved the use of the Capitol building as a church. President Dwight D. Eisenhower later stated that "without God, there could be no American form of Government, nor an American way of life. Recognition of the Supreme Being is the first—the most basic—expression of Americanism. Thus the Founding Fathers saw it, and thus, with God's help, it will continue to be." More recently, President Barack Obama defended faith in a public life in a speech in 2007 by saying, "Imagine [President] Lincoln's Second Inaugural [Address] without its reference to 'the judgments of the Lord.' Or [Martin Luther] King's 'I Have a Dream' speech without its reference to 'all of God's children.' Or President Kennedy's Inaugural [Address] without the words, 'here on Earth, God's work must truly be our own.'"

The web of theological economics becomes more entangled when various nation-states go beyond preferring a particular religion, to actually using religion as its form of governance. Twenty-two percent of recognized countries have an official state religion. Judaism has one country identified by its faith, that being Israel, which defines itself as the nation-state of the Jewish people. Thirteen countries cite a form of Christianity as the official religion, most notably the United Kingdom; granted, this is seen as more ceremonial in nature. Vatican City, which comprises only 109 acres completely surrounded by Rome, is the seat of the Catholic Church. While 94 percent of the world's Hindus live in India, India is a religiously free country,[10] and no country references Hinduism in its constitution. The most common government-endorsed faith belongs to Islam. Twenty-seven countries have anchored Islam in its constitution as the official state religion,[11] often funding and requiring certain religious functions. The majority of Islamic states are in the Middle East and northern Africa.

Nations founded on a particular religious doctrine have more solidarity in their belief system and typically can only be changed by revolution. Religiously free countries are bound to change with their people. The United States may have started as a Judeo-Christian nation, but due to its religiously free construct, it has changed over time. President Barack Obama proclaimed in 2009 while in Turkey that "although, as I mentioned, we have a very large

Christian population, we do not consider ourselves a Christian nation or a Jewish nation."[12]

Modern Religious Economies

As recently as the 1990s, 90 percent of adult Americans identified as Christian and only 6 percent as not having a religion.[13] Obama may have been on to something, as the percentage of American adults identifying as Christians dropped to 77 percent in 2009 and even further to 63 percent in 2021. Meanwhile, those identifying as nonreligious increased from 17 percent to 29 percent over the past decade. This later cohort has been led particularly by young adults; just one in three millennials attend religious services of any sort. Democrats are also noticeably less religious.[14] Similar patterns have unfolded in religious education. In 1960, 5.2 million students attended Catholic school. Despite the tremendous growth in the US population, as of 2022 less than 1.7 million students go to Catholic school.[15]

On the global scene, a worldwide study by *US News* in 2022 ranked countries by their attachment to religion. Saudi Arabia is a theocratic monarchy, meaning its god or religious leader is the monarch, and it is ranked the world's most religious country. Based on Islamic Shariah law, "any attempt to cast down on Islamic fundamentals" is illegal. Although its government is religiously free, Israel was ranked the second most religious country. The Jewish state is home to some of the most significant sites for Jews, Muslims, and Christians. India, the birthplace of both Hinduism and Buddhism, is the only country in the top 10 to not be in the Middle East. The United States is recognized as the 66th most religious country on Earth.[16]

In a world trending toward believing in not believing, the only major religion projected to experience growth in the twenty-first century, as a percentage of worldwide population, is Islam. (See Figure 8.1.) The Pew Research Center predicts Islam to grow to 29.7 percent of the world population by 2050 and then overtake Christianity as the world's largest religion. Much of Islam's anticipated growth is credited to its strong following among youth and having the highest fertility rate of all major religions (3.1. births per female). The median age of Muslims in America is 33 years old, versus the median age for all Americans of 47 years old, and 54 years old for Catholics.[17] Conversely, Christianity is projected to experience the largest net decrease in the future.[18]

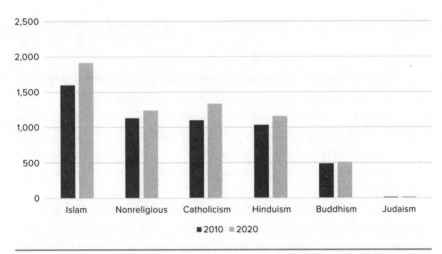

Figure 8.1   Major religions' population worldwide (millions)[19]

With a better understanding of the theological makeup of mankind, the monetary connections to religion can start to be examined. In America, Jews make up the wealthiest religion per capita. Roughly one in four Jewish households has an income in excess of $200,000, whereas the national average for households over $200,000 is only 4 percent. On the other end of the spectrum, only 1 in 10 Jewish households has an income under $30,000, versus the national average of 26 percent.[20] Of the major religions in America and in terms of household income, Jews are followed by Hindus, Muslims, Catholics, Buddhists, and Baptists, respectively.[21]

Religion can also play a vital role in someone's financial planning and investment philosophy. The trend of "socially conscious investing" is growing, with trillions of dollars managed by such funds and often guided by faith. These values-based portfolios typically avoid companies deemed to generate profits immorally, such as alcohol, gambling, tobacco, birth control, or weaponry companies. Strict followers of Sharia law follow Halal, principles that avoid interest-bearing accounts, companies with heavy debt and interest-bearing loans, or pork-related businesses.[22]

As most religions are based on faith, spirituality, and charity, it may seem taboo to examine the financial status of actual religions themselves. However, some are formal organizations with leadership structures, income and expenses, and measurable wealth.

In Islam, the organizational structure is purposefully disorganized as emphasis is placed on an individual's relationship with God. There are various sects of Islam, and at each mosque there is typically an imam who leads in prayer, but there is no single worldwide leader of Islam. Mosques can be owned by nonprofits or, in many cases in Muslim countries, by the state. American Muslims donated $1.8 billion in 2021 as zakat (the Islamic obligation to donate generally 2.5 percent of a Muslim's savings). According to the Muslim American Zakat Report of 2022, the largest recipient was international nonprofits (25.3 percent), followed by foreign Muslim-state governments (21.7 percent).[23]

Judaism is similar as it is made up of various sects and local groups that follow a rabbi or chief rabbi. Since Israel is considered the homeland for Jewish people, many followers consider the prime minister of Israel to be a top leader in the Jewish faith. Synagogues rely less on outright donations and more on annual dues that its members pay. A synagogue is typically run by a board of directors composed by its members.

The most transparent religion may also be the most complex—Catholicism. Because Catholicism has a hierarchical structure, it is possible to gain a rough calculation of its wealth. Local churches and priests report up to regional dioceses and bishops, who report to the College of Cardinals, which are all overseen by the Vatican and the pope. The Roman Curia, the Catholic Church's central administrative body, provides accounting comparable to normal corporations. The Vatican reportedly owns over 5,000 properties worldwide.[24] When including the Vatican Museums, Vatican bank, and other assets, the overall worth of the Vatican is estimated at $4.7 billion.

ECONOMIC INSIGHT

Religion is a teaching and, in that respect, is no different than any other education. Colleges need tuition money to keep the lights on, provide libraries and laboratories, and pay professors. Every college hopes to last far longer than one generation, hence their endowments driven by private giving and managed to preserve the school's legacy (see Chapter 3, Education).

Most religions meet these requirements through a form of "tithing." Religion often encourages acts of charity, considering it one of the most important virtues. Tithing means to give one-tenth of something to the organization, in this case like a suggested tax to the religion. This fits into a number of parables that promote not only familial, spiritual, and vocational responsibility, but also financial stewardship.

There are a few simple strategies that incorporate tithing. One common practice tells parishioners to donate 10 percent of their earnings, save/invest 20 percent, and spend the remaining 70 percent. Another, the third-third-third plan, teaches to save a dollar, spend a dollar, and invest a dollar for the future (this could be split between charity, college, retirement, etc.). In 2021, Americans responded by donating over $135 billion to religious organizations.[25]

Even for those who do not feel so benevolent, these ancient habits of charity still offer a positive by-product in the discipline of budgeting. In a capitalist society, a citizen might feel that every dollar spent already carries a thread of altruism—from a bill at a fancy dinner that pays a hardworking chef and the risk-taking restaurateur and ends with a tip for the waitress paying her way through college; all the way to the buyer of a Ferrari whose splurge sustained the careers of countless mechanical engineers, designers, and employees of a publicly traded company hoping to reward its shareholders.

Religious Conflict

The previous chapter revealed the links between war and the formation of economies. For all the peace and comfort religion has brought to its followers, sadly it has often been central to wars for just as long. A reader of the Old Testament can go only but a few pages before encountering the next conflict. Shortly before his death, Moses, the most revered prophet, provided this final instruction to the Israelites regarding their enemies: "And when the LORD thy God shall deliver them before thee; thou shalt smite them, *and* utterly destroy them; thou shalt make no covenant with them, nor show mercy unto them."[26]

According to the *Encyclopedia of Wars*, 123 historical conflicts were waged with religion as the primary cause. Modern violence predicated on religion has included, but is not limited to, Jews versus Muslims in Palestine, Hindus and Muslims in South Asia, Serbian forces against Muslims in Bosnia, and two decades of the Sudanese Muslim government's genocide on Christians.[27]

America is the most diverse country on Earth, as a result of immigration and protected freedoms. This lends itself to a smorgasbord of beliefs and principles among its citizens, and a natural diversification away from its founding Judeo-Christian standards. Americans can find their guiding light in a particular religion, racial identity, patriotic zeal, political affiliation, social mission, career, or any combination thereof. There is no one supreme authority to promote God, family, country, money, environment, or fun as the primary ideology (I).

The pros of such a free and fluid structure are the opportunities to discover one's true self and foster universal camaraderie, a shared opportunity for each citizen to satisfy their own MICE. The cons of this type of environment could be a fractured community in the face of opposing values. This might lead to disengagement at best or internal strife at worst. Here lies the timeless struggle between a utopia left to entirely altruistic people versus a set of controls to guide a flawed humanity. America may struggle with the discourse allowed by free thought and speech, but there is plenty of history to rebut attempts at restricting the masses.

It is ironic that the other modern superpower, China, models itself as almost the opposite of America, in terms of religion. President Xi Jinping has demanded that all members of the governing Chinese Communist Party (CCP) must be "unyielding Marxist atheists." Despite this decree, China does recognize five religions: Buddhism, Catholicism, Daoism, Islam, and Protestantism, which are allowed to participate in undefined "normal religious activities."

Religious practice is heavily regulated in China, and on January 7, 2019, the government announced a formal five-year plan of Sinicization—meaning to bring under Chinese influence. The plan shall reform all religious teachings and practice to be in line with CCP doctrine, supporting its leadership and socialist system. The US government estimates that since April 2017, the Chinese government arbitrarily detained more than one million Uyghurs, ethnic Kazakhs, Hui, and members of other Muslim groups, as well as Uyghur

Christians, in specially built or converted internment camps in Xinjiang. Detainees have reportedly been subjected to forced disappearance, political indoctrination, torture, physical and psychological abuse, including forced sterilization and sexual abuse, forced labor, and prolonged detention without trial because of their religion and ethnicity. China claims its initiatives are justified to prevent religious extremism and violent terrorism. Due to such religious persecution, the United States has designated China as a "country of particular concern" since 1999.[28]

The other notable opposition to America, Russia, has many theological similarities to China. In the tenth century, Prince Vladimir I was converted by missionaries from Byzantium and declared Christianity the national religion of Russia. The Russian Orthodox Church dominated the country's religious views for the next 1,000 years. This all changed in 1917 as the communists took control of the Soviet Union. Churches were no longer considered legal entities and lost the right to own land; as a result, monks were evicted, and most monasteries destroyed.[29]

The constitution of modern-day Russia provides for freedom of religion, equal rights irrespective of religious belief, and the right to worship and profess one's religion. The law acknowledges Christianity, Islam, Judaism, and Buddhism as the country's four "traditional" religions, and the "special role" of Russian Orthodox Christianity in the country's "history and the formation and development of its spirituality and culture."[30]

Despite this inclusive language, the US Commission on International Religious Freedom (USCIRF) has seen fit to also add Russia to its list of "countries of a particular concern." President Putin champions the Russian Orthodox Church, but has gone so far as to call Jehovah's Witness and other religious minorities "extremist," subject to fines, detention, and criminal charges. Even before the Russian invasion of Ukraine in February 2022, religious persecution provoked the United States to impose economic sanctions as a penalty, such as trade barriers, tariffs, and restricting certain financial transactions.

In summarizing this religious tour of the world, America, representing the Western way of life, is recognized as the eighth most religiously free country in the world.[31] The only notable religious hate crimes in the United States in the modern era have all been isolated incidents of citizens against other citizens. On the contrary, China and Russia place an emphasis on nationalist pride over any religious involvement.

On the other end of the spectrum, the Middle East, as a region, is ultra-religious but in one direction. As mentioned earlier, 27 countries pronounce Islam as the nationally sanctioned religion, almost all in the Middle East. Iran, Pakistan, Saudi Arabia, Tajikistan, and Turkmenistan are all deemed "countries of particular concern" for egregious violations of religious freedom.

According to the USCIRF, Iran has been cited for "scores" of Christians being "arrested, assaulted, and unjustly sentenced to years in prison." Pakistan's reputation has worsened due to a "sharp rise in targeted killings, blasphemy cases, and forced conversions" of Ahmadis, Shi'a, Hindus, Christians, and Sikhs. Women and children, particularly Christians and Hindus, are exposed to abduction, rape, forced marriage, and conversion to Islam.

From the USCIRF report, the "worst in the world and showing no signs of improvement" is Turkmenistan. "Restrictive state policies have 'virtually extinguished' the free practice of religion in the country, where the government appoints Muslim clerics, surveils and dictates religious practice, and punishes nonconformity through imprisonment, torture, and administrative harassment," the report said.[32]

Afghanistan is on the USCIRF's Tier 2 watchlist, as the Taliban has already been labeled an "entity of particular concern," reserved for non-state-sponsored groups. Afghanistan will likely move up to Tier 1 since the rapid takeover of the government by the Taliban in the summer of 2021. The all-male interim government comprises veterans of the 1990s hardline regime, including Interior Minister Sirajuddin Haqqani, who remains on the FBI's most-wanted list with a $5 million bounty. The newly reformed Taliban released a policy statement promising education "to all countrymen within the framework of Sharia [Islamic law]."[33]

While the people of Afghanistan are not in an economically prosperous position, the governing Taliban is well funded. Afghan and US officials accuse Pakistan, Iran, and Russia of providing long-standing financial aid to the regime. Private citizens from Pakistan, Saudi Arabia, the United Arab Emirates, and Qatar are also large donors. According to experts, these contributions total nearly $500 million annually. Perhaps the largest economic driver of the Taliban is opium production. Afghanistan is the world's largest opium producer and supplies 90 percent of the world's heroin. A 10 percent cultivation tax is levied on opium farmers, an illicit economy generating an estimated $1.8 to $2.7 billion annually.[34]

Over the past decade, many development and infrastructure projects in Afghanistan—roads, schools, and clinics—have been funded by the West. The Taliban tax these projects as well as workers and truckers traversing the country. Last, Afghanistan is rich in minerals and precious stones, providing a mining industry estimated at $1 billion annually.[35]

In 2021, Pope Francis carried out his vocation of global peace and made history by meeting with Grand Ayatollah Ali al-Sistani, the spiritual leader of Iraqi Shia Muslims, to speak out on twenty-first-century violence. Representing religions that have waged war for generations around the globe, they sought to stomp out hatred in Iraq, the Middle East, and all of humanity. Pope Francis also traveled to Ur, which was the city of Sumer some 5,000 years ago. There he proclaimed, "God asked Abraham to raise his eyes to heaven and count its stars," and referring to all Jews, Christians, and Muslims, continued, "In those stars, he saw the promise of his descendants; he saw us."

MICRO

He is one of 17 sons. His father is a billionaire construction mogul. He is presented with all of the opportunities for success, for wealth. But he has his own ego; he wants to escape his dad's shadow and make his own mark on the world.[36]

His journey begins in a manner fitting for a boy of his background, pursuing education among the country's elite. Civil engineering looks to be a perfect fit. New buildings are popping up everywhere, and who has more contacts than Dad? Noticeably taller than everyone in his class, motivated, and well spoken, he quickly catches the attention of a respected professor. He finds a mentor who can help him outshine even his father.

It is here, at King Abdulaziz University in Jeddah, Saudi Arabia, that Abdullah Azzam, a professor from Palestine, will educate a young Osama bin Laden on much more than civil engineering. Azzam explains to him that a godless Soviet Union is bent on destroying Afghanistan and that there's a bigger responsibility than constructing buildings; it is to unite Muslims around the world and save Afghanistan. Together Azzam and bin Laden form the Maktab al-Khidamat (MAK Services Office) and recruit over 10,000 Muslims internationally to form the Afghan Arabs. Bin Laden and his supporters lead the Islamic warriors, the Mujahideen, against the Soviets. In a David versus Goliath battle, the Afghans are desperate for help against the world's biggest country. Finding a friend in the enemy of their enemy, the US government provides money, intelligence, and advanced weaponry, including antiaircraft missiles to fend off the Soviet Union.

Osama is not an Afghan though. He breaks ties with his mentor, Azzam, and refocuses on Islam, not just Afghanistan. He uses MAK to team up with Ayman al-Zawahiri, a founding father of the Islamic Jihad of Egypt, and together they form Al-Qaeda (which translates to "the Base"). Bin Laden redirects his hatred from one superpower, the Soviet Union, to another in America, accusing the United States in 1993 of desecrating holy Saudi soil by building a military base there in the wake of the crisis in the Gulf. After he criticizes the Saudi government for not protecting the holy sites of Mecca and Medina from outsiders, Saudi Arabia revokes bin Laden's citizenship in 1994.

Bin Laden declares war against the United States in October of 1996, asserting that Islam is under attack. "The people of Islam had suffered from aggression, inequality, and injustice imposed on them by the Zionist-Crusader alliance and their collaborators to the extent that Muslims' blood became the cheapest and their wealth looted in the hands of enemies," he continues. "Their blood has spilled in Palestine and Iraq. The horrifying pictures of the massacre of Qana, in Lebanon are still fresh in our memory. Massacres in Tajikistan, Burma, Kashmir, Assam, Philippines, Somalia, Chechnya, and in Bosnia-Herzegovina took place, massacres that send shivers in the body and shake the conscience." Bin Laden goes on to issue several "fatwas," rulings by Islamic leaders, to all Muslims to kill and plunder all Americans and their allies to liberate the al-Aqsa Mosque and Mecca, in order to comply with Allah's order.

Nineteen men, mostly in their late twenties or midthirties, highly educated, financially stable, and acclimated over several years to the Western world, respond to the call. Despite the luxuries, niceties, and freedoms in a culture of sports, comedy, and Disney, their feelings of hatred are not at all deterred. They hold a deep-rooted set of beliefs that killing innocent Americans is a direct path to something far greater than could ever be experienced here on Earth. They have two targets, the seat of government and the seat of finance. On September 11, 2001, they carry out the tragic events of 9/11 in the name of Allah, forever changing the global economy.

The comments of Hassan Salam, the commander of a suicide bombing of 46 Israelis in 1996, offer the slightest bit of reasoning: "A suicide bombing is the highest level of Jihad, and highlights the depth of our faith. The bombers are holy fighters who carry out one of the more important articles of faith."

* * *

Terrorism, per its name, has one ultimate goal—instill terror in its victims. This terror affects the psychology of any economy under its influence and creates chaos amid the flow of money. Terrorists have often found the most efficient way to strengthen a small radical voice is by exploiting religion.

While Islam does not have one central voice, the Foundation for Ethnic Understanding (FFEU) created the hashtag #MuslimsAreSpeakingOut in 2011 in response to the criticism of Islam for not condemning terrorist attacks. Its goal is to highlight the overwhelming denunciation by Islamic leaders against such terrorists for hijacking the narrative of Islam. In 2014, Saudi Arabia's highest-ranking religious authority, the grand mufti, Abdulaziz Al Sheikh, said ISIS and Al-Qaeda, "are not in any way part of Islam, but are enemy number one of Islam, and Muslims are their first victims."

WHAT SHOULD I DO WITH MY MONEY?

One could posit that faith eclipses every other tool a microeconomy or macroeconomy could use. From the best to the worst, all leaders, organizations, and nations are bound to end up like those before them—history. This underscores the incomparable power of belief, of ideology (I). The wealthiest estate plan, meant to last generations, pales in comparison to the longevity of religion.

Financial rationality becomes subjective in the face of religion. For the casual believer, its teachings might be a whispering voice in the back of their head guiding everything from tithing, investing, work schedules, job choices, and friendships. For the devout, it can propel a believer surrounded in all the vanities of earthly success to give up everything, even one's life, to carry out an ultimate goal.

The power of ideology over money can be illustrated by a beautiful story about Mother Teresa of Calcutta. She was in a car with an affluent donor for her orphanages in India when she noticed a beaten homeless man on the side of the road. She asked the driver to stop, got out of the car, and began treating his maggot-infested wounds. When Mother Teresa returned to the car, the affluent donor said, "I wouldn't do what you do for a million dollars." Mother Teresa replied, "Neither would I."

None of the major religions promote evil, excess, lust, or any of the adjectives associated with economic disarray. Rather, most convey principles of peace, frugality, and charity. Therefore, it is only the human manipulation of religion that can lead economies astray. Persecution against a religious belief and persecution for a religious belief are humanity's sins, not religion's.

What you can do with your money is to think about what to do with your money. This requires looking past traditional economics and financial planning to start answering that second question, "Why?" Those answers are what form your priorities. Money (M) must go somewhere. Ideology (I) is the North Star that guides what can afford to be compromised (C) and takes charge when your ego (E) is out of line.

As St. Thomas Aquinas, the Italian Dominican friar and priest, said in the thirteenth century, "Three things are necessary for the salvation of man: to know what he ought to believe; to know what he ought to desire; and to know what he ought to do."

ECONOMIC INSIGHT

The personal choice of language can have a profound effect on manifesting one's wealth, or lack thereof. This has nothing to do with languages in the traditional sense, speaking English or Spanish, but rather the words one chooses to use in characterizing one's goals and circumstances. Some words carry immense weight to the speaker, the listener, or both. They are words ordained by society.

In word choice, there may be none greater than the word *believe*. This chapter has shown what humanity has been able to do for thousands of years, incredible goods and evils, all based on believing. The word is easily said, like all others of two syllables, but when once announced with conviction, it is almost unshakable. There is perhaps no word in finance more misused than *believe*.

As a Certified Financial Planner™ having counseled thousands of individuals on their money, I have heard people tell me they believe or do not believe in a particular financial strategy on a daily basis. "I don't believe in stocks; I only believe in funds." "I don't believe in insurance." "I believe in CDs, not bonds." "I don't believe in renting." These beliefs can come from a parent or trusted friend, something heard on a podcast or read on a blog, or from personal experience. No matter the source, once a belief is constructed and said aloud, by definition, it is near impossible to erase or alter.

Every financial belief has the ability to be right or wrong at some time. Believing solely in stocks leading up to the Great Recession may have been wrong, and after it—right. Believing in owning disability insurance throughout a perfectly healthy career may have been financially wrong, but before an accident or illness—right.

This is where belief can severely hurt a financial plan and stunt the education of any alternative options or beliefs. All financial experts agree that money and emotion never mix well. But how is one not supposed to get emotional about what they believe in? Choosing to announce a belief is best reserved for ideology (I), not money (M). It can fit within the ideology of money, like saying, "I don't believe in spending more than I earn." Or, "I believe in rewarding my employees." But when it comes to money alone, *belief* is a dangerous word.

FINANCIAL LITERACY

Money is the story within all stories. It can be a hero or nemesis, a master or a slave. It can be the ultimate goal or merely an afterthought. It can divide and conquer or reunite and rebuild. Money opens and closes every story of economics.

I'd say it's been the biggest problem all my life . . . it's money. It takes a lot of money to make these dreams come true.

—Walt Disney

illy collapses on his bed, spent from another day in the factory. Last week his parents visited from out of town, and they celebrated Billy's twenty-fifth birthday with his girlfriend. His mom brought a little chocolate cake with one candle. This week his girlfriend broke up with him; he had a feeling it was coming sooner or later.

Now he lies alone on his bed, still in his dirty jeans and work boots. It is a small apartment, a one-bedroom hardly fitting the twin bed he grew up on. The narrow hallway kitchenette leads to a bathroom that miraculously fits a sink, toilet, and shower within its walls. It's tight.

He rolls to his left and opens the blinds just enough to let a few rays of light spray across his worn body. The A/C unit kicks on and off, doing all it can to push out some relief.

"It's only temporary," Billy mutters to himself. He has been saying the same thing for three months now.

Billy knew college was a long shot. School was never his thing. His grades weren't bad, but were never really good either. He contemplated going into the service, but every time the conversation came up, he found himself in a philosophical debate on foreign affairs and was unable to understand how his service would be of service.

Uncle Jim. He loves him to death, but at moments like these, not so much. Uncle Jim is the head of their local Brotherhood of Electrical Workers 224. For as long as he could remember, Uncle Jim drove a beat-up pickup truck. Ironically enough, he is regarded as one of the most successful members of their extended family, and by success, they mean in financial terms.

The high salary, overtime, benefits, annuity, defined benefit pension. Billy has heard about all the perks of the job. But for now, their value seems a lifetime away from his apprenticeship position.

Just hang in there. You'll climb the ladder. It's nice at the top. He keeps replaying Uncle Jim's words.

After a few minutes of self-pity, Billy grabs his iPhone off his dresser. Without thinking, purely from habit, he scrolls through Snapchat and TikTok. It takes a minute to digest what he is seeing, but the mindless scrolling offers a nice escape. It's a cooldown from the day.

Once his eyes adjust, he switches to Facebook and begins scanning his newsfeed. An old buddy gets engaged. Friends vow to end friendships over political stupidity. Some smart kid from high school graduates medical school. One of his coworkers holds up a sign with her girlfriend: "It's a Boy!"

His ex-girlfriend he keeps promising himself to unfriend poses with a new puppy golden-doodle.

Billy notices every few posts is a cropped photo of stock charts—GameStop. Bitcoin. Ethereum. AMC. Underneath each screenshot is someone bragging about their latest fortune. "Yeah, whatever," he mumbles as he tries to scroll past them. It reminds him of his dad's friends showing off their winning ticket from the racetrack, knowing there were plenty of losses before and after that horse came in.

But the allure is too strong. Billy sits up in bed as if he hears his name being called. He closes Facebook and clicks his bank app, taps it a few times and impatiently waits for it to load. He already knows to within a few dollars what each balance should be, but in that split second, he imagines if his favorite "Bank Error in Your Favor" card from Monopoly could be true. Facial recognition accepted. He looks at his three accounts:

MONEY MARKET SAVINGS: $2,366
PRIME CHECKING:. $874
CREDIT CARD 01:. $3,187

Billy toggles back to the Facebook app. A new array of online brokerage services flow through his feed offering free trades, no minimums, countless services and tips. He clicks the first one. And with that, he becomes an investor, an investor with no financial plan.

MACRO

Students have long been tested in the areas of mathematics, science, and language arts, requiring certain scores to reach high school graduation. However, proving an ability to grasp the basics of personal finance has never received near the same consideration. Fortunately, the twenty-first century has ushered in a national push for financial literacy curriculum, but the shortfall in prior generations' education lingers.

The ramping up of financial literacy may be part altruistic and part necessity. Entitlements and pensions have long taken the pressure off of baby boomer employees, but the ongoing transition to the do-it-yourself approach of retirement planning (see Chapter 2, Entitlements) requires a newly educated worker. Millennials and following generations may be more likely than their parents to realize their financial mistakes in the future as safety nets fade away.

The shared responsibility of financial literacy can empower students and teachers alike. Folks in their fifties and sixties are often struggling through a financial "sandwich" of caring for young and old. In 2018, 79 percent of polled parents said they financially support their adult children. Of the estimated $500 billion transferred annually, about one-quarter goes to college education and one-quarter toward buying a first home.[1] Meanwhile, about one-third of midlife adults with parents over the age of 65 have given a parent financial support.[2] Burning the candle at both ends can put the retirement of those in between in jeopardy.

According to the Council for Economic Education 2022 Report, not much has changed. In 2011, 22 states required an economics course for high school graduation; in 2022 that number has risen only to 25. Personal finance has received slightly more attention: in 2000 six states required a personal finance course for graduation; in 2022 that number rose to 23 states. Nearly one in four millennials spend more than they earn, and 67 percent have less than three months of available emergency funds.[3]

The long-standing gap in financial education has left an enormous void to be filled. This space is occupied by thousands of "financial gurus" dominating 24/7 business television channels, magazines, self-help books, and podcasts. Through these modes of communication an unlimited amount of information is disseminated, driven by the goal of *entertaining* audiences and selling ad space based on clicks, views, and downloads.

Information by itself is never a bad thing, but it can lead to unintended ramifications. From an optimistic viewpoint, finance fans can walk away enlightened. From a cynical standpoint, the overwhelming number of conflicting opinions can lead to confusion and paralysis, or worse, a false sense of confidence to begin taking improper financial actions. Inexperienced young professionals, even students, have many of the same capabilities as a seasoned trader holding a PhD in risk management. The removal of barriers to entry can unintentionally allow the blind to lead the blind.

The explosion in financial commentary has coincided with a positive trend in professional advice. The Bureau of Labor Statistics projects the employment of personal financial advisors to grow 15 percent from 2021 to 2031, much faster than the average for all occupations.[4] However, do-it-yourself alternatives are growing even quicker. Changes are evidenced by the rise of robo-advisors and online platforms that encourage independent decision-making, often tied to the same financial commentary previously mentioned. As of 2020, robo-advisors driven by financial algorithms, also referred to as robos, manage over $460 billion. The industry is predicted to exceed $1.2 trillion by 2024. According to a study by Vanguard, millennials are more than twice as likely to use a robo-advisor than baby boomers.[5]

People who are worried by the rise of financial technology, commonly called fintech, may be comforted by viewing a broader context. While $460 billion of robo money is a big figure, this represents a tiny fraction of the $103 trillion in assets under management globally.[6] Furthermore, the overwhelming majority of these assets remain in the hands of baby boomers not yet ready to fully partner up with robots.

Change is happening rapidly. The New York Stock Exchange was once the face of international finance, with traders screaming orders on the packed floor. Today it serves primarily as a television prop set for business talk shows and photo-ops for honorary ringers of the opening and closing bells. Artificial intelligence will continue to expand, making more commentators and fewer decision makers out of humans.

MICRO

It can't buy happiness, but it puts food in the stable.
It is boring in its simpleness, yet is taught in many a fable.
It is a measure of worthiness, says each nation via cable.
It is required at any genesis, so disappoints those unable.
It is the aim of all business, yet discussed at kitchen table.
It is part of holiday messiness, so all find it relatable.
It is oft a prize of ugliness, but is a pursuit justifiable.
It is a study of iffiness, leaving the emotional unstable.
It is an illustration of sexiness, begetting sins sad to label.
It is respected for its craftiness, as its misuse will disable.
It is envied by every heiress, but has a path untraceable.
It is deceptive in its loveliness, for that is undeniable.

Millennial Millionaire detailed the "Three I's" that the fortunate are able to achieve in a fulfilled career. *Independence* is the tool that allows a worker to do what they want, where they want, and when they want without compromise (C). *Impact* is the ability to influence positive change on any and all of the other subjects of this book, satisfying one's ego (E) and ideology (I).

However, only one "I" is truly mandatory—income. The employee working overnight in a dead-end job may still find solace in meeting the bare sustenance for survival, affording food and shelter. They are working for the weekend, justifying why it is called work. Whereas, someone blindly following an urge for independence and impact can enjoy fulfilling a passion project on their own schedule, but will inevitably collide with the realization of an empty bank account. The lengths to which this person can ignore the Income part of the 3 I's is dictated by the macroeconomy they belong to and its position on givers and takers. No matter the circumstances of the economy, there is not much power behind MICE without money (M). Income separates professionals from amateurs and doers from dreamers.

ECONOMIC INSIGHT

Thomas Edison is regarded as one of the most important inventors in American history. He dominated scientific advancement in the nineteenth century, having created the lightbulb, telegraph, movie camera, and much more. The fact is, Edison himself did not invent much of what he receives credit for today. At the same time, a brilliant immigrant from Serbia by the name of Nikola Tesla was inventing the future. Believing that science was immune from economics, he solely chased impact. Independence was irrelevant for a man obsessed with his work, and he mistakenly believed income to be a pursuit of no concern for real scientists. Tesla relinquished his rights to develop and use alternating current (AC), the form of electricity still used today, to George Westinghouse. He also watched, without dismay, Guglielmo Marconi use his Tesla oscillator to patent the radio. Nikola Tesla gave much to the world, but he did not take much, eventually growing old and broke in the shadows of better businessmen. If he mastered the last I of income, there is no telling where his place in history might stand.

There are two methods to achieving the 3 I's. The first method ignores Income and requires a socialist success story. This assumes a significant portion of the population work for high incomes and then willingly give up a large enough portion of their earnings to sustain everyone else who pursues independence and impact. As discussed in Chapter 4, Economic Philosophy, most developed nations incorporate at least some of this crutch through taxation and entitlements, but never enough to allow the perpetual ignorance of income. It should come as no surprise that many of the aggressors mentioned in Chapter 7, War, were communist. Without private production fulfilling the need for money (M), expansion and capturing natural resources became the only option.

The second, and more realistic, path is to create a work situation that checks all three boxes. There are some professionals and business owners who seemingly "lucked out" in landing such roles, but further investigation often reveals that their passion hid years of very hard work. Icons of bestselling biographies attest to long days of "paying their dues," delaying the gratification found in the I's of impact and independence.

In a free and capitalist economy, the ease at which the second path can be traversed is directly tied to effort, sound financial planning, and a bit of luck. Like all things, proper exercise begins with proper education. The understanding of financial literacy can enhance the income situation of any worker, allowing them to address independence and impact sooner than later. It is the transition from simply working hard to beginning to work smart.

WHAT SHOULD I DO WITH MY MONEY?

Knowing what to do with your money concludes with investing in financial literacy. After all, it is impossible to know that which is not known. Fortunately, this is one investment that does not need to come at a price. The costs are primarily time and concentration.

Finding the right answers starts by asking the right questions. The right questions involve uncovering what your problems are and the circumstances affecting them, your microeconomy within the macroeconomy. Problems involve open-ended wants and needs. What you want may not necessarily be what you need, but what you need, if left unaddressed, will eventually become what you want most.

The first key in financial literacy is to recognize the difference between a want and a need, and then appropriately prioritize them. Ralph Waldo Emerson said, "Nothing great was ever achieved without enthusiasm." Enthusiasm is excitement, and what people want is the stimuli that create excitement.

Parallels can be found in any industry marketed toward the masses. For decades health magazines have showcased ripped models underscored by headlines that read, "Eight Minute Abs!," "Lose 20 Pounds in Two Weeks!," and "Bench Press More Now!" Their approach is timeless—sell instantaneous results through a novel method. Most doctors would agree that thousands of magazines and shows could be easily replaced by the age-old food pyramid and exercising every day. While boring may be effective and needed, boring does not excite. Boring is not wanted.

Personal financial planning contains many components. They include, but are not limited to, budgeting, insurance, estate planning, debt management, real estate and lending, wealth management, tax planning, and investing. No topic is more valuable than another. Depending on life's circumstances, each topic will have its chance to be most important. But consumer behavior shows investing in the stock market or real estate to be the most popular topics of conversation. The other aspects may be viewed as less exciting, even boring. Here is where wants interrupt needs.

While investing is a crucial part of financial planning, it should never be mistaken for financial planning. Once you agree to shelve the visions of grandeur in investing and real estate for a moment, then you can approach the true goal with a reasonable mindset—sound financial planning.

An optimal financial plan is always ready to adapt to the times, yet holds the certainty of a compass. It must be flexible enough to provide the occasional detour, but forever agree that north is north and south is south. Just as lunch follows breakfast, so must the steps of financial planning follow this order.

1. Protection first, fully, and forever
2. Liquidity
3. Debt management
4. Wealth creation
5. Growth

1. Protection First, Fully, and Forever

Protection may not receive the amount of attention it deserves for a number of reasons. Consumers may find it boring or confusing, it often comes at a price, and most people do not like thinking about the worst possible outcomes in life. However, if the unexpected event occurs without adequate protection in place, all three of these problems are realized exponentially. A family or business can find itself overwhelmingly confused, facing insurmountable costs, and no longer thinking about, but actually living through, the worst possible outcome.

The first threat to be addressed in financial planning is the chance of becoming sick or injured and unable to work. Money (M) is the beginning of MICE and the foundation of finance. When people first ask, "How do I make money?" I say, "You work." Since every other step of the financial plan is dictated by the ability to earn an income, the possible loss of that income is paramount. Getting forced out of being a giver to becoming a taker forfeits all control of your financial destiny.

Disability Coverage

Most young professionals do not think they will ever become disabled, but according to the Social Security Administration, one in four of today's 20-year-olds can expect to be out of work for at least one year because of a disabling condition before they reach their normal retirement age.[7] For those asking the question "How are people disabled from working?" the top causes are musculoskeletal disorders (27.6 percent), cancer (15.0 percent), injuries (12.0 percent), mental health issues (9.3 percent), and circulatory complications, including stroke and heart attack (8.2 percent).[8]

The consequences of disability are alarming. In 2019, 77.8 percent of bankruptcies were caused by income loss, and 44.3 percent of those were due to disability.[9] As if the loss of income is not devastating enough, it often coincides with increased healthcare costs, emotional strain, and pressure on a spouse or business partner's work-life balance.

Many people understand the financial risks of disability, but assume that they are protected by entitlements. The program most widely cited as a safety net would be Social Security Disability Insurance (SSDI), which does cover most American workers. However, over the past decade only 32 percent of disability claims were approved.[10] This can be a lengthy process even when the claimant does get approved. As of 2020 the backlog of cases exceeded 400,000.[11] Social Security uses a very strict definition of disability in which the claimant must suffer a severe medical condition expected to last at least one year or result in death. Furthermore, it must prevent the claimant from doing work they did in the past and adjusting to any other work in the future. Once approved, the benefits are quite modest. The average Social Security Disability Insurance benefit is $1,279 monthly, hardly over the poverty level.[12]

The other program sometimes relied on too heavily is workers' compensation. This covers only a disability that was directly work-related. Less than 1 percent of workers are currently receiving workers' comp.[13]

Finally, many employees assume their employer will protect them from disability. According to the Bureau of Labor Statistics, 43 percent of workers have access to group short-term disability and 35 percent to group long-term disability.[14] Having access does not imply it is automatically provided, as it may need to be enrolled into and paid for. There are a myriad of concerns with group coverage that are often overlooked. Some drawbacks include, but are not limited to, lack of portability (leave the job, leave the coverage), benefits offsetting for other income sources, definitions requiring the inability to work any occupation, lack of inflation protection or partial disability benefits, and benefit amounts that may cover only a fraction of the worker's ordinary income.

The most effective method to protect a financial plan from disability is through the use of an individually owned noncancellable guaranteed renewable true-own occupation policy. To break down this lengthy title, "individually owned" means the person owns the policy themselves, not an employer or association. "Noncancellable" means the insurance carrier cannot cancel, increase the premiums, or reduce the benefits, so long as the owner pays their premium. "Guaranteed renewable" means the owner can continue to renew their plan with the same terms every year. "True-own occupation" means the carrier must approve the disability claim if the insured cannot perform the material and substantial duties of their own occupation; benefits will not be reduced even if working in another occupation.

Life Insurance

Since death and disability are the two perils that can forever rob a worker of his or her income, the next building block of protection is life insurance. It is also worth noting that life and disability insurance may be the two most time-sensitive elements of protection, as both are dictated by the insured's age and health. Despite the odds of becoming disabled during working years being significantly higher than dying, 25 percent versus 8 percent respectively, life insurance garners more acceptance.[15] As of 2021, 52 percent of American adults own some form of life insurance, whereas only 14 percent own disability insurance.[16]

Forgoing life insurance can be a symptom of ignoring unfortunate possibilities or letting the conversation become unnecessarily complex. The first thing a consumer should consider in purchasing life insurance is how much coverage to obtain, how much of a giver do they plan on being. The industry follows an economic value called human life value (HLV) as a guideline to replace an earner's financial worth. HLV is a multiple of age and income; for instance, the generally accepted maximum amount of coverage available from ages 18 through 40 is thirty times income, twenty times income in the 40s, fifteen times income in the 50s, and then geared toward retirement and estate planning thereafter. No matter what type of product or carrier is being used, the best life insurance is the one that pays out the right amount at a time when a family or business needs it most.

After determining the appropriate amount of death benefit, the consumer can then search for the most suitable product. From a carrier standpoint, consumers should pay mind to whether the company is mutual or stock-held. There are only a few mutual carriers remaining, mutual meaning they are 100 percent owned by their policy holders and typically more sheltered from the quarterly demands of shareholders. Most other insurance carriers are stock-held, meaning they are publicly traded and have dual responsibilities to their shareholders and policyholders. Consumers can also research carriers' Comdex ranking. A Comdex ranking is a composite score of 0 to 100 from the top four rating agencies, AM Best, Fitch, Moody's, and S&P.

Last, the consumer must choose the type of policy or policies to fold into their overall plans. There are two basic types of life insurance—term and permanent. Term life insurance is meant to be temporary coverage for a specific period of years, often a 20-year term. If the insured dies within the term, their beneficiaries will receive the death benefit income-tax free. However, studies show that roughly 98 to 99 percent of all term policies never pay a claim, as fortunately the insured outlives the term and the coverage expires.

Permanent life insurance is normally designed to last for an insured's entire life. It may also have a portion of the premium invested and made available through cash values. These values can receive interest and dividends that grow tax-deferred, which can be used to pay future premiums, be withdrawn for various reasons, or be used as collateral for a loan.

Whole life insurance is the longest standing and most popular of permanent products. As of 2021, whole life insurance comprised 35 percent of market share, indexed universal life 25 percent, term 21 percent, fixed universal life 8 percent, and variable universal life 12 percent.[17]

Liability Insurance

The last major insurance domain to include in the foundation of financial planning is liability coverage. America is a very litigious country, with over 1.3 million practicing attorneys.[18] There are over 100 million cases filed every year in state trial courts plus another 400,000 in federal trial courts.[19] Consumers can protect themselves from financial damages following an accident via property and casualty insurance. This includes auto insurance, homeowner's insurance, and personal liability umbrella policies. Liability coverage kicks in whenever the insured is at fault and subject to lawsuit or paying an injured party. These oft-overlooked line items can be the difference between sheltering one's balance sheet and facing overnight bankruptcy.

Many people hope to one day self-insure, be it from the perils of death, disability, or court. However, the values of income replacement, human life value, and asset exposure to lawsuit can each be far greater than initially assumed. Creating a side fund to cover these pitfalls would require an extreme amount of income accompanied by an equally impressive savings rate. As idle money defeats the purpose of wealth in motion and achieving rates of return, these enormous reserves can be recaptured by efficiently outsourcing them to appropriate insurance plans.

Estate Planning

Beyond insurance, proper estate-planning documents are part and parcel toward being well protected. For the individual, this usually refers to drafting a will and possibly trust documents. These legal documents can offer creditor protection, tax mitigation, and guidance for how assets may be disposed in the event of death or incapacitation. They often include instructions pertaining to living wills, healthcare proxies, power of attorney, and guardians for minors. None of these conversations are exactly heartwarming, but these pieces of paper can prevent families from going to war and legacies being squandered.

2. Liquidity

Once the preceding protection boxes have been checked, an individual can proceed with a high level of confidence that major threats to a financial plan have already been addressed. The next step is budgeting to maintain adequate liquidity. Liquidity may be defined as the ease and speed of access to capital. An individual with the appropriate amount of liquidity is appealing to lenders and has the advantage of seizing opportunities when they arise. On the flip side, the individual can react to unforeseen events without having to act irrationally, such as taking on bad debt or selling investments unexpectedly.

Before becoming bogged down in a monthly budget across five Excel spreadsheets, it may be worthwhile to adhere to some simple savings strategies. Many financial experts encourage saving 20 percent of gross income every year. Where these dollars should go can be addressed later, but building this habit could be as helpful as any other financial tip.

One of the best ways to address liquidity is to maintain a safe level of cash on hand. Savings, checking, and money market accounts would all fall into the category of cash equivalents. In the United States, up to $250,000 per account is guaranteed against default by the Federal Deposit Insurance Corporation (FDIC). A good rule of thumb is to carry at least six months of fixed expenses in cash. Additionally, any certain expenses in the next couple of years should be earmarked as extra cash positions. Despite these classic mantras and tips, only 40 percent of US households have enough in liquid savings to cover at least three months of their recurring expenses, and only 28 percent can cover at least six months.[20]

Cash does not offer much in the way of growth, especially in low-interest-rate environments like the 2010s, but its safety and availability make it valuable, nonetheless. Investors may consider cash a losing proposition, eternally scorned in the face of inflation. However, the complaint of having too much cash on hand is usually one of nitpicking a good portfolio from a great one. Conversely, the complaint of having not enough cash on hand is usually dire and wrought with inferior options.

3. Debt Management

After realizing that cash is indeed king, you should then examine your debt situation. Financial treatises have forever argued whether any debt is good debt, but history has proven that debt is a tool for growth, whether it be nearly every initiative of the US government being coupled with debt, down to the three out of four homeowners who reach their dream thanks to a mortgage. Debt can make the impossible possible.

However, allowing oneself to become overleveraged is akin to skating out too far on thin ice. It can be fun for a little while, allowing one to reach parts unknown and there is the chance of coming out the other side unscathed, but should there be a crack in the ice, the results are catastrophic.

If one evil arm of debt is an unmanageable balance, the other is a seemingly unfair interest rate, the most common form of which is credit card debt. At the time of this writing, the average savings account interest rate is 0.05 percent, whereas the average credit card interest rate stands at 16.65 percent.[21] This data does represent one point in time, but the exorbitant spread between the two is perpetual.

It is fair for the onlooker to question how a bank pays its depositor a fraction of a penny each year while charging its credit card holder over 16 cents on the dollar. The justification lies in the fact that the 16.65 percent charge is not necessarily mandatory; in other words the credit card holder can always pay off their balance before the end of the month to continually avoid any interest. The bank is free of guilt in that the high interest rate is warranted by the nature of it being an unsecured debt, meaning no asset backs the loan, and there is a higher likelihood of a late payment or default on this debt. Simply put, the bank charges a higher rate to cover its higher risk.

In short, using debt, even credit card debt, is a factor in the best of financial plans; and for the average millennial with a credit score of 679, it can establish credit history and improve one's credit score.[22] However, carrying high-interest-rate debt past its due date is like a poison to a financial plan. To pursue the upcoming steps of investing before eliminating outstanding high-interest-rate debt is akin to adjusting a boat's sails while the cabin floods with water.

4. Wealth Creation

Once you are adequately protected, supported with liquidity, and void of bad debt, then you may graduate to the fourth step—wealth creation. A rich person may work very hard and make a lot of money, but the wealthy person works very hard and their money makes a lot of money. This is the phase in which becoming financially independent becomes possible.

A common flaw in investing happens before clients even begin investing; it has to do with accounts. Think of it as an investing meal plan. What good are all the right ingredients if you don't have the right pots and pans? Any investment should be looked at as a stool with three legs—liquidity, taxability, and risk. What this means is to open the correct accounts and connect each to a systematic funding strategy before settling on a favorite stock. Here are some considerations:

- Taxable accounts, such as a joint, individual, or transfer on death (TOD), can be used to invest for the future while continuing to build liquidity. Most do not carry any restrictions or penalties as to when you can withdraw your investment. The primary liquidity concern revolves around gains being taxed as income if held for less than 12 months versus taxed as capital gains if held longer than 12 months.
- Workplace retirement plans such as a 401(k) or 403(b) can be funded directly through payroll deductions and can be funded pretax or on a Roth basis. Employers may offer a company match, a valuable incentive to contribute and get extra money from your employer.
- A Roth IRA, or backdoor Roth IRA when exceeding the IRS income limits, can allow you to build a retirement bucket available tax free after age 59.5, so long as it's held for over five years. This strategy of swallowing your medicine today rather than kicking the tax can down the road can provide more certainty in retirement and allow for tax arbitrage (the practice of profiting from the various ways income and investments are taxed). This is a popular concern for those fearing rising tax rates (see Figure 9.1).
- A whole-life insurance policy can secure a permanent death benefit, accessible cash value, with possible long-term care and disability protection, and unique tax advantages.

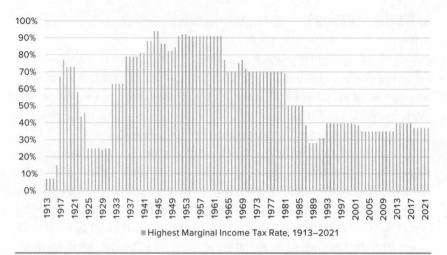

Figure 9.1   US historical marginal income tax rate[23]

Funding each of these vehicles on a systematic basis can help the financial plan move forward without too much hassle or tinkering required, while taking advantage of dollar cost averaging (DCA). DCA hedges the investor's entry points into the stock market by investing a fixed dollar amount each interval, in theory buying more positions at a low and less at a high.

To answer the common question of which of these accounts gives a better return, the chef must ponder which pot cooks a better meal. A nonqualified investment account, IRA, and 401(k) may all be able to house the exact same portfolio. It is the ingredients inside, or the investments in each account, that spell the outcome.

5. Growth

Once the overall plan has been drawn up, then the details can be filled in via step five—growth. These are the proverbial ingredients that go into baking the cake. This is the domain that undoubtedly receives the most airtime, the picking and choosing of one stock or fund over another. Step five comes after step four because while earning a 10 percent return on an investment is better than an alternative at 7 percent, other factors such as the ability or lack thereof to use that fund when needed without penalty (e.g., nonqualified account before age 59.5 versus qualified retirement account subject to IRS premature distribution penalty), or the tax ramifications of doing so, can trump a slightly better return.

During the Roaring Twenties, 1 in 10 American households owned stock. This decade of plenty ended with the beginning of the Great Depression. While no one escaped unscathed, it was the stockholders who first felt the wrath of a collapsing market. In 2022, 58 percent of American adults own stock. The all-time high was 63 percent, immediately preceding the Great Recession.[24] From a macro standpoint, the stock market serves as a measure of liquidity in the economy. From a micro standpoint, it is a measure of public confidence in particular companies' performance and results. Since the emotion of the world can instantly affect the stock market, it is considered a leading economic indicator.

There are many factors to consider in picking particular investments, and their features are constantly changing, which is part of what makes their conversation so entertaining. The easiest way to decompose the debate is by segregating investing into passive and active management.

Passive Investing

Passive investing represents a buy-and-hold type of approach. The investor may select a few stocks and then ride the wave of the market. For the investor who feels unable to achieve the right amount of diversification with their available money through stocks, they can use mutual funds or exchange traded funds (ETFs). A mutual fund is a pool of money gathered by many investors that invests in securities such as bonds, stocks, commodities, and other assets. An ETF is similar, but is traded on an exchange throughout the day and is typically more passively managed. Most ETFs are index funds, meaning they track a particular index, such as the S&P 500.

One of the more popular trends in investing has been indexing. This strategy employs investing by holding onto an index or set of indices, often through the use of ETFs, to efficiently participate in the markets. The argument being that actively managed mutual funds often do not outperform the index they are benchmarked against, so an ETF tied to the index can accomplish the same goal, if not better, with typically lower fees. Some of the most quoted indices are the DJIA ("The Dow"), S&P 500, Russell 2000, and Nasdaq. While past performance cannot guarantee future results, take a look at the hypothetical growth of buy and hold in each index over the past 40 years, 1980–2020. The Dow grew by 3,716 percent, meaning $1,000 invested in 1980 would equal $37,160 at the end of 2020. Over the same period, the S&P500— 3,341 percent and $33,410, Russell 2000—3,468 percent and $34,680, and Nasdaq—8,427 percent and $84,270.[25]

For context, it is helpful to compare these indices to other prominent asset classes and inflation. Assuming an average one-year CD rate of 4 percent over the same time frame (rates were higher in the 1980s but lower in the 2010s), the CD investor's $1,000 would have grown to $4,801. The price of gas increased from $1.22 per gallon in 1980 to $2.58 in 2020, experiencing an average annual growth rate of 1.89 percent. In regard to real estate, the median US home value in 1980 was $63,700, and in 2020 it was $358,700, providing an average annual increase of 4.42 percent.[26] It is easy to see why the stock market receives so much investor attention.

Active Investing

Active investing can use the same stocks or funds as the passive approach, but is monitored on an ongoing basis and traded to take advantage of perceived opportunities in the market. While the term "day trading"—quickly moving in and out of positions—refers to a form of active management, most active management is not day trading. Many financial advisors offer active management for an advisory fee.

For investors looking to eliminate the fees found in mutual funds and ETFs, they can become the manager of their own portfolio by choosing individual stocks and bonds. As this approach is far harder to diversify in accounts that are not of very high value, it may be deemed a riskier proposition. Winning stock pickers have been those who have exercised foresight in the financial ramifications of each chapter thus far. They have held their finger on the pulse of the world's affairs: think of Amazon in the 2010s, Tesla in the green movement, Moderna and Zoom during the Covid-19 pandemic, or the price of oil when Russia invaded Ukraine. Also consider the industries and companies that have been blessed by the US government's multitrillion-dollar checkbook or banished by taxes, tariffs, and regulation.

Financial pundits recommend a goal of retiring with 25 times annual expenses in one's portfolio. According to the Bureau of Labor Statistics, today's average retiree spends about $4,000 monthly.[27] That equates to an ideal retirement portfolio of $1.2 million. This may sound intimidating for young employees without pensions and an uncertain future for Social Security, but do not forget the power of compounding. Starting from scratch at age 22, investing $4,600 annually at a 7 percent rate of return until age 65 will create a portfolio worth over $1.2 million. Granted, inflation will make their monthly expenses more than $4,000.

Together, these five steps of financial planning provide the keys to financial literacy. Independent people can hope to impact whichever chapter of this book piques their interest, but like the original Tesla, without financial literacy, dreams will be rudely awakened. The financially uninformed stay influenced; only the informed can become the influencer.

WHY?

You asked me, "Why? Justify why I should do what I do with my money." And here we are. Do you want to invest in people? Entitlements, a nation that can't take care of its citizens is not a nation. Education, a person without knowledge is a waste of talent. Economic philosophy, a government without a treasury is only an idea. Environment, a world on fire cannot stay a home. Tech, a man without technology is a caveman. Peace, a world at war is doomed. Faith, an economy that believes in nothing stands for nothing. Or money, because if you can't afford the ticket, you can't come inside. Are the costs worth it? I can give all the insight in the world, but now it is finally your turn. As the great philosopher, Seneca, said before his death in 65 BC, "Most powerful is he who has himself in his own power." It's time to be in power of your MICE and obtain your well-being, your wealth . . .

If it feels like a lot, don't fret, there are eight billion people here to help you. Every one of them is a renter and a user, a guest of Earth, just like you and me. Some are givers and some are takers. They are us. But don't wait. Please do not wait any longer. History is being written each day by people just like you. There are good chapters and there are bad chapters, and books at some point come to an end.

So remember that virtually anything can be put off until tomorrow, until one day it can't. Of all the commodities, the most important is time. A malady early on is hard to detect, but easy to fix. However, to let the malady grow may someday find it easy to detect, but impossible to fix. You know how money (M) works, and you've seen how humanity has used it to guide ideology (I), compromise (C), and ego (E). All you have to decide is how you are going to use it.

Next time you ask that second question, "Why?" reflect on the economic maze we have traveled through this book. People will get lost, they will change directions, they will hit dead ends, some might cheat, and others will give up. Some will find what they're looking for and win the day, while others may never know the feeling before the sun runs out. But if you know what to do with your money, you can cut right to the center and maybe show another the way.[28]

ACKNOWLEDGMENTS

Sometimes it feels like writing a book is enough to make you go crazy, and without friends, family, and a supportive team, it just might be. Fortunately for me, I've been blessed by God to be surrounded with people who not only made this book possible, but made it an awesome journey all the way through. There are too many kind souls to mention by name, so if I missed you here, please know that your friendship and support are never forgotten.

First off, I'd like to thank my editor at McGraw Hill, Michele Matrisciani. After completing the original manuscript of this book, I searched and interviewed for the perfect publisher to bring it home, and lo and behold a LinkedIn message created a whole new team. Month after month, with each marked-up chapter you returned to me, I wondered how I'd ever find the right words to make my book all that I envisioned. Yet, without fail, we worked together to make each sentence, paragraph, and chapter all that it could be. Thank you for bringing out the best writer in me, and thank you to everyone else at MH for being my guide.

Thank you, Steve Straus, to you and your team at THINK Book Works for proofreading my book. You were meticulous in your work and I believe the end result shows.

To all my friends who were a sounding board for me throughout this process, it was much appreciated. Little did you know that through our random conversations on current affairs, political debates, and world history, you were helping me craft a story.

To my clients, my professional career is as much my success as it is yours. Since 2008, when I was a young kid cold-calling for business I hardly yet understood, each and every one of you taught me something new about your life and your dreams, which forced me to always find the best financial solutions to achieve the wealth we all desire. To every guest who appeared on The Kuderna Podcast, not only have you helped make my show a success, but every interview truly opened my eyes to the world. To my friends and colleagues at International Planning Alliance and Kuderna Financial Team, from the staff to fellow advisors and mentors, you have all helped me develop a business that allowed me to also pursue my passion as an author.

Last but certainly not least, my family. Thank you to my children— Alexis, Josh, and Jared, you are the subtle reminder to me why this book is so important, in that the future is all we have to look forward to. To my wife, Anita, there are no words to express my love and gratitude; you make our house a home. To my parents and my big brother, Jeff, your lifelong lessons are unmistakable throughout this book and all that I try to do.

NOTES

POPULATION

1. NASA, "NASA Research Confirms It's a Small World, After All," https://www.jpl.nasa.gov/news/nasa-research-confirms-its-a-small-world-after-all.

2. Max Roser, Hannah Ritchie, and Esteban Ortiz-Ospina, 2013, "World Population Growth," OurWorldInData.org, https://ourworldindata.org/world-population-growth.

3. World Population Review (original source: Historical Estimates of World Population—US Census Bureau), https://worldpopulationreview.com/continents/world-population.

4. The World Bank, data 2020, https://data.worldbank.org/indicator/SP.DYN.LE00.IN and https://data.worldbank.org/indicator/SP.DYN.IMRT.IN.

5. *Smithsonian Magazine*, "Top 10 Nation-Building Real Estate Deals," https://www.smithsonianmag.com/history/top-10-nation-building-real-estate-deals-135815933/.

6. Kahn Academy, "America Moves to the City," https://www.khanacademy.org/humanities/us-history/the-gilded-age/gilded-age/a/america-moves-to-the-city.

7. https://myhome.freddiemac.com/blog/research-and-analysis/20210208-suburbs-vs-cities#:~:text=Over%20the%20past%20few%20years,the%20suburbs%20than%20in%20cities.

8. https://constructioncoverage.com/research/cities-spending-most-on-residential-construction-2021.

9. CDC, *National Vital Statistics Report 2019*, https://www.cdc.gov/nchs/data/nvsr/nvsr70/nvsr70-17.pdf.

10. https://news.bloomberglaw.com/pharma-and-life-sciences/investor-owned-nursing-homes-draw-scrutiny-as-deals-flourish.

11. https://morningconsult.com/2022/05/19/private-equity-in-health-care-exclusive-data/#:~:text=Private%20equity%20investors%20disclosed%20spending,owned%20by%20private%20equity%20firms.

12. World Bank, "Population, Total" (original source: United Nations Population Division, census reports).

13. *Straits Times*, "10 Famous Slums in the World and the Challenges They Face," statistic from 2011–2014, https://www.straitstimes.com/world/africa/10-famous-slums-in-the-world-and-the-challenges-they-face.
14. Smithsonian Magazine, "Book That Incited a Worldwide Fear of Overpopulation," https://www.smithsonianmag.com/innovation/book-incited-worldwide-fear-overpopulation-180967499/.
15. World Bank, "Fertility Rate, Total" (original source: UN Population Division, census reports).
16. World Population Review, "Most Dangerous Cities in the US 2022," https://worldpopulationreview.com/us-city-rankings/most-dangerous-cities-in-the-us.
17. Urban Calculator, 2018.
18. https://www.pewresearch.org/hispanic/2016/09/20/overall-number-of-u-s-unauthorized-immigrants-holds-steady-since-2009/.
19. https://worldpopulationreview.com/country-rankings/immigration-by-country.

ENTITLEMENTS

1. Constitutional Rights Foundation, Bill of Rights in Action 14 3 a "How Welfare Began in the United States," https://www.crf-usa.org/bill-of-rights-in-action/bria-14-3-a-how-welfare-began-in-the-united-states.html.
2. History.com, "Six People Who Made Big Money During the Great Depression," https://www.history.com/news/great-depression-people-who-made-money.
3. Britannica, "Brain Trust," https://www.britannica.com/topic/Brain-Trust.
4. Concord Coalition (original source: Congressional Budget Office), https://www.concordcoalition.org/What-is-an-Entitlement.
5. Social Security Administration, Research Note #23, Luther Gulick Memorandum re: Famous FDR Quote, https://www.ssa.gov/history/Gulick.html.
6. AARP, Social Security Resource Center, https://www.aarp.org/retirement/social-security/.
7. Social Security Administration, August 2022, Average Monthly Retirement Benefit × 12, https://www.ssa.gov/policy/docs/quickfacts/stat_snapshot/.
8. GoBankingRates, "American Workers Get Less Social Security and Less Paid Time Off Than Workers in Other Countries," https://www.gobankingrates.com/retirement/social-security/american-workers-get-less-social-security-and-less-paid-time-off-than-workers-in-other-countries/.
9. Center on Budget and Policy Priorities, "Social Security Lifts More Americans Above Poverty Than Any Other Program," https://www.cbpp.org/research/social-security/social-security-lifts-more-people-above-the-poverty-line-than-any-other#:~:text=Social%20Security%20benefits%20play%20a,March%202021%20Current%20Population%20Survey.
10. OECD 2020, "G20 Pension Replacement Rates," https://data.oecd.org/pension/net-pension-replacement-rates.htm.
11. Social Security Administration, "Annual Report of the Supplemental Security Income Program, 2021," https://www.ssa.gov/oact/ssir/SSI21/index.html.
12. Social Security Administration, Disability Evaluation Under Social Security, https://www.ssa.gov/disability/professionals/bluebook/.

13. William C. Greenough and Francis P. King, *Pension Plans and Public Policy* (New York: Columbia University Press, 1976) 27.

14. Victor Reuther, *The Brothers Reuther and the Story of UAW* (Boston: Houghton Mifflin Company, 1976), 310.

15. NCPERS, "The Evolution of Public Pension Plans: Past, Present and Future,"https://www.ncpers.org/files/ncpers-evolution-of-public-pensions-2008 .pdf.

16. Foundation for Economic Education, "The 5 States with the Most Underfunded Public Employee Pensions," https://fee.org/articles/the-5-states-with-the-most -underfunded-public-employee-pensions/.

17. https://www.pewtrusts.org/en/research-and-analysis/articles/2022/07/07/states -unfunded-pension-liabilities-persist-as-major-long-term-challenge#:~:text=A %20state%2Dby%2Dstate%20review,and%20New%20Mexico%20(15.7%25).

18. https://www.pewtrusts.org/en/research-and-analysis/issue-briefs/2021/09/the -state-pension-funding-gap-plans-have-stabilized-in-wake-of-pandemic.

19. Empire Center, "Newest Pensions for Retirees of Police and Fire Careers Average $86,852," https://www.empirecenter.org/publications/newest-pensions -for-police-and-fire-careers/#:~:text=Newest%20Pensions%20for%20Retirees %20of%20Police%20and%20Fire%20Careers%20Average%20%2486%2C852 ,-September%2014%2C%202021&text=Full%20career%20police%20and %20firemen,average%20award%20of%20%2486%2C852%20annually.

20. https://www.nj.gov/treasury/pensions/documents/factsheets/fact16.pdf.

21. Congressional Research Service, "Medicare: Insolvency Projections," https:// sgp.fas.org/crs/misc/RS20946.pdf.

22. https://www.kff.org/medicare/issue-brief/how-much-more-than-medicare-do -private-insurers-pay-a-review-of-the-literature/.

23. US Census, 2020.

24. Center on Budget and Policy Priorities, "Policy Basics: Introduction to Medicaid," 2020, cbpp.org/research/health/introduction-to-medicaid.

25. World Bank, "Population Ages 65 and Above (% of total population)," https://data .worldbank.org/indicator/SP.POP.65UP.TO.ZS.

26. USDA, "A Short History of SNAP," https://www.fns.usda.gov/snap/short-history -snap.

27. USDA, "Foods Typically Purchased by Supplemental Nutrition Assistance Program (SNAP) Households (Summary)," https://www.foodpolitics.com/wp -content/uploads/SNAPFoodsTypicallyPurchased_16.pdf.

28. CNBC, "Pandemic's $794 Billion Unemployment Benefits Were Historic. Here's a Look Back at Their Scope," https://www.cnbc.com/2021/09/02/pandemics-794 -billion-unemployment-benefits-were-historic-heres-why.html.

29. US Census Bureau, *Current Population Survey, 2020 and 2021 Annual Social and Economic Supplements.* NOTE: The differences between the values above are not all statistically significant at the confidence level used by the Census Bureau. © 2021 Peter G. Peterson Foundation, https://www.brookings.edu/research /an-analysis-of-out-of-wedlock-births-in-the-united-states/; for national average: https://sgp.fas.org/crs/misc/R43667.pdf.

30. Budget of the US Government Fiscal Year 2023, Table S-4 Proposed Budget by Category, https://www.whitehouse.gov/wp-content/uploads/2022/03/budget_fy2023.pdf.

31. The Social Security estimate is based on the highest payout at age 70 in 2022 and the pension plan estimates are based on NJDPB calculations.

32. https://www.statista.com/statistics/187894/traditional-ira-total-assets-in-the-us-since-2000/#:~:text=A%20traditional%20IRA%20is%20a,trillion%20U.S.%20dollars%20in%202021, and https://www.propublica.org/article/the-number-of-people-with-iras-worth-5-million-or-more-has-tripled-congress-says.

33. IRS, "Exceptions to Tax on Early Distributions."

34. IRS, "Roth IRAs."

35. IRS, "US Individual Income Tax."

36. SSA-1495.

37. Athene Holding Ltd., https://www.ge.com/news/press-releases/ge-transfers-17-billion-in-us-pension-plan-obligations-to-athene#:~:text=Approximately%2070%2C000%20of%20GE's%20retirees,as%20part%20of%20this%20transfer.

38. Mercer US Pension Buyout Index, June 30, 2021, https://www.mercer.us/our-thinking/wealth/mercer-us-pension-buyout-index.html.

39. SSA.gov, 2020.

40. SSA, "Research Note #4 Inter-Fund Borrowing Among the Trust Funds."

EDUCATION

1. *Smith v. Regents of the University of California.*

2. College Consensus, https://www.collegeconsensus.com/features/most-in-demand-degrees/.

3. NCES, Fast Facts, 2019, https://nces.ed.gov/programs/raceindicators/indicator_red.asp.

4. Bureau of Labor Statistics, 2020, https://www.bls.gov/news.release/hsgec.nr0.htm.

5. NCES, Fast Facts, 2019.

6. https://nces.ed.gov/programs/coe/indicator/cba/annual-earnings.

7. https://www.usnews.com/education/best-colleges/paying-for-college/articles/2019-06-25/the-cost-of-private-vs-public-colleges#:~:text=The%20average%20cost%20of%20tuition,out%2Dof%2Dstate%20students.

8. https://commonslibrary.parliament.uk/research-briefings/sn01079/.

9. Federal Reserve Bank of New York, https://www.theatlantic.com/business/archive/2013/05/just-27-of-bas-have-jobs-related-to-their-major-dont-believe-the-feds-new-stat/276080/.

10. Federal Reserve Bank of New York, https://ips-dc.org/the-federal-government-owns-92-of-student-debt-will-biden-wipe-it-out/.

11. CBO, "Estimates of the Cost of Federal Credit Programs in 2022."

12. American Federation of Teachers, 2020, https://www.aft.org/news/report-shows-alarming-poverty-among-adjunct-faculty.

13. *The Chronicle for Higher Education*, 2019, https://www.chronicle.com/newsletter/weekly-briefing/2020-07-18.

14. https://www.cbssports.com/college-football/news/nick-saban-contract-extension
    -alabama-coach-regains-highest-paid-spot-with-deal-worth-93-6-million/#:~:
    text=With%20the%20new%20contract%2C%20Saban,paid%20coach%20in
    %20college%20football.
15. *USA Today*, https://www.bizjournals.com/austin/news/2020/01/27/ut-has-another
    -record-year-for-sports-revenue.html.
16. National Center for Education Statistics, *U.S. News & World Report*. Note: Tuition
    and fees are in constant 2018–2019 dollars. For public schools, in-state tuition and
    fees are used. All CPI percent change values calculated for the month of January.
17. 2021 NACUBO, TIAA Study of Endowments, https://www.nacubo.org/research
    /2021/nacubo-tiaa-study-of-endowments.
18. Data USA, Harvard University, enrollment 2020, https://datausa.io/profile
    /university/harvard-university#:~:text=Harvard%20University%20has%20a
    %20total,University%20are%20enrolled%20full%2Dtime.
19. "College Endowments Boomed in Fiscal 2021," *Inside Higher Ed*, https://www
    .insidehighered.com/news/2022/02/18/college-endowments-boomed-fiscal
    -year-2021-study-shows#:~:text=College%20and%20university%20endowments
    %20posted,size%20swelled%20to%20%24200%20million.
20. "Understanding College and University Endowments," American Council on
    Education, https://www.acenet.edu/Documents/Understanding-College-and
    -University-Endowments.pdf.
21. https://www.firstthings.com/article/1991/04/the-decline-and-fall-of-the-christian
    -college.
22. Greenspan and Wooldridge, *Capitalism in America*, 281.
23. American Council on Education, "Minorities in Higher Education," https://www
    .acenet.edu/Documents/Minorities-in-Higher-Education-2009-Supplement-23rd
    .pdf.
24. Merriam-Webster Dictionary.
25. *Britanica*, "Affirmative Action," https://www.britannica.com/topic/affirmative
    -action.
26. US Department of Commerce, Census Bureau, Current Population Survey (CPS),
    October Supplement, 2010 and 2019. See *Digest of Education Statistics 2020*, table
    302.60.
27. *Students for Fair Admissions, Inc. v. President and Fellows of Harvard College.*
28. Best Colleges,"A History of Affirmative Action in College Admissions" (original
    source: Gallup), https://www.bestcolleges.com/news/analysis/2020/08/10/history
    -affirmative-action-college/.
29. Education Data Initiative, College Enrollment and Student Demographic Initia-
    tive, https://educationdata.org/college-enrollment-statistics.
30. US Bureau of Labor Statistics, https://www.bls.gov/ooh/construction-and
    -extraction/elevator-installers-and-repairers.htm.
31. Melanie Hanson, "Average Cost of Community College," EducationData.org, July
    25, 2021.
32. University World News, "Why China wants 'Western-style' Liberal Arts
    Education," https://www.universityworldnews.com/post.php?story=
    20171202052059445.

33. PISA 2018 results, https://factsmaps.com/pisa-2018-worldwide-ranking-average -score-of-mathematics-science-reading/.

34. https://betteraccounting.com/small-businesses-are-the-backbone-of-the -economy/#:~:text=Small%20businesses%20create%20two%2Dthirds,than %20large%20patenting%20firms%20do.

35. Smith Family Business Initiative at Cornell, Family Business Facts, https://www .johnson.cornell.edu/smith-family-business-initiative-at-cornell/resources/family -business-facts/.

36. Studentaid.gov, https://tamingthehighcostofcollege.com/2022-23-federal-student -loan-interest-rates/.

ECONOMIC PHILOSOPHY

1. https://www.washingtonpost.com/news/the-fix/wp/2018/03/21/as-americans -become-more-educated-the-gop-is-moving-in-the-opposite-direction/.

2. *Merriam-Webster Dictionary.*

3. *Merriam-Webster Dictionary.*

4. *Moscow Time,* "Russia's 500 Super Rich Wealthier Than Poorest 99.8%—Report," The Boston Consulting Group, https://www.themoscowtimes.com/2021/06/10 /russias-500-super-rich-wealthier-than-poorest-998-report-a74180.

5. Alan Greenspan and Adrian Wooldridge, *Capitalism in America*, 250.

6. Bureau of Labor Statistics, Unemployment Rate.

7. DJIA, Federal Reserve Public Data.

8. Bureau of Labor Statistics, end of year Unemployment Rate, 1929–2021.

9. Treasury Direct. (https://www.treasurydirect.gov/govt/reports/pd/histdebt /histdebt.htm)

10. Economic Freedom of the World Index- 2022.

11. *Merriam-Webster Dictionary.*

12. https://tradingeconomics.com/china/personal-income-tax-rate.

13. Ministry of National Defense of the People's Republic of China, http://eng.mod .gov.cn/news/2022-03/05/content_4906161.htm

14. https://www.cnbc.com/2022/03/05/china-defense-spending-to-rise-by -7point1percent-in-2022-says-finance-ministry.html.

15. UN Conference on Trade and Development, https://unctad.org/news/china-rise -trade-titan.

16. World Bank, 2020.

17. Hurun Report, 2020.

18. The World Bank, GDP Growth.

19. UN, Department of Economic and Social Affairs: Population Dynamics, 2019.

20. World Bank, "GDP Current US$."

21. World Bank, "GDP per capita (current US$)."

22. Kenneth Rogoff, "Can China's Outsized Real Estate Sector Amplify a Delta-Induced Slowdown?," VoxEU.

23. National Association of Realtors, "How Do Home Sales Affect the Economy and the Job Market in Your State," 2021, https://www.nar.realtor/blogs/economists -outlook/how-do-home-sales-affect-the-economy-and-the-job-market-in-your -state.

24. Ibid., 209.
25. The Heritage Foundation.
26. Federalreserve.gov, https://www.federalreserve.gov/monetarypolicy/bst _recenttrends.htm.
27. OECD, 2021, https://www.oecd.org/tax/revenue-statistics-united-states.pdf.
28. Trading Economics, December 2020.
29. OECD, Tax to GDP 2020.
30. OECD, General Government Spending 2020.
31. America's SBDC, 2017, https://americassbdc.org/wp-content/uploads/2017/05 /White-Paper-GenStudy-6-1-2017.pdf.
32. Gallup, 2020, https://www.seattletimes.com/business/this-eras-capitalism-is -driving-many-among-the-young-to-socialism/.
33. https://www.businessinsider.com/millennials-would-vote-socialist-bernie -sanders-elizabeth-warren-debt-2019-10.
34. CDC, "Antidepressant Use Among Adults 2015–2018."
35. Transparency International, Corruption Perceptions Index.
36. Open Secrets, Industry Profiles, 2020.
37. Athletic Business, "How Stadium Construction Costs Reached the Billions," https://www.athleticbusiness.com/facilities/stadium-arena/article/15142672/how -stadium-construction-costs-reached-the-billions.
38. Open Secrets, "Super PACs," https://www.opensecrets.org/political-action -committees-pacs/super-pacs/2022.
39. Open Secrets, "2020 Election to Cost $14 Billion, Blowing Away Spending Records."

ENVIRONMENT

1. https://www.macrotrends.net/1333/historical-gold-prices-100-year-chart.
2. https://www.federalreservehistory.org/essays/oil-shock-of-1973-74#:~:text =The%20embargo%20ceased%20U.S.%20oil,a%20barrel%20in%20January %201974.
3. *The American Oil & Gas Reporter*, "Estimated Global Oil Reserves," https:// www.aogr.com/web-exclusives/exclusive-story/u.s.-holds-most-recoverable-oil -reserves#:~:text=Total%20global%20oil%20reserves%20are,barrels%20of%20oil %20a%20year.
4. Bloomberg, "Britain, China Lead Way in New Saudi Business Licenses," https:// www.bnnbloomberg.ca/britain-china-lead-way-in-new-saudi-business-licenses -1.1250504.
5. Inside Climate News, "Biden Plan Could Allow New Offshore Drilling in Gulf of Mexico," https://www.texastribune.org/2022/07/02/biden-gulf-drilling-leasing -oil/.
6. World Atlas, "Countries with the Most Natural Resources," https://www .worldatlas.com/articles/countries-with-the-most-natural-resources.html.
7. Worldbank, GDP per Capita, 2020.
8. *World Population Review*, "Oil Reserves by Country 2022."
9. NASA, "Climate Change: How Do We Know?" https://climate.nasa.gov/evidence/.
10. World Bank, "CO2 Emissions" (original source Climate Watch Data 2020).

11. NASA, "Four Decades and Counting: New NASA Instrument Continues Measuring Solar Energy Input to Earth," https://climate.nasa.gov/news/2659/four-decades-and-counting-new-nasa-instrument-continues-measuring-solar-energy-input-to-earth/#:~:text=November%2028%2C%202017-,Four%20decades%20and%20counting%3A%20New%20NASA%20instrument%20continues%20measuring%20solar,flare%20activity%20in%20September%202017.

12. NCDC, "Billion-Dollar Weather and Climate Disasters," https://www.ncei.noaa.gov/access/billions/#:~:text=References-,Overview,332%20events%20exceeds%20%242.275%20trillion.

13. NHC, "Costliest US Tropical Cyclones," https://www.ncei.noaa.gov/access/billions/dcmi.pdf.

14. World Meteorological Organization, "Top Ten Disasters," https://public.wmo.int/en/media/press-release/weather-related-disasters-increase-over-past-50-years-causing-more-damage-fewer.

15. OFDA/CRED International Disaster Data, https://ourworldindata.org/ofdacred-international-disaster-data.

16. Insurance Information Institute, https://www.iii.org/fact-statistic/facts-statistics-us-catastrophes.

17. National Geographic, "The World's Plastic Pollution Crisis Explained," https://education.nationalgeographic.org/resource/worlds-plastic-pollution-crisis-explained.

18. Science Direct, "Human Footprint in the Abyss: 30-Year Records of Deep-Sea Plastic Debris," https://www.sciencedirect.com/science/article/pii/S0308597X17305195.

19. Ecocrab, "Plastic Production Is Increasing," https://www.oecd.org/environment/plastic-pollution-is-growing-relentlessly-as-waste-management-and-recycling-fall-short.htm.

20. BLS and BEA.

21. American Lung Association, "State of the Air," 2020.

22. Climate Action Tracker, https://climateactiontracker.org/documents/989/state_climate_action_2021.pdf.

23. Alan Olmstead, ed., "Agriculture," in *Economic Sectors*, vol. 4 of *Historical Statistics of the United States: Millennial Edition*, ed. Susan Carter.

24. Hedges and Company, 2022, https://hedgescompany.com/blog/2018/10/number-of-licensed-drivers-usa/.

25. https://www.usatoday.com/story/money/cars/2022/04/02/tesla-sales-record-310-000-vehicles/7257188001/.

26. "EV Battery Recycling: Makes Cars Cheaper and Helps Solve the Microchip Shortage Crisis," Motor Biscuit, https://www.motorbiscuit.com/ev-battery-recycling-makes-cars-cheaper-helps-solve-microchip-shortage-crisis/.

27. CNBC, "Tesla Stock Is up More Than 4,000 Percent Since Its Debut 10 Years Ago," https://www.cnbc.com/2020/06/29/tesla-stock-up-4125percent-since-ipo-ten-years-ago.html.

28. Motley Fool, "The 25 Hottest IPOs of 2010," https://www.fool.com/investing/general/2011/01/04/the-25-hottest-ipos-of-2010.aspx._

29. EPA, "About Nuclear Submarines and Aircraft Carriers," https://www.epa.gov/radtown/nuclear-submarines-and-aircraft-carriers#:~:text=Nuclear%20submarines%20and%20aircraft%20carriers%20are%20powered%20by%20onboard%20nuclear,power%20to%20turn%20the%20propeller.
30. Energy.gov, Ultimate Fast Facts.
31. Jonah Goldberg, "To Fight Climate Change Seriously, Nuclear Power Must Be on the Table," *News Herald,* 2021.
32. US Department of Energy, "The Ultimate Facts Guide About Nuclear Energy."
33. Forbes, "After 48 Years Democrats Endorse Nuclear Energy in Platform," https://www.forbes.com/sites/robertbryce/2020/08/23/after-48-years-democrats-endorse-nuclear-energy-in-platform/.

TECH

1. Marketing Charts: Social Apps Average Hours per User per Month, January 2021.
2. Encyclopedia, "Barnes & Noble," https://www.encyclopedia.com/economics/economics-magazines/barnes-noble-inc#:~:text=From%20fiscal%201994%20through%20fiscal,and%20%242.8%20billion%20in%201998.
3. https://www.statista.com/statistics/266289/net-revenue-of-amazon-by-region/#:~:text=In%202021%2C%20Amazon's%20total%20consolidated,generated%20through%20international%20revenue%20channels.
4. https://variety.com/2022/tv/news/the-cw-age-average-viewer-broadcast-1235342962/.
5. *Journal of Youth and Adolescence,* https://news.byu.edu/intellect/10-year-byu-study-shows-elevated-suicide-risk-from-excess-social-media-time-for-young-teen-girls.
6. Insider Intelligence, "More Gen-Zers now use TikTok than Instagram in the US," https://www.insiderintelligence.com/content/more-us-gen-zers-now-use-tiktok-than-instagram.
7. https://www.ic3.gov/Media/PDF/AnnualReport/2021_IC3Report.pdf.
8. FTC in the Consumer Sentinel Network database from January 1, 2021, through March 31, 2022.
9. Library of Congress, "Regulation of Cryptocurrency Around the World: November 2021 Update," https://tile.loc.gov/storage-services/service/ll/llglrd/2021687419/2021687419.pdf.
10. People's Bank of China, July 2021, "Progress of Research & Development of E-CNY in China," http://www.pbc.gov.cn/en/3688110/3688172/4157443/4293696/2021071614584691871.pdf.
11. US SEC, "SEC Nearly Doubles Size of Enforcement's Crypto Assets and Cyber Unit."
12. FBI Internet Crime Report 2021.
13. Treasury's Financial Crimes Enforcement Network (FinCEN), 2021, https://www.fincen.gov/sites/default/files/2021-10/Financial%20Trend%20Analysis_Ransomware%20508%20FINAL.pdf.
14. World Bank, "High Technology Exports (current US$) 2020" (original source: UN and Comtrade database through WITS).

15. https://www.voanews.com/a/race-for-semiconductors-influences-taiwan-conflict -/6696432.html#:~:text=Taiwan%20makes%2065%25%20of%20the,90%25%20of %20the%20advanced%20chips.

16. https://www.usatoday.com/story/money/cars/2022/02/13/used-cars-cost-more /6778705001/.

17. CNBC, "Nissan to Make Half a Million Fewer Cars in 2021 Due to Chip Shortage," https://www.cnbc.com/2021/05/13/nissan-to-make-half-a-million-fewer-cars-in -2021-due-to-chip-shortage.html#:~:text=Japanese%20car%20maker%20Nissan %20is,surge%20in%20raw%20material%20prices.

18. Semiconductor Industry Association, https://www.semiconductors.org/global -semiconductor-sales-increase-13-2-year-to-year-in-january/.

19. https://www.nytimes.com/2021/08/30/business/media/china-online-games .html#:~:text=China's%20strict%20limits%20on%20how,under%20government %20rules%20issued%20Monday.

20. https://psnet.ahrq.gov/perspective/artificial-intelligence-and-diagnostic-errors.

21. https://www.whitehouse.gov/wp-content/uploads/2018/05/Cybersecurity-Risk -Determination-Report-FINAL_May-2018-Release.pdf.

22. Mordor Intelligence, "Cyber Security Insurance Market—Growth, Trends, Covid-19 Impact, and Forecasts (2021–2026)."

WAR

1. https://www.worldhistory.org/war/.

2. Genesis 10:22.

3. Office of the Historian, "U.S. Debt and Foreign Loans, 1775–1795," https://history .state.gov/milestones/1784-1800/loans.

4. David Hacker, "A Census-Based Count of Civil War Dead," https://www.history .com/news/american-civil-war-deaths#:~:text=David%20Hacker%20published %20%E2%80%9CA%20Census,as%20many%20as%20850%2C000%20dead.

5. Treasury Direct, "The History of US Public Debt—the Civil War," https://www .treasurydirect.gov/kids/history/history_civilwar.htm.

6. Alan Greenspan and Adrian Wooldridge, "The Two Americas," *Capitalism in America*, Penguin Press: 2018.

7. American Battlefield Trust, "Small Arms Across Three Wars," https://www .battlefields.org/learn/articles/small-arms-across-three-wars.

8. Department of Veterans' Affairs, "America's Wars." (https://www.va.gov/opa /publications/factsheets/fs_americas_wars.pdf)

9. National Park Service and Eastern National, "Industry and Economy During the Civil War," *The Civil War Remembered*, https://www.nps.gov/articles/industry -and-economy-during-the-civil-war.htm.

10. Office of the Historian, "U.S. Debt and Foreign Loans, 1775–1795."

11. https://www.britannica.com/event/World-War-I/Killed-wounded-and-missing.

12. Steven Lobell, "The Political Economy of War Mobilization: From Britain's Limited Liability to a Continental Commitment," *International Politics* (2006).

13. Harold F. Williamson, *The American Petroleum Industry: The Age of Energy 1899– 1959*, Northwestern University Press: 1963, 267.

14. T. Balderston, "War Finance and Inflation in Britain and Germany, 1914–1918," *Economic History Review* (1989).
15. National Bureau of Economic Research, "The Economics of World War I," https://www.nber.org/digest/jan05/economics-world-war-i.
16. Fouquin and Hugot, "Value of Exported Goods as Share of GDP" (CEPII 2016), https://ourworldindata.org/grapher/merchandise-exports-gdp-cepii.
17. Treasury Direct, "History of US Public Debt—World War I."
18. History Channel, "John Maynard Keynes Predicts Economic Chaos," https://www .history.com/this-day-in-history/keynes-predicts-economic-chaos#:~:text=In %20his%20The%20Economic%20Consequences,repercussions%20on%20Europe %20and%20the.
19. National World War II Museum, https://www.nationalww2museum.org/war /articles/great-debate.
20. Library of Congress, The Lend-Lease Act.
21. Iowa PBS, "IMPACT OF WORLD WAR II ON THE U.S. ECONOMY AND WORKFORCE," https://www.iowapbs.org/iowapathways/artifact/1590/impact -world-war-ii-us-economy-and-workforce.
22. Prospect, "The Way We Won: America's Economic Breakthrough During World War II," https://prospect.org/health/way-won-america-s-economic-breakthrough -world-war-ii/.
23. Moneywise, "The Financial Facts You Never Learned About World War II," https://moneywise.com/a/ch-b/financial-facts-about-world-war-ii/p-12.
24. St. Louis Fed, "Which War Saw the Highest Defense Spending? Depends How It's Measured."
25. Institute for Economics and Peace, "Economic Consequences of War on the US Economy," https://www.economicsandpeace.org/wp-content/uploads/2015/06 /The-Economic-Consequences-of-War-on-US-Economy_0.pdf.
26. Norwich University Online, "The Cost of U.S. Wars Then and Now," https://online .norwich.edu/academic-programs/resources/cost-us-wars-then-and-now.
27. History.com, "GI Bill," https://www.history.com/topics/world-war-ii/gi-bill.
28. Tony Judt, *Postwar: A History of Europe Since 1945.*
29. http://news.bbc.co.uk/2/hi/6215847.stm.
30. The Library of Economics and Liberty, German Economic Miracle, https://www .econlib.org/library/Enc/GermanEconomicMiracle.html.
31. US National Archives and Records Administration, "Joint Intelligence Objectives Agency," https://www.archives.gov/iwg/declassified-records/rg-330-defense -secretary.
32. Robert Murphy, "Diplomat Among Warriors" (London: 1964), 251.
33. Department of State, Office of the Historian, "The Dawes Plan, the Young Plan, German Reparations, and Inter-Allied War Debts," https://history.state.gov /milestones/1921-1936/dawes.
34. "The Epic Gold Heist That Financed the War for Hitler," Knowledge at Wharton, https://knowledge.wharton.upenn.edu/article/the-epic-gold-heist-that-financed -the-war-for-hitler/.
35. https://history.state.gov/milestones/1945-1952/truman-doctrine.
36. The Report on the Covert Activities of the Central Intelligence Agency.

37. BBC, "Vietnam War," https://www.bbc.co.uk/bitesize/guides/zv7bkqt/revision/2.

38. History, "Vietnam War Protests," https://www.history.com/topics/vietnam-war/vietnam-war-protests.

39. BLS.gov, "The Vietnam-era cohort: employment and earnings."

40. Military.com, "6 Things to Know About Operation Desert Storm," https://www.military.com/history/operation-desert-storm-6-things-know.

41. Institute for Economics and Peace, "Economic Consequences of War on the US Economy," (https://www.economicsandpeace.org/wp-content/uploads/2015/06/The-Economic-Consequences-of-War-on-US-Economy_0.pdf).

42. Naval History and Heritage Command (through 06/30/2008), War on Terror from Watson Institute 2022, "Costs of Major US Wars," https://www.history.navy.mil/research/library/online-reading-room/title-list-alphabetically/c/costs-major-us-wars.html.

43. Jörg Baten, *A History of the Global Economy. From 1500 to the Present.* Cambridge University Press: 2016, 25.

44. Bloomberg, Cato Institute Senior Fellow Johan Norberg, 2019.

45. "Insights into the Tax Systems of Scandinavian Countries," Tax Foundation 2021, https://taxfoundation.org/scandinavian-countries-taxes-2021/#:~:text=Top%20personal%20income%20tax%20rates,of%20Scandinavian%20income%20tax%20systems.

46. Heritage, "2021 Index of Economic Freedom."

47. US News, "The 15 Richest Counties in the US," July 11, 2022, https://www.usnews.com/news/healthiest-communities/slideshows/richest-counties-in-america.

48. Department of Defense.

49. World Bank, "Military expenditure (% of GDP) United States 1960–2020."

50. Brown University, "Costs of War," https://www.brown.edu/news/2021-09-01/costsofwar.

51. FRED, "Federal Debt Held by Foreign and International Investors," https://fred.stlouisfed.org/series/FDHBFIN.

52. Brown University, "The Cost of Debt Financed War," https://open.bu.edu/handle/2144/40916?show=full.

53. "The Total Cost of U.S. Tariffs," American Action Forum, https://www.americanactionforum.org/research/the-total-cost-of-tariffs/.

54. Government Technology, "Microsoft: Russia Launched 58 percent of State-Backed Cyber Attacks," https://www.govtech.com/security/microsoft-russia-launched-58-of-state-backed-cyber-attacks.

55. Reuters, "Suspected Russian Hackers Spied on U.S. Treasury Emails," https://www.reuters.com/news/picture/suspected-russian-hackers-spied-on-us-tr-idUSKBN28N0PG.

56. World Population Review, "US Foreign Aid by Country 2019."

57. Philanthropy Network, "Giving USA 2021: In a year of unprecedented events and challenges, charitable giving reached a record $471.44 billion in 2020," https://givingusa.org/wp-content/uploads/2021/06/GUSA2021_Infographic_Digital.pdf.

58. JICA Ogata Sadako Research Institute, "Estimating China's Foreign Aid 2019–2020," https://www.jica.go.jp/jica-ri/publication/other/l75nbg000019o0pq-att/Estimating_Chinas_Foreign_Aid_2019-2020.pdf.

59. Foreign Policy, "Russia Is the Biggest Recipient of Chinese Foreign Aid," https://foreignpolicy.com/2017/10/11/russia-is-the-biggest-recipient-of-chinese-foreign-aid-north-korea/.
60. https://ustr.gov/countries-regions/china-mongolia-taiwan/peoples-republic-china.
61. *Harvard Business Review*, "Americans Don't Know How Capitalist China Is," https://hbr.org/2021/05/americans-dont-know-how-capitalist-china-is.
62. Soviet (and CCP) Subversion of the Free World Press, "1984 Complete Interview—Yuri Bezmenov Yuri Bezmenov: The Life and Legacy of the Influential KGB Informant Who Defected to the West," https://cosmolearning.org/documentaries/yuri-bezmenov-interview-soviet-subversion-of-the-free-world-press-1984/.
63. https://immigration.procon.org/us-undocumented-immigrant-population-estimates/
64. Migration Policy Institute, "Chinese Immigrants in the United States," https://www.migrationpolicy.org/article/chinese-immigrants-united-states-2018.
65. Macrotrends, "China Immigration Statistics 1960–2021."
66. Genesis 8:21.

RELIGION

1. Exodus 24:12–13, New International Version.
2. History.com, "Russia—a Timeline," https://www.history.com/topics/russia/russia-timeline.
3. World Atlas, "The Oldest Companies Still Operating Today," https://www.worldatlas.com/articles/the-oldest-companies-still-operating-today.html.
4. History.com, "Ancient Rome," https://www.history.com/topics/ancient-rome/ancient-rome.
5. History.com, "Hinduism," https://www.history.com/topics/religion/hinduism.
6. Jewish Data Bank, 2019, https://www.jewishdatabank.org/content/upload/bjdb/2019_World_Jewish_Population_(AJYB,_DellaPergola)_DataBank_Final.pdf.
7. Chronological Life Application Study Bible, New Living Translation.
8. CIA Factbook, 2020.
9. History.com, "Islam," https://www.history.com/topics/religion/islam.
10. Pew Research Center, "5 Facts About Religion in India," https://www.pewresearch.org/fact-tank/2018/06/29/5-facts-about-religion-in-india/.
11. Pew Research Center, "Many Countries Favor Specific Religions, Officially or Unofficially," https://www.pewresearch.org/religion/2017/10/03/many-countries-favor-specific-religions-officially-or-unofficially/#:~:text=More%20than%2080%20countries%20favor,and%20territories%20around%20the%20world.
12. US News & World Report, "Obama Is Wrong When He Says We're Not a Judeo-Christian Nation," https://www.usnews.com/opinion/articles/2009/05/07/obama-is-wrong-when-he-says-were-not-a-judeo-christian-nation.
13. https://www.pewresearch.org/religion/2022/09/13/how-u-s-religious-composition-has-changed-in-recent-decades/.
14. Pew Research Center, 2019.

15. NCEA, https://www.ncea.org/NCEA/Who_We_Are/About_Catholic_Schools /Catholic_School_Data/Highlights/NCEA/Who_We_Are/About_Catholic _Schools/Catholic_School_Data/Highlights.aspx?hkey=e0456a55-420d-475d -8480-c07f7f090431.

16. https://www.usnews.com/news/best-countries/slideshows/the-10-most-religious -countries.

17. PRRI, "The 2020 Census of American Religion," https://www.prri.org/research /2020-census-of-american-religion/.

18. Pew Research Center, "The Future of World Religions," https://www.pewresearch .org/religion/2015/04/02/religious-projections-2010-2050/.

19. Pew Research Center 2010. World Population Review 2020.

20. Pew Research Center, "Economics and Well-Being Among US Jews," https://www .pewresearch.org/religion/2021/05/11/economics-and-well-being-among-u-s -jews/.

21. Pew Research Center, "2014 Religious Landscape Study," https://www.pewresearch .org/religion/religious-landscape-study/.

22. Saturna Capital, "Halal Investing," https://www.saturna.com/amana/halal -investing.

23. IUPUI, "Muslim American Zakat Report 2022," https://scholarworks.iupui.edu /handle/1805/28468.

24. Administration of the Patrimony of the Holy See (APSA), 2021, https://www .vaticannews.va/en/vatican-city/news/2021-11/administration-of-the-patrimony -of-the-apostolic-see.html.

25. Lilly Family School of Philanthropy, Giving USA: Total U.S. Charitable Giv- ing Remained Strong in 2021, Reaching $484.85 Billion," https://philanthropy .iupui.edu/news-events/news-item/giving-usa:--total-u.s.-charitable-giving -remained-strong-in-2021,-reaching-$484.85-billion.html?id=392#:~:text= Highlights%20and%20Numbers%20for%202021%20Charitable%20Giving%20to %20Recipients%3A,0.7%25%20adjusted%20for%20inflation.

26. Deuteronomy 7:2 (KJV).

27. Modern Diplomacy, "Religious Conflicts Around the Globe and a Solution," https://moderndiplomacy.eu/2020/10/15/religious-conflicts-around-the-globe -and-a-solution/.

28. US Department of State, "2019 Report on International Religious Freedom: China (Includes Tibet, Xinjiang, Hong Kong, and Macau)," https://www.state.gov/reports /2019-report-on-international-religious-freedom/china/.

29. Encyclopedia Britannica, https://www.britannica.com/place/Russia/Religion.

30. US Department of State, "2020 Report on International Religious Freedom: Russia," https://www.state.gov/reports/2020-report-on-international-religious -freedom/russia/.

31. https://www.usnews.com/news/best-countries/rankings/religious-freedom.

32. USCIRF 2021 Annual Report.

33. Associated Press, "Taliban Form All-Male Afghan Government of Old Guard Members," September 7, 2021, https://apnews.com/article/middle-east-pakistan -afghanistan-arrests-islamabad-d50b1b490d27d32eb20cc11b77c12c87.

34. https://www.unodc.org/documents/data-and-analysis/tocta/5.Heroin.pdf

34. BBC, "Afghanistan: How Do the Taliban Make Money?" https://www.bbc.com/news/world-46554097.
35. The Counterproliferation Papers established by the USAF Counterproliferation Center.

FINANCIAL LITERACY

1. https://www.businessinsider.com/adulthood-most-expensive-for-parents-merrill-lynch-report-2018-10
2. https://www.aarp.org/research/topics/economics/info-2020/midlife-adults-providing-financial-support-to-family-members.html
3. Council for Economic Education, 2022 Survey of the States, https://www.councilforeconed.org/wp-content/uploads/2022/03/2022-SURVEY-OF-THE-STATES.pdf).
4. Bureau of Labor Statistics, https://www.bls.gov/ooh/business-and-financial/personal-financial-advisors.htm#:~:text=in%20May%202021.-,Job%20Outlook,on%20average%2C%20over%20the%20decade.
5. CNBC, "Why Robo-Advisors Are Striving Toward a 'Hybrid Model,' as the Industry Passes the $460 Billion Mark," April 12, 2021, https://www.cnbc.com/2021/04/12/why-robo-advisors-may-never-replace-human-financial-advisors.html.
6. Boston Consulting Group, "The $100 Trillion Machine," https://www.bcg.com/publications/2021/global-asset-management-industry-report.
7. Social Security Administration, "Disability and Death Probability Tables for Insured Workers Born in 1999," https://www.ssa.gov/oact/NOTES/ran6/an2020-6.pdf, Table A.
8. Integrated Benefits Institute, "Health and Productivity Benchmarking 2019" (released September 2020), Long-Term Disability, All Employers, Condition-specific results.
9. David U. Himmelstein, Robert M. Lawless, Deborah Thorne, Pamela Foohey, and Steffie Woolhandler, "Medical Bankruptcy: Still Common Despite the Affordable Care Act," *American Journal of Public Health* 109, no. 3 (March 1, 2019): 431–433. See Table 1, https://www.ncbi.nlm.nih.gov/pmc/articles/PMC6366487/.
10. Social Security Administration, "Annual Statistical Report on the Social Security Disability Insurance Program, 2019."
11. Social Security Administration, "Age Distribution of Pending Hearings (FY 2016–FYTD 2020 Q4)."
12. SSA.gov, 2021, https://www.ssa.gov/disabilityfacts/facts.html#:~:text=Social%20Security%20disability%20payments%20are,poverty%20level%20(%2412%2C140%20annually.
13. Bureau of Labor Statistics, *Employer-Reported Workplace Injuries and Illnesses (Annual)*, 2018, Table 1, Incidence rates of nonfatal occupational injuries and illnesses by industry and case types, cases with days away from work.
14. Bls.gov, 2022, https://www.bls.gov/news.release/ebs2.htm.
15. The life expectancy information is based on the 2015 VBT Preferred Class Structure Mortality Table.

16. Life Insurance Marketing and Research Association, https://www.limra.com/en/newsroom/industry-trends/2022/disability-insurance-and-a-secure-retirement-go-hand-in-hand/.

17. LIMRA, https://www.limra.com/en/newsroom/news-releases/2022/limra-2021-annual-u.s.-life-insurance-sales-growth-highest-since-1983/.

18. American Bar Association, 2020, https://www.americanbar.org/news/abanews/aba-news-archives/2019/08/profile-of-the-profession-report/.

19. IAALS, Judges in the United States, 2019, https://iaals.du.edu/sites/default/files/documents/publications/judge_faq.pdf.

20. Federal Reserve, "Money in the Bank? Assessing Families' Liquid Savings Using the Survey of Consumer Finance," *FEDS Notes*, November 19, 2018.

21. Federal Reserve, May 2022, https://www.forbes.com/advisor/credit-cards/average-credit-card-interest-rate/#:~:text=The%20Federal%20Reserve%20keeps%20tabs,that%20assessed%20interest%20was%2016.65%25.

22. Experian, 2020 Q3, https://www.experian.com/blogs/ask-experian/research/millennials-record-highest-credit-score-increase/.

23. Tax Policy Center, "Historical Highest Marginal Income Tax Rates."

24. Gallup, "What Percentage of Americans Owns Stock?", 2021, https://news.gallup.com/poll/266807/percentage-americans-owns-stock.aspx.

25. Yahoo Finance, January 1, 1980–December 31, 2020.

26. Federal Reserve Bank of St. Louis, "Median Sales Price of Houses Sold for the United States," https://fred.stlouisfed.org/series/MSPUS.

27. BLS, 2020, https://www.fool.com/retirement/2019/03/02/the-average-american-spends-nearly-4000-per-month.aspx#:~:text=And%20according%20to%20the%20Bureau,or%20around%20%243%2C800%20per%20month.&text=Spending%20more%20during%20retirement%20than,t%20necessarily%20a%20bad%20thing.

28. Registered Representative and Financial Advisor of Park Avenue Securities LLC (PAS). OSJ: 1040 BROAD STREET, 2ND FLOOR, SUITE 202, SHREWSBURY NJ, 07702, 973-2444420. Securities products and advisory services offered through PAS, member FINRA, SIPC. Financial Representative of The Guardian Life Insurance Company of America® (Guardian), New York, NY. PAS is a wholly owned subsidiary of Guardian. KUDERNA FINANCIAL TEAM is not an affiliate or subsidiary of PAS or Guardian. CA Insurance License Number - 0K04194.

INDEX

ABOUT THE AUTHOR

Bryan M. Kuderna grew up in Ocean Township, New Jersey. He went on to graduate from The College of New Jersey with a Bachelor of Science in finance and a minor in economics, and later obtained a Master of Science in Financial Services (MSFS) from The American College. He credits his time spent studying at the University of Economics in Prague, Czech Republic, as one of his most formative college experiences.

Bryan began his career as a financial advisor in 2008 amid the Great Recession. He became a Certified Financial Planner™ in 2013 and founded Kuderna Financial Team, a New Jersey–based financial services firm. He has since been named one of New Jersey's Leaders in Finance* and routinely qualifies for Million Dollar Round Table (MDRT®) and other industry honors.

He is the host of *The Kuderna Podcast*, a show dedicated to helping listeners build wealth in its original meaning. His previous books include *Millennial Millionaire: A Guide to Become a Millionaire by 30*, and a foray into fiction with his young adult fantasy novel, *ANOROC*.

Bryan resides in New Jersey with his wife, Anita, and their three children. In his spare time he enjoys rooting for the Dallas Cowboys, training Brazilian Jiu-Jitsu, and has completed endurance races including the Rock N' Roll Marathon in Washington, DC, and International Ironman in Mont Tremblant, Quebec, Canada. Bryan stays grounded through his Catholic faith and involvement with the Rotary Club of Asbury Park.

---

* NJBiz 2021 Leaders in Finance Honorees